WEEDS OF THE NORTHERN U.S. AND CANADA

A Guide for Identification

Weeds

of the Northern U.S.

and Canada

FRANCE ROYER & RICHARD DICKINSON

LONE PINE PUBLISHING

THE UNIVERSITY OF ALBERTA PRESS

Published by
The University of Alberta Press
Ring House 2
Edmonton, Alberta, Canada   T6G 2E1
	and
Lone Pine Publishing
1901 Raymond Avenue SW, Suite C
Renton, Washington
USA   98055

First edition, fourth printing, 2004
Copyright © France Royer and Richard Dickinson 1999
ISBN 1–55105–221–0

CANADIAN CATALOGUING IN PUBLICATION DATA

Dickinson, Richard, 1960–
	Weeds of the northern U.S. and Canada

	Includes bibliographical references and index.
ISBN 1–55105–221–0

	1. Weeds—Canada—Identification. 2. Weeds—United States—
Identification. I. Royer, France, 1951– II. Title.
SB613.C2D522 1999   581.6'52'0971   C99–910332–6

Printed on acid-free paper.
Colour separations and filmwork by Elite Lithographers Co. Ltd.,
Edmonton, Canada
Printed and bound in Canada by Kromar Printing Ltd., Winnipeg,
Manitoba.

The University of Alberta Press acknowledges the financial support
of the Government of Canada through the Book Publishing Industry
Development Program for its publishing activities. The Press also
gratefully acknowledges the support received for its program from
the Canada Council for the Arts.

THE CANADA COUNCIL | LE CONSEIL DES ARTS
FOR THE ARTS | DU CANADA
SINCE 1957 | DEPUIS 1957

To farmers everywhere

Contents

Acknowledgements

wild cucumber,
Echinocystis lobata
(Michx.) T. & G.

The authors would like to thank friends and family for their support and encouragement throughout this project. As well, our thanks go to Glenn Rollans, Director of the University of Alberta Press, for believing in this project; to Leslie Vermeer, our editor, for help in organizing and presenting this information and making sure all the loose ends were tied; to Alan Brownoff, the designer, for making the photographs look good; and to Lana Kelly for complementing the text with her line drawings. We are also grateful to those who provided technical support and comments: Debbie Bigelow, Denise Maurice, Cathy Cross, Shaffeek Ali, and the staff with the Plant Industry Division, Agriculture and Agri-Food Canada.

Foreword

spotted knapweed,
Centurea maculosa Lam.

Richard Dickinson and France Royer have produced an excellent guide for weed identification. *Weeds of the Northern U.S. and Canada* provides a comprehensive description of each weed species in a concise and user-friendly form. The photographs are superb, and the close-ups emphasize the identifying features of each weed species at different growth stages.

It is often necessary to identify weeds before they flower to control them effectively, and the seedling pictures meet that need. The Quick ID and Similar Species write-ups will help to make weed identification an easy and pleasant experience and will minimize the need for advanced knowledge in botanical terminologies. The Weed Designation section is a useful addition for alerting readers to the legal status of each weed and, by raising awareness, can help prevent the movement of these plants to other areas.

Weeds of the Northern U.S. and Canada is a welcome addition as an aid to weed identification. This book will be a useful text to the student, the weed professional, the botanist, or anyone who has an interest in weeds and wild plants.

SHAFFEEK ALI
Provincial Weed Specialist
Alberta Agriculture, Food and Rural Development

Annual sow thistle,
Sonchus asper (L.) Hill

What is a weed? According to the poet Ralph Waldo
Emerson, a weed is "a plant whose virtues have not
yet been discovered." But ask a gardener, farmer, or
weed control specialist, and the answers will range
from "a plant of little value" to "a species that
competes with crops" to "a troublesome pest that
affects the health of livestock and humans." A weed
might best be defined as any plant growing in an
area where it is not wanted. Weeds affect all of us,
whether we cultivate large tracts of cropland or
small backyard gardens, and in our efforts to
encourage more desirable plants, our strategy is
normally to control competing species.

Humans are intimately linked with the plant life that
surrounds us. We raise crops for food, harvest fibres
for our clothing, extract chemicals for our indus-
tries, and enjoy the many environmental benefits

that plants give us. Yet to reap these rewards, we must favour some plants over others. The less-favoured species become weeds, something we must control. In the past, we attempted to eradicate weed species through extreme measures; today, our practices lean increasingly to control through gentler methods. But changing agricultural practices lead to changing weed problems, which means we must always be working to adapt our solutions to the current situation.

Some species compete too well with desirable plants; other species produce noxious substances that can harm other plants, animals, or humans. For these and many other reasons, weed control is an important and necessary component of our world.

To control a weed, we must be able to identify the species, understand its biology, and implement the most appropriate control method. *Weeds of the Northern U.S. and Canada* has been designed to assist readers with the identification of more than 175 species from 48 plant families. The families are arranged in alphabetical order of their English family names. An introductory family page describes the general characteristics of each family, including references to well-known, representative ornamental and produce species, to help readers learn to distinguish important traits in familiar species.

Within each family, species are listed alphabetically by their scientific names, because local common names can vary widely. (A list of regional names is included in the text and index for easy cross-reference.) Each species account includes detailed descriptions of the seed, seedling, leaves, flower, mature plant, and fruit for easy recognition. More than 750 colour photographs complement the text and aid in identification. Closely related or similar species are also described, highlighting the most distinctive and distinguishing characteristics of each species.

Non-technical terms have been used whenever possible, to make the text easier for novices. Nonetheless, readers with formal training will find the text a fluent blend of technical accuracy and plain language. The book includes an extensive illustrated glossary and a broad list of references, for those readers seeking additional information. Novice readers will also find the quick-reference identification keys for seedlings, mature plants, and grasses helpful; the keys use thumbnail images for easy visual matching. These keys are intended to be instructive, to help readers learn to identify plants easily. Seeing the characteristics while reading their verbal description helps to secure important traits in memory.

◢

Why do we need another book on weeds? One reason is that current weed literature is widely dispersed and has been largely organized by region and nation. *Weeds of the Northern U.S. and Canada* examines weeds from across the continent, from Alaska to Newfoundland and from northern California to Virginia, including representative species from the many provinces and states in-between. Another reason is that many weed publications are too technical for the average user. A third limitation is the lack of detailed colour images in many weed publications. *Weeds of the Northern U.S. and Canada* features colour photos of weeds at every stage, allowing users to identify and match species immediately, right in the field. This book presents a complete, single-source reference, offering useful information at a glance on its two-page spreads.

Weeds of the Northern U.S. and Canada was written to promote thoughtful awareness of weeds and their qualities at all stages. It presents an array of important technical information, including germination temperature, seed dimensions, seed production, and distribution. The book is intended to create knowledgeable readers who can apply selective and appropriate controls and avoid broad-spectrum treatments that may be inefficient or even harmful.

The 175 species presented here represent a manageable number of important weeds. Future editions may include more and different species, as control concerns, agricultural practices, and weed legislation change. The species included in this edition were chosen to represent a diversity of control issues and the spectrum of species distribution. Our species choices were also guided by geography, in an effort to include plants from all the major regions of northern North America. Most species listed here are quite common and widely distributed, with well-established control regimes. Other species are less common but still deserve our attention: if left untreated, these species could become a major problem because of inadequate control mechanisms.

Some of the plants listed here as weeds have not been officially classified as such by legislation. "Noxious weeds," like any other biological form, live in dynamic systems: legislation can either anticipate or respond to problem weeds. For example, purple loosestrife (*Lythrum salicaria* L.) has been listed as a noxious weed in Alberta, where it is established in only a few sites; this is an act of preventive legislation that recognizes the long-term potential for harm of this prolific species. Green amaranth (*Amaranthus hybridus* L.), often confused with redroot pigweed, is not yet listed, but its incidence is on the rise; this is a species for concern. Legislation information is presented right in the text, allowing landowners to become aware of concerns in their regions and to plan control strategies before a problem gets out of hand.

No matter what we might think of them, weeds will always be with us. *Weeds of the Northern U.S. and Canada* is a comprehensive guide to living with them.

Abbreviations
for Provincial and State Names

CANADA

AB	Alberta
BC	British Columbia
MB	Manitoba
NB	New Brunswick
NF	Newfoundland
NS	Nova Scotia
NT	Northwest Territories
ON	Ontario
PE	Prince Edward Island
PQ	Quebec
SK	Saskatchewan
YK	Yukon

UNITED STATES OF AMERICA

AK	Alaska
AL	Alabama
AR	Arkansas
AZ	Arizona
CA	California
CO	Colorado
CT	Connecticut
DC	District of Columbia
DE	Delaware
FL	Florida
GA	Georgia
HI	Hawaii
IA	Iowa
ID	Idaho
IL	Illinois
IN	Indiana
KS	Kansas
KY	Kentucky
LA	Louisianna
ME	Maine
MD	Maryland
MA	Massachusetts
MI	Michigan
MN	Minnesota
MS	Mississippi
MO	Missouri
MT	Montana
NB	Nebraska
NV	Nevada
NH	New Hampshire
NJ	New Jersey
NM	New Mexico
NY	New York
NC	North Carolina
ND	North Dakota
OH	Ohio
OK	Oklahoma
OR	Oregon
PA	Pennsylvania
RI	Rhode Island
SC	South Carolina
SD	South Dakota
TN	Tennessee
TX	Texas
UT	Utah
VA	Virginia
VT	Vermont
WA	Washington
WI	Wisconsin
WV	West Virginia
WY	Wyoming

Flower Structure

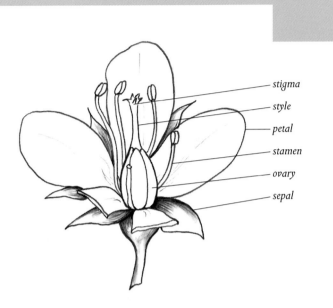

- stigma
- style
- petal
- stamen
- ovary
- sepal

Leaf Types

simple

pinnately compound

bipinnately compound

palmately compound

Key to Mature Plants

Mature plants are identified by leaf arrangement and flower colour. Flowers are grouped by colour and listed alphabetically. Species with more than one type of leaf arrangement are identified in each of the respective groups.

basal   **alternate**   **opposite**   **whorled**

1. Plants without leaves or with leaves reduced to small scales

Cuscuta spp.
pp 260–61

Lemna trisulca
pp 126–27

2. Plants with alternate leaf arrangement

Echium vulgare
pp 76–77

Lappula squarrosa
pp 78–79

Medicago sativa
pp 308–09

BLUE

GREEN

Amaranthus graecizans F
pp 4–5

Amaranthus hybridus
pp 6–7

Amaranthus retroflexus
pp 8–9

Ambrosia trifida M
pp 18–19

Artemisia absinthium
pp 24–25

Atriplex hortensis
pp 150–51

Axyris amaranthoides M
pp 152–53

Axyris amaranthoides F
pp 152–53

Chenopodium album
pp 154–55

Chenopodium gigantospermum
pp 156–57

Iva axillaris
pp 42–43

Kochia scoparia M
pp 158–59

Monolepis nuttalliana
pp 160–61

Potamogeton richardsonii
pp 344–45

Salsola kali
pp 162–63

Xanthium strumarium F
pp 64–65

PINK

Carduus nutans
pp 26–27

Centaurea maculosa
pp 28–29

Hesperis matronalis
pp 282–83

Ipomoea hederacea
pp 262–63

Polygonum coccineum
pp 86–87

Polygonum convolvulus
pp 88–89

Rosa arkansana
pp 358–59

Arctium minus
pp 20–21

Arctium tomentosum
pp 22–23

Campanula rapunculoides
pp 204–05

Chaenorrhinum minus
pp 134–35

Cirsium arvense
pp 32–33

Delphinium bicolor
pp 114–15

Rumex crispus
pp 92–93

Achillea millefolium
pp 16–17

Capsella bursa-pastoris
pp 270–71

Cardaria chalapensis
pp 272–73

Chrysanthemum leucanthemum
pp 30–31

Cicuta maculata
pp 104–05

Convolvulus arvensis
pp 256–57

Convolvulus sepium
pp 258–59

Datura stramonium
pp 296–97

Daucus carota
pp 106–07

Echinocystis lobata M
pp 166–67

Erigeron canadensis
pp 36–37

Fagopyrum tartaricum
pp 82–83

Gnaphalium palustre
pp 38–39

Lepidium densiflorum
pp 284–85

Malva rotundifolia
pp 232–33

Matricaria perforata
pp 48–49

WHITE

Melilotus alba
pp 310–11

Polygonum arenastrum
pp 84–85

Polygonum lapathifolium
pp 90–91

Rhus radicans
pp 378–79

Solanum nigrum
pp 300–01

Solanum triflorum
pp 302–03

Symphoricarpos occidentalis
pp 208–09

Thlapsi arvense
pp 292–93

Trifolium repens
pp 314–15

YELLOW/ORANGE

Abutilon theophrasti
pp 228–29

Berberis vulgaris
pp 68–69

Brassica kaber
pp 266–67

Camelina microcarpa
pp 268–69

Crepis tectorum
pp 34–35

Descurainia sophia
pp 274–75

Erucastrum gallicum
pp 278–79

Erysimum cheiranthoides
pp 280–81

Euphorbia cyparissias
pp 366–67

Euphorbia esula
pp 368–69

Hibiscus trionum
pp 230–31

Hyoscyamus niger
pp 298–99

Lactuca serriola
pp 44–45

Linaria dalmatica
pp 136–37

Linaria vulgaris
pp 138–39

Matricaria matricarioides
pp 46–47

Medicago lupulina
pp 306–07

Neslia paniculata
pp 286–87

Oenothera biennis
pp 130–31

Oxalis corniculata
pp 394–95

Portulaca oleracea
pp 352–53

Potentilla norvegica
pp 356–57

Ranunculus acris
pp 116–17

Raphanus raphanistrum
pp 288–89

Senecio viscosus
pp 50–51

Senecio vulgaris
pp 52–53

Sisymbrium altissimum
pp 290–91

Sonchus arvensis
pp 54–55

Sonchus asper
pp 56–57

Tanacetum vulgare
pp 58–59

Tragopogon dubius
pp 62–63

Tribulus terrestris
pp 96–97

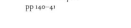

Verbascum thapsus
pp 140–41

3. Plants with basal leaf arrangement

GREEN

Plantago major
pp 338–39

Triglochin maritima
pp 12–13

Typha latifolia
pp 110–111

ORANGE

Hieracium aurantiacum
pp 40–41

PINK/BLUE

Delphinium bicolor
pp 114–15

Plantago media
pp 340–41

WHITE

Androsace septentrionalis
pp 348–49

Zigadenus venenosus
pp 220–21

YELLOW

Draba nemerosa
pp 276–77

Oxytropis monticola
pp 312–13

Taraxacum officinale
pp 60–61

4. Plants with opposite leaf arrangement

BLUE

Knautia arvensis
pp 382–83

GREEN

Euphorbia glyptosperma
pp 370–71

Iva axillaris
pp 42–43

Scleranthus annuus
pp 322–23

Urtica dioica
pp 374–75

PINK

Asclepias speciosa
pp 242–43

Dracocephalum parviflorum
pp 246–47

Erodium cicutarium
pp 144–45

Galeopsis tetrahit
pp 248–49

Geranium bicknellii
pp 146–47

Lamium amplexicaule
pp 250–51

Stachys palustris
pp 252–53

Vaccaria pyramidata
pp 334–35

PURPLE

Chaenorrhinum minus
pp 134–35

Lythrum salicaria
pp 224–25

Apocynum androsaemifolium
pp 120–21

Apocynum cannabinum
pp 122–23

Cerastium arvense
pp 318–19

Gypsophila paniculata
pp 320–21

Silene cucubalus
pp 324–25

Silene noctiflora
pp 326–27

Silene pratensis
pp 328–29

Spergula arvensis
pp 330–31

Stellaria media
pp 332–33

Euphorbia esula
pp 368–69

5. Plants with whorled leaf arrangement

Ceratophyllum demersum
pp 212–13

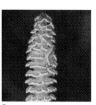

Equisetum arvense
pp 216–17

Galium aparine
pp 72–73

Hippuris vulgaris
pp 238–39

GREEN

Lythrum salicaria
pp 224–25

PURPLE

Elodea canadensis
pp 390–91

Mollugo verticillata
pp 100–01

Myriophyllum exalbescens F
pp 386–87

WHITE

Euphorbia esula
pp 368–69

YELLOW

Key to Seedlings

Identification of seedlings is based on the shape of
the cotyledons (seed leaves). This key does not
include all species in this book, as some species
rarely produce seedlings in nature.

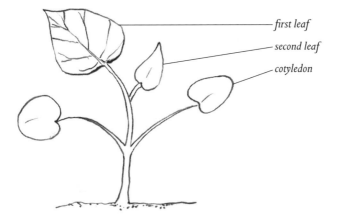

— first leaf
— second leaf
— cotyledon

1. Seedlings with grass-like cotyledons

Cyperus esculentus
pp 362–63

Tragopogon dubius
pp 62–63

Triglochin maritima
pp 12–13

2. Seedlings with heart or kidney-shaped cotyledons

Brassica kaber
pp 266–67

Convolvulus arvensis
pp 256–57

Malva rotundifolia
pp 232–33

Raphanus raphanistrum
pp 288–89

3. Seedlings with lance-shaped cotyledons

Amaranthus graecizans
pp 4–5

Amaranthus hybridus
pp 6–7

Amaranthus retroflexus
pp 8–9

Atriplex hortensis
pp 150–51

Axyris amaranthoides
pp 152–53

Carduus nutans
pp 26–27

Chaenorrhinum minus
pp 134–35

Chenopodium album
pp 154–55

Chenopodium gigantospermum
pp 156–57

Datura stramonium
pp 296–97

Euphorbia esula
pp 368–69

Euphorbia glyptosperma
pp 370–71

Gypsophila paniculata
pp 320–21

Monolepis nuttalliana
pp 160–61

Polygonum arenastrum
pp 84–85

Polygonum coccineum
pp 86–87

Polygonum convolvulus
pp 88–89

Portulaca oleracea
pp 352–53

Ranunculus acris
pp 116–17

Solanum nigrum
pp 300–01

LANCE

Solanum triflorum
pp 302–03

Xanthium strumarium
pp 64–65

4. Seedlings with needle-like cotyledons

NEEDLE

Daucus carota
pp 106–07

Salsola kali
pp 162–63

Scleranthus annuus
pp 322–23

Spergula arvensis
pp 330–31

5. Seedlings with oblong-shaped cotyledons

OBLONG

Descurainia sophia
pp 274–75

Kochia scoparia
pp 158–59

Melilotus alba
pp 310–11

Mollugo verticillata
pp 100–01

Rumex crispus
pp 92–93

Senecio viscosus
pp 50–51

Senecio vulgaris
pp 52–53

Tribulus terrestris
pp 96–97

Urtica dioica
pp 374–75

Vaccaria pyramidata
pp 334–35

6. Seedlings with oval-shaped cotyledons

Arctium minus
pp 20–21

Arctium tomentosum
pp 22–23

Artemisia absinthium
pp 24–25

Asclepias speciosa
pp 242–43

Capsella bursa-pastoris
pp 270–71

Chrysanthemum leucanthemum
pp 30–31

Cirsium arvense
pp 32–33

Crepis tectorum
pp 34–35

Draba nemerosa
pp 276-77

Echinocystis lobata
pp 166–67

Echium vulgare
pp 76–77

Erigeron canadensis
pp 36–37

Galium aparine
pp 72–73

Gnaphalium palustre
pp 38–39

Hieracium aurantiacum
pp 40–41

Hyoscyamus niger
pp 298–99

Lactuca serriola
pp 44–45

Lappula squarrosa
pp 78–79

Lepidium densiflorum
pp 284–85

Linaria dalmatica
pp 136–37

OVAL

Linaria vulgaris
pp 138–39

Matricaria matricarioides
pp 46–47

Matricaria perforata
pp 48–49

Medicago lupulina
pp 306–07

Medicago sativa
pp 308–09

Oxalis corniculata
pp 394–95

Polygonum lapathifolium
pp 90–91

Potentilla norvegica
pp 356–57

Sida spinosa
pp 234–35

Silene noctiflora
pp 326–27

Silene pratensis
pp 328–29

Sonchus arvensis
pp 54–55

Sonchus asper
pp 56–57

Stellaria media
pp 332–33

Tanacetum vulgare
pp 58–59

Taraxacum officinale
pp 60–61

Thlapsi arvense
pp 292–93

Verbascum thapsus
pp 140–41

7. Seedlings with round cotyledons

ROUND

Abutilon theophrasti
pp 228–29

Camelina microcarpa
pp 268–69

Campanula rapunculoides
pp 204–05

Geranium bicknellii
pp 146–47

Hibiscus trionum
pp 230–31

Lythrum salicaria
pp 224–25

Neslia paniculata
pp 286–87

8. Seedlings with spatula or spoon-shaped cotyledons

SPATULA

Achillea millefolium
pp 16–17

Ambrosia trifida
pp 18–19

Dracocephalum parviflorum
pp 246–47

Erucastrum gallicum
pp 278–79

Erysimum cheiranthoides
pp 280–81

Fagopyrum tartaricum
pp 82–83

Galeopsis tetrahit
pp 248–49

Hesperis matronalis
pp 282–83

Knautia arvensis
pp 382–83

Lamium amplexicaule
pp 250–51

Oenothera biennis
pp 130–31

Plantago major
pp 338–39

SPOON

Plantago media
pp 340–41

Sisymbrium altissimum
pp 290–91

9. Seedlings with irregularly shaped cotyledons

IRREGULAR

Convolvulus sepium
pp 258–59

Cuscuta spp.
pp 260–62

Equisetum arvense
pp 216–17

Erodium cicutarium
pp 144–45

Ipomoea hederacea
pp 262–63

Key to Grasses

Grasses in this key have been arranged according to their leaf base and inflorescence.

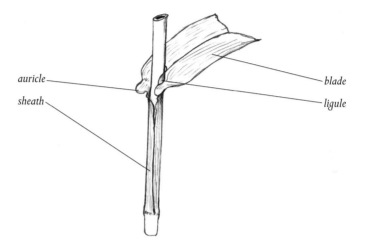

auricle

sheath

blade

ligule

1. Grasses without ligules or auricles

Cyperus esculentus
pp 362–63

Cyperus esculentus
pp 362–63

Echinochloa crusgalli
pp 180–81

Echinochloa crusgalli
pp 180–81

NO LIGULES OR AURICLES

2. Grasses with ligules and no auricles

Avena fatua
pp 172–73

Avena fatua
pp 172–73

Bromus inermis
pp 174–75

Bromus inermis
pp 174–75

LIGULES / NO AURICLES

Bromus tectorum
pp 176–77

Bromus tectorum
pp 176–77

Digitaria sanguinalis
pp 178–79

Digitaria sanguinalis
pp 178–79

Hordeum jubatum
pp 182–83

Hordeum jubatum
pp 182–83

Panicum capillare
pp 186–87

Panicum capillare
pp 186–87

Panicum miliaceum
pp 188–89

Panicum miliaceum
pp 188–89

Poa annua
pp 190–91

Poa annua
pp 190–91

Setaria faberi
pp 192–93

Setaria faberi
pp 192–93

Setaria glauca
pp 194–95

Setaria glauca
pp 194–95

Setaria verticillata
pp 196–97

Setaria verticillata
pp 196–97

Setaria viridis
pp 198–99

Setaria viridis
pp 198–99

Sorghum halapense
pp 200–01

Sorghum halapense
pp 200–01

3. Grasses with ligules and auricles

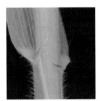

Agropyron repens
pp 170–71

Agropyron repens
pp 170–71

Lolium persicum
pp 184–85

Lolium persicum
pp 184–85

Family and Species Descriptions

marsh smartweed,
Polygonum coccineum Muhl.

tumbling mustard,
Sisymbrium altissimum L.

female flower

male flower

fruit

The amaranth family is a small, diverse group of plants containing more than 900 species native to tropical and subtropical areas of the world. They are primarily annuals, with stalked alternate leaves. Several species have both male and female plants, as well as plants with both sexes. The small, non-showy flowers are usually greenish purple and are found in terminal or axillary clusters. The 3 bracts found below each flower are the distinguishing feature of this family. Flowers have 2 to 5 sepals, no petals, 2 to 5 stamens opposite the sepals, and 2 to 3 stigmas.

The amaranth family is of little economic importance. Many amaranth species have a weedy growth habit.

Amaranth Family

redroot pigweed,
Amaranthus retroflexus L.

Amaranthaceae

prostrate pigweed

Amaranthus graecizans L.

An annual native to western North America.

Also known as: prostrate amaranth, spreading pigweed, mat amaranth, tumbleweed

French names: amarante fausse-blite, amarante étalée, amarante basse, amarante charnue

Scientific synonyms: *A. blitoides* S. Wats.

QUICK ID
- Prostrate growth habit
- Leaves with prominent white veins on the underside
- Greenish flowers in leaf axils

Distribution: Found throughout Canada (except in the Atlantic provinces) and the northern two-thirds of the United States.

Weed Designation
Canada: MB

DESCRIPTION

Seed: Seeds are disc-shaped, black, 1.5 to 1.7 mm across. The surface of the seed is smooth and shiny. Each plant is capable of producing more than 15,000 seeds.

Seedling: Cotyledons are narrow, 4 to 10 mm long and 1 to 1.5 mm wide, pale green with a reddish purple underside. The stem below the cotyledons is often reddish purple. The first leaf is ovate with a shallow notch at the tip.

Leaves: Leaves are alternate, ovate to spoon-shaped, 5 to 50 mm long. Leaf tips usually have a slight indentation. Prominent white veins are found on the underside of the shiny, dark-green leaves.

Flower: Flowers are greenish, 1.5 to 3 mm across, and appear in clusters of 2 or more in the leaf axils. Flowers are of 2 types: male and female. Male flowers are composed of 4 to 5 sepals and 3 to 4 stamens. Female flowers have 4 to 5 sepals and a single pistil. Petals are absent. Small, leaf-like structures below each flower, called bracts, are sharp-pointed and soft.

Plant: This species has green to reddish purple stems, 15 to 120 cm long, with numerous branches that form thick, circular mats. The stems are somewhat fleshy and do not root at the leaf nodes.

Fruit: The fruit is a lens-shaped capsule, about 2.5 mm long. It contains a single seed.

REASONS FOR CONCERN

A common weed of gardens, roadsides, and waste areas, prostrate pigweed is a serious weed of row crops. It competes with the crop for moisture and nutrients. Prostrate pigweed is an alternate host for beet curly top, beet yellows, and tobacco mosaic viruses. Prostrate pigweed is also capable of accumulating large amounts of nitrogen, which MAY CAUSE NITRATE POISONING in cattle.

SIMILAR SPECIES

Purslane (*Portulaca oleracea* L.) is often confused with prostrate pigweed. It is distinguished by its thick, fleshy leaves and yellow flowers (see pp 352-53). The prostrate reddish stems often root at leaf nodes.

purslane

green amaranth

Amaranthus hybridus L.

An annual introduced from tropical North America.

Also known as: prince's feather, wild beet, smooth pigweed, slender pigweed

French names: amarante hybride, amarante verte

Scientific synonyms: *A. hypochondriacus* L.

QUICK ID
 Leaves alternate
Base of the stem reddish
Flower cluster soft and papery

Distribution: Found from Quebec to Manitoba and throughout the northern half of the United States.

Weed Designation
None

DESCRIPTION

Seed: Black, ovate seeds are 1 to 1.1 mm long and 0.8 to 0.9 mm wide. The surface of the seed is smooth and shiny.

Seedling: Cotyledons, 3 to 12 mm long and 1 to 3 mm wide, are dull green above and tinged with magenta underneath. The upper surface of the cotyledons has several prominent veins. The stem below the cotyledons is often purplish red. The first leaves are ovate and have a few hairs on the stalks.

Leaves: Leaves are alternate, ovate to diamond-shaped, and up to 15 cm long. These long-stalked leaves are dull green and prominently veined.

Flower: Flowers of 2 types, male and female, are borne in terminal and axillary clusters. The terminal clusters, up to 15 cm long, and axillary clusters, 1 to 8 cm long, point upwards. Male flowers are composed of 1 to 5 sepals and 1 to 5 stamens. The female flowers have 1 to 5 sepals and a single pistil. Petals are absent. Flowers are about 2 mm across. Floral bracts below each flower are 3 to 4 mm long and soft.

Plant: Green amaranth is a common weed of gardens, fields, and waste areas. It is a slender plant with erect reddish stems up to 2 m tall. The mature plant is hairless, giving rise to another common name, smooth pigweed.

Fruit: The fruit, a capsule 1.5 to 2 mm long, splits around the middle, releasing a single, shiny black seed.

REASONS FOR CONCERN

Green amaranth is a common weed of cultivated fields, gardens, and waste areas. In New Zealand, green amaranth has caused significant losses in cultivated crops. Green amaranth is an alternate host for tobacco mosaic virus. It is also capable of accumulating large amounts of nitrogen, which MAY CAUSE NITRATE POISONING in cattle.

SIMILAR SPECIES

Redroot pigweed (*A. retroflexus* L.) is similar in appearance to green amaranth. Redroot pigweed is distinguished by leaves with scattered hairs, and a spiny flower cluster (see pp 8-9). Hybridization between the 2 species is known to occur, producing plants with intermediate characteristics.

redroot pigweed

redroot pigweed

Amaranthus retroflexus L.

An annual introduced from the southern United States, first observed in eastern Canada prior to 1900; it had spread to British Columbia by 1942.

Also known as: red-root, rough pigweed, green amaranth, redroot amaranth, Chinaman's greens, careless weed

French names: amarante à racine rouge, amarante réfléchie, amarante pied rouge

QUICK ID
⌀ Reddish pink taproot
⌀ Dense flower clusters at the ends of branches
⌀ Plant has bristly rough texture

Distribution: Found throughout Canada (except Newfoundland) and the United States.

Weed Designation
Canada: AB, MB, PQ

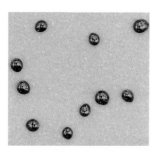

DESCRIPTION

Seed: Seeds are disc-shaped, shiny black, about 1.2 mm wide. Each plant is capable of producing 150,000 seeds that may remain dormant in the soil for up to 40 years. Seeds germinate very late in spring, often after cultivated crops have emerged. Seeds below 2.5 cm of the soil surface will not germinate.

Seedling: Cotyledons are lance-shaped, 3.5 to 10 mm long and 1 to 2 mm wide, and reddish purple below. The stem below the cotyledons is dark red near the soil surface. The first leaves are ovate, prominently veined, and slightly notched at the tip. Hairs on the leaf stalk and margin appear by the third leaf stage.

Leaves: Leaves are alternate, ovate to diamond-shaped, 4 to 15 cm long and 6 cm wide. The margins are smooth to wavy. Leaves often appear drooping because of the long leaf

stalks. The leaf underside has prominent white veins.

Flower: Small greenish flowers, 2 to 4 mm wide, appear in dense terminal clusters, up to 20 cm long. Flowers are wind-pollinated and of 2 types: male and female. Male flowers consist of 1 to 5 greenish purple, spine-tipped sepals, each 4 to 8 mm long, and 5 stamens. Female flowers are composed of similar sepals and a single pistil. Petals are absent in both flower types. Each flower has 1 to 3 spine-tipped bracts (about 8 mm long) at the base, giving the flower cluster a bristly appearance. Flowers are produced from June to September.

Plant: Redroot pigweed has an indeterminate growth habit, which means that it flowers and produces seed until killed by frost. Pale-green or reddish stems, up to 1 m tall, are branched and have a rough texture. The taproot is pinkish red, short, and fleshy. Plants are capable of producing seed within 8 weeks of germination. In most climates, this allows the possibility of 2 generations in a single growing season.

Fruit: The fruit, a capsule, 1.5 to 2 mm long, contains a single seed.

REASONS FOR CONCERN

Redroot pigweed is a large, fast-growing weed that can cause significant crop yield reductions because of the large seed production and viability. It is a host for tarnished plant bug and European corn borer (pests of vegetables and ornamentals), *Orobanche ramosa* L. (a parasitic plant of tomatoes), and green peach aphid. It is also host to several viral diseases in vegetable crops.

SIMILAR SPECIES

Prostrate pigweed (*A. graecizans* L.) is distinguished from redroot pigweed by its growth habit. As the common name implies, prostrate pigweed forms large, flat mats on the soil surface (see pp 4-5).

flower

The arrow-grass family consists of about 20 species of herbaceous plants found in moist alkaline areas throughout temperate regions of the world. The dark-green leaves are basal and somewhat fleshy. The erect flowering stem is leafless, with numerous small greenish purple flowers. The flowers have 3 sepals and 3 petals, all similar in appearance, 6 short stalked stamens, and 3 to 6 feathery stigmas. The sepals and petals often fall off when the flower opens. The feathery stigmas, a trait commonly found in wind-pollinated plants, collect pollen from the wind for fertilization.

Many species of this family contain triglochinin and are POISONOUS to humans and livestock.

Arrow-grass Family

seaside arrow-grass,
Triglochin maritima L.

Juncaginaceae

seaside arrow-grass

Triglochin maritima L.

A perennial native to North America.

Also known as: arrow-grass, spike-grass, salt-marsh arrowgrass

French names: troscart maritime

QUICK ID
🍃 Leaves grass-like, basal, somewhat fleshy
🍃 Flowers greenish white
🍃 Plants prefer moist habitats

Distribution: Found throughout Canada and the United States.

Weed Designation
Canada: MB

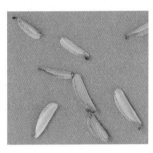

DESCRIPTION

Seed: Seeds are elliptical and yellow-brown, 3 mm long and 0.5 mm wide. Each plant is capable of producing up to 600 seeds.

Seedling: Seaside arrow-grass has a single dark-green cotyledon, 3 to 6 mm long, almost round in cross-section, and grass-like. The tip of the cotyledon is bent or hooked.

Leaves: Leaves are grass-like, basal, and somewhat fleshy. The leaves, up to 50 cm long and less than 6 mm wide, are semi-circular in cross-section. Four to 10 dark-green leaves emerge from the sheaths of the previous year's growth.

Flower: Small, greenish white flowers, 1 to 2 mm wide, appear in a terminal spike-like cluster, 10 to 50 cm long. Flowers are composed of 3 sepals and 3 petals, all similar in appearance, 6 stamens, and a single style. The pistil has 6 feathery stigmas that collect pollen from the wind.

Plant: A plant of moist alkaline areas, arrowgrass has a stout rootstalk with numerous fibrous roots. The stems, up to 100 cm tall, usually have the previous year's leaf bases present. The flowering stem and leaves rise from the same point.

Fruit: The fruit is an oblong capsule, about 6 mm long. Each capsule contains a single seed. Each flower produces 3 to 6 capsules.

REASONS FOR CONCERN

Seaside arrow-grass contains triglochinin and taxiphillin, TOXIC SUBSTANCES that release hydrogen cyanide when ingested causing respiratory failure. Plants are most dangerous in the early spring when livestock are feeding on new growth. Livestock deaths have occurred when 0.5% of body weight in plant material had been ingested.

SIMILAR SPECIES

Slender arrow-grass (*T. palustris* L.), a native perennial, is easily distinguished from seaside arrow-grass. The plant is smaller and has flowering stems, 10 to 20 cm tall. Each flower produces 3 single-seeded capsules. Slender arrow-grass is often found growing alongside seaside arrow-grass. It is less poisonous than seaside arrow-grass.

slender arrow-grass

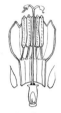

radiate head

disc floret

achene

Aster Family

Often called the daisy, sunflower, or composite family, the aster family is one of the largest plant families in the world. With over 22,000 species, it is a diverse group of plants ranging from herbs to shrubs. The common trait among the members of this family is the flower cluster, referred to as a head or capitulum. It resembles a single flower with 1 or more rows of involucral bracts. The head is composed of several small flowers of 1 or 2 types. The ray florets are often strap-like and resemble the rays of the sun. The disc florets are tubular and often make up the "button" or centre of the flower head. These florets produce 3 types of flower heads. Flower heads composed of disc florets only are referred to as *discoid*, while those composed of ray florets are called *ligulate*. When both types of florets are present in the same head, it is referred to as *radiate*. Plants with ligulate heads often have white, milky juice.

Florets usually contain both male and female reproductive parts, but occasionally only female. Florets lack sepals, but have 5 united petals and 5 stamens that are fused at the top to form a tube around the single style. The style is often split into 2 lobes at the tip. In the aster family, the sepals are highly modified into a structure referred to as the

pappus. The pappus may be represented by scales, hairs, or bristles.

The fruit is called an achene, with or without pappus. The type of pappus is a characteristic often used in identification of the species. Some of the economically important plants of this family include sunflowers, artichokes, lettuce, and calendulas. Hundreds of other species are grown for ornamental value. There are several weed species in the aster family.

Clockwise from top:
nodding beggar-ticks,
Bidens cernua L.;
common groundsel,
Senecio vulgaris L.;
orange hawkweed,
Hieracium aurantiacum L.

Asteraceae

yarrow

Achillea millefolium L.

A perennial native to North America.

Also known as: thousand-leaf, bloodwort, old man's pepper, milfoil, fernweed

French names: achillée mille-feuille, herbe à dinde, mille-feuille

Scientific synonyms: *A. lanulosa* Nutt.; *A. borealis* Bong.

QUICK ID
- Leaves divided 2 to 3 times into narrow segments
- Plants aromatic
- Flowers white

Distribution: Found throughout Canada and the United States, except for the southwestern states.

Weed Designation
Canada: MB

DESCRIPTION

Seed: Seeds are ovate to egg-shaped, dark brown, 1.6 to 1.8 mm long and less than 0.5 mm wide. The surface has fine lines and a slight sheen. There is no pappus. Each plant is capable of producing 4,000 seeds. Germination takes place in the top 3 cm of soil when soil temperatures reach 25 °C. Research has shown that after 9 years, 41% of all seeds are still viable.

Seedling: Cotyledons are club-shaped, 2 to 4 mm long and less than 1.5 mm wide, with 3 prominent veins. The first 2 leaves appear opposite, 3-lobed, with scattered long hairs on the upper surface. Later leaves are deeply lobed and divided into numerous narrow segments.

Leaves: Leaves are alternate, 4 to 15 cm long, and divided 2 to 3 times into numerous narrow segments. They are woolly, bluish green, and aromatic. Basal leaves are feather-like and numerous. Stem leaves, usually 8 to 20, are reduced in size upwards.

Flower: Flower heads appear in terminal round or flat-topped clusters, 6 to 30 cm across. Each head, 3 to 7 mm across, consists of 5 white, sterile ray florets (1.5 to 3 mm long), and 10 to 30 yellow disc florets. There are about 20 floral bracts below the flowers. They appear in 3 to 4 overlapping rows. Each bract is 4 to 5 mm long with pale to dark margins.

Plant: Yarrow has woolly stems and strongly scented leaves. Plants, up to 1 m tall, are rarely branched and very leafy. An extensively branched rhizome allows the plant to form large colonies.

Fruit: The single-seeded fruit is called an achene. Each disc floret produces a single fruit.

REASONS FOR CONCERN

Dairy cattle that ingest yarrow are reported to produce off-flavoured milk. Yarrow is an alternate host for chrysanthemum stunt virus.

SIMILAR SPECIES

Siberian yarrow (*A. sibirica* Ledeb.), a perennial native to western North America, has comb-like leaves and is not as aromatic as common yarrow. Flower heads are composed of 6 to 12 white ray florets (1 to 2 mm long) and 25 to 30 yellow disc florets. Siberian yarrow has stems up to 80 cm tall. It is not as woolly as common yarrow.

Siberian yarrow

great ragweed

Ambrosia trifida L.

An annual native to North America.

Also known as: kinghead, giant ragweed, crown-weed, wild hemp, horse-weed, bitter-weed, tall ambrosia, buffalo-weed

French names: grande herbe à poux, ambrosie trifide

DESCRIPTION

Seed: Egg-shaped, greyish brown seeds are 6 to 8 mm long and 2 to 3 mm wide. The surface of the seed is smooth. Each plant can produce over 275 seeds. Optimal depth for germination is 2 cm. Germination usually occurs when soil temperatures reach 20 to 30 °C.

Seedling: Cotyledons are spoon-shaped, 2 to 4 cm long and 1 to 1.5 cm wide. The stem below the cotyledons is shiny green with purple blotches. The first 2 leaves are lance-shaped with toothed margins. The second 2 leaves are deeply 3-lobed and rough-hairy.

Leaves: Lower leaves are opposite and upper leaves are alternate. Leaves are 5 to 25 cm across and 3 to 5-lobed with 3 prominent veins. Leaves are long-stalked and have a rough, sandpapery texture, with coarsely toothed margins.

Flower: Flower heads are greenish and of 2 types, male and female. Male flower heads are produced in terminal spikes. The head is surrounded by 5 to 12 bracts, each with 3 prominent black ribs. Female flower heads contain 1 flower and appear in clusters of 1 to 4 at the base of male clusters or in leaf axils. Female heads are 6 to 13 mm long.

Plant: Great ragweed is wind-pollinated and produces large amounts of pollen. Plants may be up to 6 m tall on fertile soils, but 2 to 4 m is common. Stems have several branches and are rough hairy. Populations have increased over the last 200 years, coinciding with agricultural expansion in North America. Great ragweed has a high nutritive forage value.

Fruit: An egg-shaped woody bur, 5.6 to 6.3 mm long, greenish tan with purple streaks on the upper portion. It is round to 5-sided and contains a single seed. A beak or spine can be found at the centre of the widest end. Five spines encircle the central beak. One to 3 smaller spines may be found between the outer ring and the central beak.

REASONS FOR CONCERN

Great ragweed is a highly competitive species in moist cropland and pastures. It is the major cause of hay fever in late summer and early fall. Great ragweed is also an alternate host for aster yellows, chrysanthemum stunt, tobacco mosaic, tobacco ring spot, and tobacco streak viruses.

SIMILAR SPECIES

Common ragweed (*A. artemisiifolia* L.) is distinguished from great ragweed by leaves that are divided into several narrow segments.

common ragweed
(flower heads)

common ragweed *(seeds)*

common burdock

Arctium minus (Hill) Bernh.

A biennial introduced from northern Europe, first reported from New England in 1638 and common in Ontario by 1860.

Also known as: lesser burdock, wild rhubarb, clothbur, beggar's-buttons, smaller burdock, cuckoo button, cockle button, hardock, hurr-burr, cuckold dock

French names: bardane, petit bardane, bardane mineure, rapace, rhubarbe sauvage, toques

QUICK ID
- Floral bracts with hooked bristles
- Stems hollow
- Fruiting heads remain closed at maturity

Distribution: Found throughout Canada and the northern two-thirds of the United States, except a small area around the western Great Lakes.

Weed Designation
Canada: BC, MB, PQ
USA: WY

DESCRIPTION

Seed: The club-shaped, mottled brown seeds are 5.7 to 6.1 mm long and 2.2 to 2.4 mm wide. The pappus, consisting of barbed yellow bristles about 1.5 mm long, is deciduous. Each plant may produce up to 18,000 seeds. Seeds are viable for up to 3 years. Alternating temperatures and daylength are reported to increase germination.

Seedling: Cotyledons are dull green, elliptical, 15 to 29 mm long and 6 to 7 mm wide. The stem below the cotyledons is often purplish green. The first leaf is ovate with prominent veins visible on the upper surface. The leaf underside is covered with downy hairs.

Leaves: A basal rosette of leaves is produced in the first year of growth. Basal leaves are up to 50 cm long and 40 cm wide, and white woolly beneath. Stem leaves are alternate and reduced in size upwards. They are usually ovate to oblong.

Flower: Flower heads appear in spike-like clusters in the axils of the upper leaves. Heads are short-stalked, 1 to 3 cm across, and composed of purple disc florets surrounded by several rows of overlapping hooked bracts. The bracts are reduced in size inward and shorter than the disc florets. Bracts do not spread and release seeds at maturity.

Plant: A biennial, common burdock produces a basal rosette of leaves during its first year of growth. The rosette may be up to 1 m wide. Flowering stems appear in the second year and may be up to 2 m tall. The stem is thick, hollow, and grooved. Common burdock has a large fleshy taproot. In Japan, common burdock roots are harvested as a vegetable.

Fruit: The single-seeded fruit is called an achene. Fruiting heads (about 1.4 cm across) attach themselves to clothing and fur with the aid of hooked bristles on the floral bracts.

REASONS FOR CONCERN

Common burdock is not a problem in cultivated land or pastures. It is found growing along fencelines, river banks, and waste areas. Common burdock is an alternate host for cucumber mosaic and tobacco streak viruses.

SIMILAR SPECIES

Greater burdock (*A. lappa* L.) is distinguished from common burdock by flower heads that are 3 to 4.5 cm across. At maturity, the outer bracts spread and release seeds. Each plant may produce up to 10,500 seeds. Another species, woolly burdock (*A. tomentosum* Mill.), is distinguished from common burdock by floral bracts covered with soft woolly hairs and heads 2 to 3 cm across (see pp 22-23).

woolly burdock

Arctium tomentosum Mill.

A biennial introduced from northern Europe.

Also known as: cotton burdock

French names: bardane, bardane tomenteuse

QUICK ID
- Floral bracts covered with soft hairs
- Floral bracts spread at maturity
- Florets have sticky hairs

Distribution: Found throughout Canada and the northern two-thirds of the United States.

Weed Designation: Canada: BC, MB, PQ

DESCRIPTION
Seed: Seeds are club-shaped, mottled brown, 5 to 6.5 mm long. The pappus, consisting of barbed yellow bristles about 1.5 mm long, is deciduous. Each plant may produce up to 12,000 seeds. Seeds are viable for up to 3 years.

Seedling: Cotyledons are dull green, elliptical, 9 to 25 mm long and 5 to 8 mm wide. The stem below the cotyledons is often purplish green. The first leaf is ovate with prominent veins visible on the upper surface. The leaf underside is covered with downy hairs.

Leaves: A basal rosette of leaves is produced in the first year of growth. Basal leaves are up to 45 cm long and 40 cm wide, and white woolly beneath. Lower leaves have hollow stalks. Stem leaves, produced in the second season, are alternate, reduced in size upwards, and ovate with a heart-shaped base.

Flower: Flower heads appear in rounded or flat-topped clusters at the ends of the branches. Heads, 3 to 4.5 cm across, are composed of purple disc florets and are surrounded by several rows of overlapping hooked bracts. These bracts are as long as or longer than the disc florets, and spread when the seeds have matured.

Plant: Woolly burdock is a robust plant that grows to 3 m in height. At maturity, the plant is umbrella-shaped with flower heads at the tips of the branches. A large fleshy taproot is produced during the first year of its life cycle. Stems are often striped with red and green.

Fruit: The single-seeded fruit, called an achene, is about 6 mm long.

REASONS FOR CONCERN

Woolly burdock is common in waste areas, fencelines, and stream banks. The hooked bristles on the floral bracts aid in dispersal of seeds.

SIMILAR SPECIES

Common burdock (*A. minus* (Hill) Bernh.) is distinguished from woolly burdock by its floral bracts. The bracts of common burdock are hairless and do not spread when the seeds have matured. The flower heads are 2 to 2.5 cm across. It is also found throughout Canada and the northern United States (see pp 20-21).

absinthe

Artemisia absinthium L.

A perennial introduced from Europe as a garden plant: its seed was available for sale in the United States in 1832, and the weed had spread to Manitoba by 1860.

Also known as: wormwood, absinthium, madderwort, warmot, vermooth

French names: armoise absinthe, absinthe

QUICK ID
- Plant has characteristic sage odour
- Nodding flower heads
- Leaves greyish green, divided 2 to 3 times into narrow segments

Distribution: Found throughout Canada and the northern two-thirds of the United States.

Weed Designation
Canada: MB
USA: ND

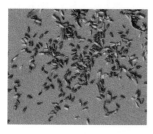

DESCRIPTION

Seed: Seeds are club-shaped, light brown, 0.8 to 1.1 mm long and less than 0.4 mm wide. The surface of the seed is smooth. Each plant may produce up to 50,000 seeds that may remain dormant in the soil for several years.

Seedling: Cotyledons are ovate, 2 mm long and 1 mm wide. The cotyledons have a powdery appearance on the upper surface. The first 2 or 3 leaves are ovate with a few tooth-like lobes on the margin. Later leaves are deeply lobed and covered with dense, soft hairs. Seedlings emerge throughout the growing season.

Leaves: Leaves are alternate, 3 to 10 cm long and wide, and greyish green on both sides. Basal and lower stem leaves are long-stalked and

divided 2 to 3 times into narrow segments.
Each segment is 1.5 to 4 mm wide. Leaf
segments have smooth margins and rounded
tips. Leaves are reduced in size upwards. The
uppermost leaves are lance-shaped, simple, 1
to 2 cm long; they are stalkless.

Flower: Small, nodding flower heads, 2 to 3 mm
high and 3 to 5 mm wide, appear in the axils
of the upper leaves. The flower clusters form
a large panicle. Flower heads are composed
of an outer row of greyish floral bracts and
numerous disc florets. Inside the floral
bracts, a ring of female disc florets surrounds
the inner perfect florets. Flower heads are
usually greyish green with yellowish brown
centres. Each plant may produce up to 1,500
heads, each averaging 36 florets per head.

Plant: A shrubby perennial, absinthe rises from
a woody root that can be 1.25 cm in diameter.
Plants are silvery grey throughout with
several stems rising from the base. The stems,
up to 2 m tall, are hairy when young and
become hairless with age. It was not recognized as a weed until the mid-1950s. The
plant has a strong, sage-like odour.

Fruit: The single-seeded fruit is called an achene.

plains wormwood

REASONS FOR CONCERN
Absinthe is not a problem in cultivated crops,
but is a serious weed in pastures and increases
as livestock graze on more palatable species.
Cattle that consume absinthe produce off-
flavoured milk and dairy products. Small
amounts of absinthe seed in grain have
caused shipments to be rejected for export.

SIMILAR SPECIES
Biennial wormwood (*A. biennis* Willd.), an annual
or biennial sage-like plant, is easily distinguished from absinthe. The stems of biennial
wormwood, 30 to 100 cm tall, are reddish. The
leaf segments have toothed margins. Another
native species, plains wormwood (*A. campestris*
L.), is found throughout North America. A
perennial herb, it is distinguished from
absinthe by its larger flower heads (2 to 4 mm
wide) and narrower leaf segments.

nodding thistle

Carduus nutans L.

A biennial (occasionally an annual), introduced from Europe, Asia, and north Africa in the early 1900s.

Also known as: musk thistle, Italian thistle, plumeless thistle, buck thistle, Queen Anne's thistle, musk bristle thistle

French names: chardon penché

QUICK ID
- Plants spiny
- Flower heads purple
- Leaf bases extend down the stems, producing a spiny wing

Distribution: Found throughout Canada (except Prince Edward Island) and the United States.

Weed Designation
Canada: AB, MB, ON, PQ, SK
USA: CA, CO, DE, HI, ID, KS, MD, MI, MN, MO, ND, NE, OK, OR, SD, TN, UT, VA, WY

DESCRIPTION

Seed: Seeds are elliptical, pale yellow to orange-brown, 3.4 to 4.5 mm long and 1.3 to 1.9 mm wide. The surface of the seed is smooth and glossy, with several ridges running its length. The pappus, which consists of straight white hairs about 25 mm long, is deciduous.

Seedling: Cotyledons are lance-shaped, dull green, 7.5 to 15 mm long and 2.5 to 6 mm wide. Seed leaves have broad white veins. The first leaf is lance-shaped, with numerous prickles on the margin. Later leaves are spatula-shaped and irregularly toothed, with each tooth ending in a prickle.

Leaves: A basal rosette of 6 to 8 leaves is produced in the first season of growth. These leaves are up to 30 cm long and 15 cm wide. Both surfaces of the leaves are covered with fine, woolly hairs. Stem leaves are alternate, deeply lobed, up to 40 cm long and 15 cm wide. The lobes have 3 to 5 spiny points, with 1 prominent yellow or white spine at the tip. Leaves are dark green with a white midrib. The bases of the leaves extend down the stem, giving it a spiny, winged appearance.

Flower: Nodding flower heads, composed of red to purple disc florets, are 1.5 to 8 cm across and appear at the end of stems in groups of 1 to 3. Floral bracts with purplish spiny tips appear in several rows. The outer row of bracts is 2 to 8 mm wide and reflexed. The stalk of the flower head is covered with soft white hairs. It is not spiny or prickly.

Plant: Nodding thistle has a large, fleshy taproot that is often hollow near the soil surface. The unbranched stems are up to 2.5 m tall and densely spiny. Large, flat basal rosettes are formed in the first year and flowers appear in the second year of growth. The plant is so spiny that livestock often avoid grazing near it.

Fruit: The fruit, called an achene, is single-seeded.

REASONS FOR CONCERN

Nodding thistle is capable of reducing yield on pastures and rangeland up to 100%. Once established, nodding thistle forms large colonies that crowd out forage plants.

SIMILAR SPECIES

Plumeless thistle (*C. acanthoides* L.), a close relative of nodding thistle, is distinguished by its erect flower heads that are less than 2.5 cm across. The stem below the flower heads is densely spiny. Plumeless thistle is not as widely distributed as nodding thistle.

spotted knapweed

Centaurea maculosa Lam.

A biennial or short-lived perennial, introduced from Europe into Victoria, British Columbia in 1893.

Also known as: diffuse knapweed, Russian knapweed, yellow star-thistle

French names: centaurée maculée, centaurée tachetée

QUICK ID
- Floral bracts black-tipped, not spiny
- Flowers purple, rarely white
- Leaves covered with translucent dots

Distribution: Found in Nova Scotia, New Brunswick, Ontario, Quebec, Alberta, and British Columbia. It is found in the northeastern United States and along the Pacific Coast, inland to central Montana.

Weed Designation
  Canada: FEDERAL, AB, BC, MB
  USA: CO, ID, MI, MT, ND, NE, OR, SD, TX, UT, WA, WY

DESCRIPTION

Seed: Oblong, greyish brown seeds are 2.8 to 3.3 mm long and 1.2 to 1.6 mm wide. The surface has 10 to 15 faint ridges and several white hairs about 0.2 mm long. The pappus consists of numerous white feathery or comb-like bristles, each up to 2 mm long. Each plant may produce over 20,000 seeds. Research has shown that light reduces germination.

Seedling: Cotyledons are ovate. The first leaves are lance-shaped, undivided, and hairless. Later leaves are deeply lobed.

Leaves: Leaves of the first-year rosette are compound with several irregularly lobed segments. Leaves are alternate, 5 to 15 cm long, somewhat hairy, and covered with translucent dots. Lower leaves are divided into narrow segments while the upper leaves are undivided. Basal leaves, when present, are long-stalked.

Flower: Flower heads, 1.5 to 2.5 cm across, are composed of purplish disc florets. Heads are produced at the ends of branches and in leaf axils. The outer ring of disc florets is sterile and does not produce any seeds. Floral bracts, 1 to 1.4 cm long, have comb-like margins with 5 to 7 pairs of black hairs, each 1 to 2 mm long.

Plant: Spotted knapweed spreads only by seed. The stems, up to 180 cm tall, are often green and purple-striped. Plants have numerous branches that have a slightly sandpapery texture. Unlike diffuse knapweed (*C. diffusa* Lam.), this species does not produce tumbleweeds.

Fruit: Each floret produces a single-seeded fruit, called an achene.

REASONS FOR CONCERN

Spotted knapweed is not a serious concern in cropland as cultivation provides good control. In pastures, spotted knapweed's early spring growth allows it to out-compete other plants for moisture and nutrients. It also produces a chemical that prevents other species from growing in the immediate area. This has enabled spotted knapweed to infest over 8,500 acres of rangeland in British Columbia and hundreds of thousands of acres in the northwestern United States.

SIMILAR SPECIES

Diffuse or spreading knapweed (*C. diffusa* Lam.) is distinguished from spotted knapweed by its spine-tipped floral bracts. Flower heads are white to pale pink, 5 mm across. Two other species of knapweed are found in Canada and the United States. Russian knapweed (*C. repens* L.) has green bracts with white margins and purplish pink flowers. Yellow star-thistle (*C. solstitialis* L.) has yellow flowers and floral bracts tipped with yellow spines.

Russian knapweed

diffuse knapweed

yellow star-thistle

ox-eye daisy

Chrysanthemum leucanthemum L.

A perennial introduced from Europe as a garden plant.

Also known as: white daisy, white weed, field daisy, mid-summer daisy, marguerite, poorland flower, moon-penny, poverty weed, dog daisy

French names: marguerite blanche, grande marguerite, chrysanthème leucanthème

Scientific synonyms: *Leucanthemum vulgare* Lam.

QUICK ID
- Daisy-like flower with white ray florets and yellow disc florets
- Leaves with wavy to lobed margins
- Leaves with clasping bases

Distribution: Found throughout Canada and the United States, except for the north-central plains.

Weed Designation
Canada: FEDERAL, BC, MB, PQ
USA: HI, IL, IN, KS, KY, WI, WV, WY

DESCRIPTION
Seed: Seeds are ovate, brown to black, 1 to 2 mm long. The surface of the seed has 10 prominent ribs. There is no pappus.

Seedling: Cotyledons, 3 to 5.5 mm long and 1 to 2.5 mm wide, are ovate and hairless. The first leaves appear opposite, spoon-shaped, and wavy-margined. Later leaves are toothed.

Leaves: Stalked basal leaves are spatula-shaped, 4 to 15 cm long and 5 cm wide. The leaf edges can be toothed to deeply lobed. The stem leaves are alternate, smooth, and glossy. Leaves are reduced in size upwards. The leaf stalks are short and clasp the stem. The margins are toothed to shallowly lobed and are lacerated near the base.

Flower: Solitary heads, composed of white ray florets and yellow disc florets, are 2 to 6 cm across and appear at the ends of stems. The 15 to 35 white ray florets are 10 to 20 mm long; the yellow disc florets are about 3 mm long. Both types of florets are capable of producing seed. Ray florets are female and do not produce pollen. The floral bracts are green with brown margins and appear in several overlapping rows.

Plant: Ox-eye daisy is a shallow-rooted plant with numerous stems rising from the base. Stems are hairless and can reach heights of 1 m. Reproduction is by both seed and creeping rhizomes.

Fruit: A single-seeded fruit, called an achene, is produced by each floret.

REASONS FOR CONCERN

Once established, ox-eye daisy can quickly replace up to 50% of the grass in a pasture. It is not a problem in cultivated crops as it has a shallow root system that is easily damaged by cultivation. Ox-eye daisy is an alternate host for chrysanthemum stunt, aster yellows, and tomato aspermy viruses.

SIMILAR SPECIES

Although the flowers of scentless chamomile (*Matricaria perforata* Merat; see pp 48-49) resemble those of ox-eye daisy, the leaves are quite different. The leaves of scentless chamomile are feathery or fern-like, while those of ox-eye daisy are broad with few divisions. The white ray florets of scentless chamomile are slightly shorter (8 to 16 mm long) than those of ox-eye daisy. A widely grown ornamental plant, shasta daisy (*C. maximum* L.) has flower heads 5 to 8 cm across and stems up to 90 cm tall. Shasta daisy is very difficult to distinguish from ox-eye daisy. The 2 species are almost identical, except for a few microscopic differences.

Canada thistle

Cirsium arvense (L.) Scop.

A perennial introduced from France in the late 1700s.

Also known as: creeping thistle, field thistle, cursed thistle, corn thistle, small-flowered thistle, green thistle

French names: chardon des champs, chardon du Canada

QUICK ID

- Prickly stems and leaves
- Extensive creeping rhizome
- Purplish pink flowers less than 2.5 cm across

Distribution: Found throughout Canada and the northern half of the United States.

Weed Designation

Canada: FEDERAL, AB, BC, MB, ON, PQ, SK
USA: FEDERAL, AND ALL EXCEPT AR

DESCRIPTION

Seed: Elliptical, light-brown seeds are 3.3 to 4 mm long and 1 to 1.2 mm wide. The pappus is composed of numerous feathery bristles, about 2.8 cm long, and is often shed before the seed has matured. An individual plant may produce over 40,000 seeds. Germination takes place in the top 1 cm of the soil. New seeds will germinate in bright light. Seeds are viable in soil for up to 21 years.

Seedling: Cotyledons, 6 to 14 mm long and 3 to 5.5 mm wide, are ovate, stalkless, and hairless. The first leaves are slightly hairy and irregularly lobed with spiny margins. By the 2-leaf stage, the root system may be up to 15 cm long. Thirty-four days after germination (approximately the 3-leaf stage), an extensive root system with numerous buds has developed. At 4 months, the seedling has a rhizome over 100 cm long. The rhizome bears buds that will produce new shoots in future growing seasons.

Leaves: Leaves are alternate, oblong, 5 to 15 cm long. These stalkless leaves have a curled, wavy surface and several prickly toothed, irregularly shaped lobes. The leaf underside is often covered with soft, woolly hairs.

Flower: Flower heads are terminal or axillary and composed of numerous pinkish purple (occasionally white) disc florets. Male and female flower heads appear on separate plants. Male flower heads are oblong, about 12 mm across. Female flower heads are flask-shaped, up to 25 mm across. A single female flower head can produce about 45 viable seeds. There are several rows of overlapping spiny floral bracts surrounding the male and female flower heads.

Plant: Canada thistle has a deep creeping rhizome that allows it to survive below the cultivation zone. There are approximately 8 buds for every metre of rhizome and a year-old plant may have as many as 200 buds. A single plant is capable of producing over 6 m of rhizome per year. The stems, up to 120 cm tall, are leafy and hollow, becoming hairy with age. The northern limits of Canada thistle's range roughly coincides with those areas where the average January temperature is -18°C.

juvenile

Fruit: Each floret in the female flower heads produces a single-seeded fruit called an achene. No fruit are produced by the male flower heads.

REASONS FOR CONCERN

Canada thistle is an aggressive weed and has the potential to reduce crop yields by 100%. The rhizomes are unaffected by cultivation as they grow below normal tillage depths.

narrow-leaved hawk's-beard

Crepis tectorum L.

An annual or winter annual introduced from Siberia into North America prior to 1890; the first Canadian report was from New Brunswick in 1877.

Also known as: annual hawk's-beard, yellow hawk's-beard

French names: crépis des toits

QUICK ID
- Milky juice
- Flowers yellow, 10 to 15 mm across
- Leaves with backward pointing lobes

Distribution: Found throughout Canada (except Newfoundland) and the northeastern United States.

Weed Designation
Canada: AB, MB

DESCRIPTION

Seed: Seeds are spindle-shaped, 3 to 4 mm long, dark purplish brown. The seed has 10 prominent ribs that are rough to touch. The pappus is composed of numerous white bristles which aid in seed dispersal. Each plant is capable of producing over 49,000 seeds. No dormant period is required for germination.

Seedling: Cotyledons are ovate, 10 to 12 mm long and 2 to 3 mm wide, and hairless. The first leaves are spatula-shaped with a few sharp downward-pointing teeth.

Leaves: Basal leaves are stalked, lance-shaped, 10 to 15 cm long and 4 cm wide. The margins vary from numerous backward-pointing teeth to deeply lobed segments. The stalkless stem leaves are alternate, less than 1 cm wide; they clasp the stem. The leaf margins often roll under towards the midrib.

Flower: Flower heads, 10 to 15 mm across, are composed of 30 to 70 yellow ray florets. Branches usually yield flower heads in groups of 5. There are 1 or 2 rows of floral bracts, each 6 to 9 mm long. The inner row of 12 to 15 bracts has numerous black, bristly hairs. The basal rosette of leaves disappears by the time flowers appear.

Plant: A prolific seed producer, narrow-leaved hawk's-beard can reach a height of 1 m. All parts of the plant exude a milky latex sap when broken. The taproot is branched and extends deep into the soil. Stems are hairless and quite leafy.

Fruit: A single-seeded fruit, called an achene, is produced by each floret.

REASONS FOR CONCERN

Narrow-leaved hawk's-beard is primarily a weed of forage crops, pastures, roadsides, and waste areas. It is occasionally a serious weed in fall-sown crops where the winter annual phase is not controlled by spring cultivation.

SIMILAR SPECIES

Narrow-leaved hawkweed (*Hieracium umbellatum* L.) is often confused with narrow-leaved hawk's-beard. Narrow-leaved hawkweed is an erect perennial plant with numerous yellow flower heads, 20 to 25 mm across. The floral bracts are dark green to black. Seeds are about 3 mm long and have a brownish or tawny pappus.

winter annual rosette

narrow-leaved hawkweed

Canada fleabane

Erigeron canadensis L.

An annual, winter annual, or occasionally biennial native to North America.

Also known as: horseweed, fleabane, bitterweed, hog-weed, mare's-tail, blood stanch, colt's-tail, fireweed

French names: vergerette du Canada, vergerolle du Canada, érigéron du Canada, queue de renard

Scientific synonyms: *Conyza canadensis* (L.) Cronq.; *Leptilon canadense* (L.) Britt.

QUICK ID
- Flowers white to yellow, 3 to 5 mm across
- Stems with numerous branches
- Crushed leaves and stems have a carrot scent

Distribution: Found throughout Canada and the United States.

Weed Designation
Canada: MB

DESCRIPTION
Seed: Seeds are oblong, flattened, yellowish brown, less than 2 mm long. Pappus is greyish white to tan. Each plant may produce up to 10,000 seeds.

Seedling: Cotyledons, 2 to 3.5 mm long and 1 to 2 mm wide, are ovate and hairless. The first leaves are spatula-shaped and hairy on the upper surface and leaf margin.

Leaves: Leaves are alternate, oblong to lance-shaped, 2 to 10 cm long. Lower leaves are short-stalked and often bristly haired, especially near the base. Leaves are reduced in size upwards. The middle and upper leaves, up to 8 cm long and 1 cm wide, are stalkless with smooth margins.

Flower: Numerous flower heads, 3 to 5 mm across, are crowded into branched terminal clusters. Flower heads are composed of white ray and yellow disc florets. The ray florets are short and usually hidden by the floral bracts. Each head contains about 20 disc florets. Floral bracts are 2 to 4 mm long and appear in 2 to 3 overlapping rows.

Plant: A profusely branched and leafy annual, Canada fleabane ranges from 7.5 to 180 cm tall. The stem and branches, which rise from a fibrous root system, are covered with short, bristly hairs. Crushed leaves and stem are reported to have a carrot-like scent.

Fruit: A single-seeded fruit called an achene is produced by each floret.

REASONS FOR CONCERN

Canada fleabane is a serious weed in cultivated crops, pastures, and meadows. The leaves and flowers contain herpene, a chemical that IRRITATES the nostrils of horses. The leaves of Canada fleabane may cause SKIN IRRITATIONS for some people. It is also an alternate host for aster yellows, tobacco mosaic, and tobacco ring spot viruses.

SIMILAR SPECIES

Philadelphia fleabane (*E. philadelphicus* L.), also called skevish, daisy fleabane, or sweet scabious, is easily distinguished from Canada fleabane. The flower heads of Philadelphia fleabane have more than 150 white to purplish ray florets 5 to 10 mm long. This plant is also found throughout North America.

Philadelphia fleabane

marsh cudweed

Gnaphalium palustre Nutt.

An annual native to North America.

Also known as: low cudweed, western marsh cudweed, wartwort, mouse-ear, everlasting, lowland cudweed

French names: gnaphale des vases

QUICK ID
- Plants less than 20 cm tall
- Plants covered with dense woolly hairs
- Flowers whitish to brownish green

Distribution: Found throughout Canada and the western United States.

Weed Designation
Canada: MB

DESCRIPTION
Seed: Seeds are ovate, brown, less than 1 mm long. The pappus is composed of simple white hairs that are deciduous. Each plant is capable of producing over 500 seeds.

Seedling: Cotyledons, 1 to 2 mm long and less than 1 mm wide, are lance-shaped and pale green. The first leaves are opposite and similar in shape and size to the cotyledons.

Leaves: Leaves are alternate, oblong to lance-shaped, 1 to 3 cm long. Leaves have a single vein, are stalkless, and are covered with loose, felt-like hairs. Leaf margins are smooth to slightly wavy.

Flower: Flower heads appear in small, leafy terminal or axillary clusters of 3 to 10. The floral bracts are scale-like, pale brown with white tips, 3 to 4 mm long. The whitish to brownish green or straw-coloured heads are composed of yellowish white disc florets. Ray florets are absent. The outer florets are female, while the inner florets have both male and female reproductive structures.

Plant: An annual of moist areas, marsh cudweed is usually 5 to 20 cm tall. Leafy stems are erect and branched near the base. The whole plant is covered with tufts of loose, white woolly hairs.

Fruit: Each floret produces a single-seeded fruit, called an achene.

REASONS FOR CONCERN

Marsh cudweed is a serious weed in low-lying areas of cultivated cropland. It is also found in roadside ditches and on the banks of irrigation canals.

SIMILAR SPECIES

Low cudweed (*G. uliginosum* L.) is often confused with marsh cudweed. The floral bracts of low cudweed are brownish green, and the leaves are narrower. The whole plant is covered with fine white hairs. An annual plant of moist areas, low cudweed is less than 20 cm tall. Low cudweed is found throughout Canada and the northern United States.

orange hawkweed

Hieracium aurantiacum L.

A perennial introduced from Europe.

Also known as: devil's paintbrush, orange paint-brush, red daisy, missionary-weed, king devil

French names: épervière orangée, bouquet rouge

QUICK ID
- Milky juice
- Flowers orange
- Leaves basal

Distribution: Found throughout Canada and the northern half of the United States.

Weed Designation
    Canada: BC, MB, PQ
    USA: WV

DESCRIPTION
Seed: Seeds are oblong, purplish black, about 2 mm long. The surface has ridges running lengthwise. The pappus consists of simple, dirty-white hairs about 3 mm long.

Seedling: Cotyledons, 2 to 3.5 mm long and 1 to 2 mm wide, are ovate, hairless, and short-stalked. The stem below the cotyledons is often reddish purple. The first 3 leaves are spatula-shaped with a channelled leaf stalk. The upper surface of the leaves has a few long hairs, while the lower surface is hairless. Long hairs are also found on the leaf margin.

Leaves: Leaves are basal, club-shaped, 5 to 15 cm long and 1 to 3.5 cm wide. Both surfaces of the leaves are covered with stiff hairs. The leaf margins are smooth. One or 2 small leaves may be present on the flowering stem.

Flower: Heads appear in compact terminal clusters of 5 to 25. Flower heads, 2 to 2.5 cm across, are composed of burnt-orange ray florets. Floral bracts, 6 to 8 mm long, appear in 2 or 3 overlapping rows. The bracts are covered with black bristly hairs.

Plant: Orange hawkweed reproduces by seed, long-spreading rhizomes, and above-ground runners. The flowering stalk is 20 to 70 cm tall and covered with stiff black hairs. The stem and leaves exude milky juice when broken.

Fruit: Each floret produces a single-seeded fruit, called an achene.

REASONS FOR CONCERN
Orange hawkweed is a serious weed of lawns, pastures, and roadsides.

SIMILAR SPECIES
King devil (*H. pratense* Tausch.) is similar to orange hawkweed. The stems of king devil, up to 80 cm tall, are leafless and covered with black hairs. The 2 species are distinguished by the king devil's yellow flowers. The heads are about 1 cm across. It is found throughout Canada (except Saskatchewan and Manitoba) and in the northern third of the United States.

king devil

poverty-weed

Iva axillaris Pursh

A perennial native to North America.

Also known as: death weed, devil's-weed, small-flowered marsh elder, bozzleweed, poverty sumpweed

French names: herbe de pauvreté

QUICK ID
- Lower leaves opposite and upper leaves alternate
- Flower heads appearing in leaf axils
- Flower heads nodding, less than 5 mm across

Distribution: Found throughout western Canada and the United States.

Weed Designation
Canada: MB, SK
USA: CA, CO, ID, WA, WY

DESCRIPTION
Seed: The egg-shaped seeds are reddish brown to black, 2.6 to 3.3 mm long and 1.6 to 2.2 mm wide. The surface is dull and scaly. There is no pappus. Seeds are rarely produced in nature, and have a very low germination rate.

Seedling: Seedlings are rarely produced in nature. New plants are produced primarily from buds on the creeping root system.

Leaves: Lower leaves are opposite, while the upper leaves are alternate. The leaves are pale green, thick, and oblong, 0.5 to 4 cm long and less than 1 cm wide. Each leaf has 1 to 3 prominent veins at the base. These stalkless leaves are rough-haired.

Flower: Nodding flower heads appear singly in leaf axils. Heads, less than 5 mm across, are composed of 5 to 8 female and 12 to 20 male greenish disc florets. The outer florets are female and the inner male. Flowers are wind-pollinated and produce large amounts of pollen. Floral bracts, 3 to 4 mm long, are united into a 4 to 5-lobed cup.

Plant: Common in highly alkaline areas, poverty-weed forms large colonies and has been known to drastically reduce crop yield. A highly adaptive plant, it can remain dormant under severe weather conditions. The roots are up to 1.8 m deep, cork-like, and impervious to moisture. Under favourable conditions, a single plant may spread over 18 m in diameter. Stems, up to 60 cm tall, are rarely branched. The whole plant has an unpleasant odour.

Fruit: Each female floret produces a single-seeded fruit, called an achene.

REASONS FOR CONCERN

An occasional weed of cultivated cropland, poverty-weed is found primarily on road-sides, railways, pastures, and waste areas. Large amounts of pollen are produced by poverty-weed and may cause hay fever.

SIMILAR SPECIES

False ragweed (*I. xanthifolia* Nutt.) is closely related to poverty-weed. False ragweed, a robust annual with stems up to 2 m tall, has large-stalked leaves, 5 to 20 cm long. Small, greenish white flower heads are borne in large terminal clusters. When not in flower, false ragweed resembles sunflowers. It is found throughout Canada (except the Atlantic provinces) and the United States.

false ragweed

prickly lettuce

Lactuca serriola L.

An annual, winter annual, or biennial introduced from Europe.

Also known as: common wild lettuce, compass plant, milk thistle, horse thistle, wild opium

French names: laitue scariole, laitue vireuse, scariole

Scientific synonyms: *L. scariola* L.

QUICK ID
- Milky juice
- Leaves with a prickly midrib on the leaf under side
- Flowers yellow

Distribution: Found throughout Canada (except Newfoundland) and the United States, except northern Maine and southern Florida.

Weed Designation
Canada: MB

DESCRIPTION

Seed: Lance-shaped seeds are olive-brown, 2.7 to 3 mm long and less than 1 mm wide. Five to 7 lengthwise ribs can be found on each side of the seed; these ribs have minute white hairs or barbs that point towards the pappus. The pappus, about 3 mm long, is composed of numerous white bristles.

Seedling: Cotyledons are ovate, 5 to 9 mm long and 2 to 3 mm wide. The upper surface and margin of the cotyledons are hairy. The first leaf is ovate, prominently veined, and hairy.

Leaves: Leaves are alternate, oblong, 5 to 30 cm long and 2.5 to 10 cm wide. These bluish green leaves are deeply lobed with backward-pointing lobes. The margins are sharply toothed to prickly. Stem leaves clasp the stem with a pair of pointed basal lobes. The midvein on the underside of the leaf has a row of sharp yellowish spines. Leaves often point east and west, giving rise to another common name, compass plant.

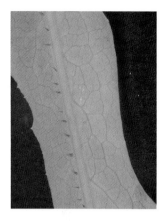

Flower: Flower heads, 3 to 10 mm across and 8 to 10 mm high, appear in a large terminal pyramid-shaped clusters. Heads are composed of 5 to 12 yellow ray florets. Disc florets are absent. Floral bracts, appearing in 3 or 4 overlapping rows, are hairless and 9 to 16 mm long.

Plant: Prickly lettuce has hollow woody stems up to 1.8 m tall, and reproduces by seed only. It has a large taproot that may grow to 2 m deep. The pale green stems are often prickly near the ground surface.

Fruit: Each floret produces a single-seeded fruit, called an achene.

REASONS FOR CONCERN

A serious weed of cropland, orchards, and gardens, prickly lettuce has been reported to reduce crop yields drastically. Reports indicate that cattle feeding on large amounts of prickly lettuce will develop pulmonary emphysema, a chronic respiratory condition. Prickly lettuce is also an alternate host for cucumber mosaic, tomato spotted wilt, aster yellows, lettuce mosaic, and tobacco ring spot viruses.

SIMILAR SPECIES

Common blue lettuce (*L. pulchella* (Pursh) DC.), a deep-rooted perennial, is distinguished from prickly lettuce by its blue flowers and non-prickly leaves. A native plant of central and western North America, common blue lettuce has stems up to 60 cm tall.

common blue lettuce

pineapple-weed

Matricaria matricarioides
(Less.) Porter

An annual native to western North America.

Also known as: rayless mayweed, rayless dog fennel

French names: matricaire odorante, matricaire suave

Scientific synonyms: *Chamomilla suaveolens* Rydb.

QUICK ID
- Plants with a pineapple scent
- Cone-shaped flower heads
- Stems less than 40 cm tall with numerous branches

Distribution: Found throughout Canada and the United States. It is a common weed in northern communities of Yukon, Northwest Territories, and Alaska.

Weed Designation
Canada: MB

DESCRIPTION
Seed: Egg-shaped, light-brown seeds are 1.3 to 1.6 mm long and less than 0.7 mm wide. Seeds are often 5-sided. The surface is glossy with a few dark orange to brown ribs. There is no pappus.

Seedling: Cotyledons are spatula-shaped (about 3 mm long and 1 mm wide) and short-stalked. The first leaves appear opposite and have a pair of pointed lobes near the base. The second set of leaves has several pairs of lobes. All following leaves are alternate.

Leaves: Leaves are alternate, 1 to 5 cm long, and divided several times into narrow segments. These segments, 1 to 2 mm wide, are hairless. The fern-like leaves give off a pineapple scent when crushed.

Flower: Small yellow disc florets, about 1 mm across, are arranged in a cone-shaped head, 5 to 10 mm across. Ray florets are absent. The flower head is surrounded by 2 to 3 rows of greenish yellow floral bracts; these bracts have translucent papery edges. Pineapple-weed blooms from early spring to late autumn.

Plant: A low-branching annual with leafy stems, pineapple-weed grows up to 40 cm tall. The plant is hairless and gives off a pineapple scent when crushed. The characteristic odour aids in identification.

Fruit: A single-seeded fruit, called an achene, is produced by each floret.

REASONS FOR CONCERN

Pineapple-weed is often found growing on compacted soil in farmyards, waste areas, and roadsides. It is also an alternate host for raspberry Scottish leaf curl virus.

SIMILAR SPECIES

Scentless chamomile (*M. perforata* Merat) is closely related to pineapple-weed. It is distinguished from pineapple-weed by its white ray florets (see pp 48-49). As the common name implies, the crushed leaves of scentless chamomile are odourless.

scentless chamomile

scentless chamomile

Matricaria perforata Merat.

An annual, biennial, or short-lived perennial introduced from northern Europe and western Asia.

Also known as: mayweed, false chamomile, scentless mayweed

French names: matricaire inodore, matricaire maritime

Scientific synonyms: *M. maritima* L.; *M. inodora* L.

QUICK ID
- Flowers are white and daisy-like
- Leaves divided into narrow segments
- Leaves are odourless when crushed

Distribution: Found throughout Canada, in the eastern United States, and on the Pacific Coast.

Weed Designation
Canada: AB, BC, MB, PQ, SK
USA: WA

DESCRIPTION
Seed: Seeds are rectangular, dark brown, 2 mm long with 3 prominent ribs. The pappus is composed of small scales; it may be absent. Each plant is capable of producing over 300,000 seeds that may remain dormant for several years. The seeds of scentless chamomile require light for germination.

Seedling: Cotyledons are ovate, stalkless, 2 to 3 mm long. The first leaves are divided into narrow segments. Later leaves are divided into several branched segments.

Leaves: Leaves are alternate, 2 to 8 cm long, and odourless when crushed. The hairless leaves are divided into numerous narrow or thread-like branched segments. Leaves are short-stalked or stalkless.

Flower: Terminal flower heads, 3 to 4 cm wide, are composed of 12 to 20 white ray florets, 8 to 16 mm long, and numerous yellow disc florets, 2 to 3 mm long. The disc florets form a flattened central button. Both types of florets are capable of producing seed. Below each flower head are 2 or 3 rows of overlapping bracts.

Plant: A prolific seed producer, scentless chamomile grows from a fibrous root system. The stems, up to 1 m tall, are hairless and have numerous branches. Scentless chamomile usually flowers in its first year of growth.

rosette

Fruit: Each floret produces a single-seeded fruit called an achene.

REASONS FOR CONCERN

Scentless chamomile is an aggressive weed in forage and non-cropland areas. It has recently been found in cultivated crops. Care should be taken to ensure that plants in cultivated crops do not set seed.

SIMILAR SPECIES

Ox-eye daisy (*Chrysanthemum leucanthemum* L.) is often confused with scentless chamomile. While the flowers are similar in appearance, the leaves are very different (see pp 30-31). The leaves of ox-eye daisy are lobed and not narrowly dissected like those of scentless chamomile. Stinking mayweed (*Anthemis cotula* L.) and wild chamomile (*M. recutita* L.) are similar in appearance but have a strong odour when crushed. Stinking mayweed, as the common name implies, is malodorous. Wild chamomile is pineapple-scented and has flower heads about 2 cm across.

ox-eye daisy

sticky groundsel

Senecio viscosus L.

An annual, winter annual, or biennial introduced from Europe.

Also known as: viscous groundsel

French names: séneçon visqueux

QUICK ID

- Flower heads yellow, composed of disc florets
- Stems hollow
- Stems, leaves, and flower heads with sticky hairs

Distribution: Found throughout Canada and the northeastern United States.

Weed Designation Canada: MB

DESCRIPTION

Seed: Seeds are ovate, tan, 2 to 3 mm long. The surface of the seed has 5 to 10 prominent veins. The pappus is composed of short white bristles, 3 to 4 mm long. Each plant is capable of producing over 1,500 seeds.

Seedling: Cotyledons are oblong, 3 to 11 mm long and 1 to 3 mm wide, hairless. The stalks of the cotyledons are prominently grooved. The first leaves are irregularly toothed with

teeth pointing towards the tip of the leaf. A
few hairs are found on the stalk of the leaf.

Leaves: Leaves are alternate, oblong, 3 to 12 cm
long and 1 to 5 cm wide. Lower leaves are
wavy-margined to deeply lobed. Leaves are
not reduced in size upwards. The upper
leaves are stalkless, clasping, and coarsely
toothed to irregularly lobed. All leaves are
covered with short, sticky hairs.

Flower: Flower heads, 7 to 15 mm across, are
composed of yellow disc florets, 6 to 9 mm
long, and appear at the ends of branches. The
yellow ray florets are small and inconspicuous. A row of yellowish green floral bracts
surrounds the disc florets. The bracts are
usually the same length as the florets and
may be black-tipped.

Plant: Sticky groundsel can be found growing
on roadsides, railway grades, and waste areas.
Sticky groundsel, as the common name
implies, is sticky-haired throughout and has a
strong odour. The stems, up to 75 cm tall,
have numerous branches.

Fruit: Each floret produces a single-seeded fruit,
called an achene.

SIMILAR SPECIES

Common groundsel (*S. vulgaris* L.), a more
common introduced species, is found in
cropland, gardens, and waste ground. The
plant is hairless, which distinguishes it from
sticky groundsel. Common groundsel is
found throughout Canada and the United
States (see pp 52-53).

common groundsel

common groundsel

Senecio vulgaris L.

An annual, winter annual, or biennial introduced from Europe in 1620: the Pilgrims brought the plant to North America as a treatment for the early stages of cholera.

Also known as: groundsel, grimsel, simson, bird-seed, ragwort, chickenweed

French names: séneçon vulgaire, séneçon commun

QUICK ID
- Flower heads yellow composed of disc florets
- Stems hollow
- Stems, leaves and flower heads are hairless

Distribution: Found throughout Canada and the United States, including Alaska.

Weed Designation
Canada: MB
USA: TN

DESCRIPTION

Seed: Seeds are spindle-shaped, tan, about 2.5 mm long. The pappus is composed of a tuft of short white bristles, 3 to 4 mm long. Seeds are sticky during wet weather and attach themselves to fur and clothing. Each plant is capable of producing over 1,700 seeds.

Seedling: Cotyledons are oblong, hairless, 3 to 11 mm long and 1 to 3 mm wide. The stalks of the cotyledons are prominently grooved. The first leaves are irregularly toothed with teeth pointing towards the tip of the leaf. A few hairs may be found at the base of the leaf stalk.

Leaves: Leaves are alternate, oblong, 5 to 15 cm long and 1 to 4 cm wide. Lower leaves are wavy-margined to deeply lobed. They often have a purplish green underside and are prominently veined. The upper leaves are stalkless, clasping, and coarsely toothed to irregularly lobed. Leaves are somewhat fleshy.

Flower: Flower heads, 5 to 10 mm across, are composed of yellow disc florets, 5 to 8 mm long, and appear at the ends of branches. There are no ray florets. A row of yellowish green floral bracts surrounds the disc florets; the bracts are usually the same length as the florets and black-tipped.

Plant: Common groundsel has several branches. The hollow stems, up to 60 cm tall, are hairless and somewhat succulent. Plants are capable of producing seeds within 5 weeks of germination. With a possibility of 4 generations in a growing season, a single seed has the potential to produce over 1 billion seeds.

Fruit: Each floret produces a single-seeded fruit, called an achene.

REASONS FOR CONCERN

A prolific seed producer with the ability to flower at temperatures below 0 °C, common groundsel is a serious weed of cultivated crops and gardens. It is also an alternate host for beet mildew yellowing, beet western yellow, aster yellows, beet curly top, beet ring spot, and lettuce mosaic viruses. Common groundsel contains senecionine, an alkaloid that causes IRREVERSIBLE LIVER DAMAGE IN LIVESTOCK that feed on plants over an extended period of time. The highest levels of toxins are present in flowers, the lowest in the roots.

rosette

SIMILAR SPECIES

Sticky groundsel (*S. viscosus* L.), a less common introduced species, is found occasionally on railway grades and waste areas. The plant is sticky-hairy throughout, which distinguishes it from common groundsel. Sticky groundsel is found throughout Canada and the United States (see pp 50-51).

perennial sow thistle

Sonchus arvensis L.

A perennial introduced from Europe and the Caucasus region of Asia.

Also known as: creeping sow thistle, field sow thistle, field milk thistle, gutweed, swine thistle, marsh sowthistle

French names: laiteron des champs, laiteron vivace, crève-z-yeux

QUICK ID
- Milky juice
- Flower heads yellow, greater than 2.5 cm across
- Stems below flower heads have yellow hairs

Distribution: Found throughout Canada and the northern half of the United States.

Weed Designation
Canada: FEDERAL, AB, BC, MB, ON, PQ
USA: FEDERAL, AK, AZ, CA, CO, CT, HI, IA, ID, IL, IN, KS, MA, ME, MI, MN, MT, ND, NV, OH, OR, PA, RI, SD, VT, WA, WI, WV, WY

DESCRIPTION
Seed: Rectangular, reddish brown seeds are 2.5 to 3.0 mm long and 1 mm wide. The surface has 12 to 15 prominent ribs, each with several coarse teeth. The pappus consists of numerous white hairs, 8 to 10 mm long, which may be shed at maturity. Each plant can produce up to 4,000 seeds, which may remain dormant in the soil for several years. Seeds germinate at 0.5 to 3 cm depth.

Seedling: Cotyledons, 4 to 8 mm long and 1 to 5 mm wide, are ovate with a small indentation at the tip. The cotyledons are somewhat fleshy and contain milky juice. The first leaves are spatula-shaped and irregularly toothed. These teeth point downward and

are tipped by a weak prickle. Cotyledons
wither soon after the first leaves appear.

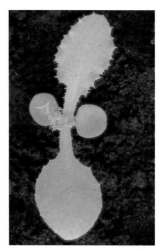

Leaves: Leaves are alternate, lance-shaped, 6 to
40 cm long. Lower leaves are deeply lobed
with soft prickly margins. The leaf stalks are
winged and curled back. The upper leaves
are less deeply lobed, with spine-tipped
teeth. These leaves clasp the stem and have 2
to 7 backward-pointing lobes per side. Stem
leaves are stalkless with rounded lobes at the
base. Most leaves are found on the lower half
of the stem.

Flower: Numerous bright-yellow flower heads, 3
to 5 cm wide, are composed of ray florets.
The dark-green floral bracts below the
flower head are 14 to 25 mm long and
covered with yellow hairs. These yellow hairs
are also present on the stem below the
flower head.

Plant: Perennial sow thistle has an extensive
horizontal root system that grows below the
cultivation zone. The root system, up to 3 m
deep, is easily broken and gives rise to new
plants from buds on the rhizome near 60 cm
depth. Succulent, hollow stems, up to 2 m
tall, may be branched near the top, except
below the flower head. All parts of the plant
contain white milky sap.

Fruit: Each floret produces a single-seeded fruit,
called an achene.

REASONS FOR CONCERN

It has been reported that mild infestations of
perennial sow thistle can drastically reduce
crop yields. Perennial sow thistle competes
with the crop for moisture, nutrients
(primarily nitrogen), light, and space.
Perennial sow thistle is an alternate host for
aster yellows and beet mosaic viruses.

SIMILAR SPECIES

S. uliginosus Bieb., also called perennial sow
thistle, is often mistaken for *S. arvensis*. *S. uliginosus* does not have yellow hairs on the floral
bracts or stem. The floral bracts are green
with white margins. Both are common
throughout the same range.

S. uliginosus

annual
sow thistle

Sonchus asper (L.) Hill

An annual introduced from Europe and north Africa; first collected in Canada in Ontario in 1877.

Also known as: spiny-leaved sow thistle, spiny annual sow thistle, spiny milk thistle, prickly sow thistle, sharp-fringed sow thistle

French names: laiteron rude, laiteron âpre, laiteron épineux

QUICK ID

⊘ Milky juice
⊘ Yellow flower head less than 2.5 cm across
⊘ Leaves with a large rounded lobe at the stem

Distribution: Found throughout Canada and the United States.

Weed Designation
  Canada: AB, MB, ON, SK

DESCRIPTION

Seed: Seeds are elliptical, reddish brown, 2.5 to 3 mm long and 1.3 to 1.5 mm wide. Seeds have 6 prominent ribs, each with a few minute barbs. The pappus consists of soft, white hairs about 7 mm long. Each plant is capable of producing 26,000 seeds that are viable for up to 8 years. The plant requires shallow soil for germination.

Seedling: Cotyledons, 5 mm long and 2 mm wide, are ovate with a shiny midvein on the underside. The first leaf is spatula-shaped with a few pointed lobes. Later leaves have downward-pointing soft prickles. Milky juice is evident by the fourth leaf stage.

Leaves: Leaves are alternate, 6 to 30 cm long, stalkless. They are shallowly lobed with spiny and toothed margins. The base of the clasping stem leaves have large rounded lobes. Leaves are reduced in size upwards, and often have 5 to 11 lobes per side. Leaves are dark, glossy green above and pale green below. In late summer, the leaves turn purplish green and become stiff and prickly.

Flower: Flowering heads are 1.5 to 2.5 cm wide and composed of numerous light-yellow ray florets. The flower head is pear-shaped to round, 9 to 12 mm long. Floral bracts are 9 to 16 mm high.

Plant: Annual sow thistle has hairless stems that are often reddish green. The stems rising from a short taproot grow up to 1.5 m, and are hollow and leafy. All parts of the plant contain a white milky sap.

Fruit: Each floret produces a single-seeded fruit, called an achene.

REASONS FOR CONCERN

Annual sow thistle is a problem weed in cultivated crops, gardens, and roadsides. It is an alternate host for beet curly top, tobacco streak, cucumber mosaic, lettuce necrotic yellow, lucerne dwarf, and aster yellows viruses.

SIMILAR SPECIES

S. oleraceus L., also called annual sow thistle, is often confused with *S. asper*. *S. oleraceus* is distinguished by the shape of the base of the leaf and by the number of ribs on the seed. The base of the leaves is pointed. The seed has 3 to 5 faint ribs on the surface. This species is found throughout Canada and the United States. Some of its other common names are hare's-lettuce, colewort, milk thistle, and milk tassel.

S. oleraceus

common tansy

Tanacetum vulgare L.

A perennial introduced from Europe as a medicinal garden herb.

Also known as: golden buttons, garden tansy, bitter buttons, hind-head, parsley-fern, ginger-plant

French names: tanaisie vulgaire, tanaisie commune

QUICK ID

- Leaves aromatic when crushed
- Stems with numerous yellow button-like flower heads
- Stems somewhat woody and purplish red

Distribution: Found throughout Canada (including the Northwest Territories) and the United States.

Weed Designation

Canada: AB, BC, MB

USA: WY

DESCRIPTION

Seed: Oblong, grey to tan seeds are 1.5 mm long with longitudinal ribs. The pappus is reduced to a short 5-lobed crown. Each plant is capable of producing over 50,000 seeds. Optimal germination occurs in the top 2 cm of soil.

Seedling: Cotyledons are ovate, 2.3 to 4 mm long and 1 to 2 mm wide. The first 2 or 3 leaves are ovate with small teeth on the margin. Later leaves are deeply lobed into narrow segments. Star-shaped hairs are evident on leaves from the first to fourth leaf stage. After the fifth leaf stage, leaves are hairless.

Leaves: Leaves are alternate, 5 to 25 cm long and 4 to 8 cm wide. The leaves are twice-divided into narrow, toothed segments. The leaves have numerous small glands which give the plant its strong odour.

Flower: Flat-topped clusters of 20 to 200 heads are composed of small yellow disc florets. Ray florets are minute or absent. Each flower head is button-like, 5 to 10 mm wide. Overlapping floral bracts are greenish brown with papery tips.

Plant: A somewhat woody aromatic plant, common tansy has a stout rhizome and hairless stems that grow up to 1.8 m tall. The stems are often purplish red near the ground. Common tansy reproduces by both seed and its creeping root.

Fruit: Each floret produces a single-seeded fruit, called an achene.

REASONS FOR CONCERN

Tansy is not a problem in cultivated crops because it cannot withstand cultivation. It is a problem in pastures, however, where it tends to increase because livestock find it unpalatable. Some reports indicate that common tansy is SOMEWHAT POISONOUS to livestock, although it may be eaten when no other food source is available. Tansy is also an alternate host for chrysanthemum stunt virus.

SIMILAR SPECIES

Tansy ragwort (*Senecio jacobaea* L.), an introduced biennial or perennial from Europe, resembles common tansy. Tansy ragwort has ray florets and seeds with a pappus. Leaves and stem are similar in appearance. Tansy ragwort is found throughout Canada (except in the prairie provinces) and on the east and west coasts of the United States. Tansy ragwort contains a TOXIC compound that has resulted in considerable loss of livestock. Ingestion of the plant causes livestock to stagger, hence another common name, staggerwort.

leaf

dandelion

Taraxacum officinale
Weber

QUICK ID
- Milky juice
- Basal leaves
- Flowering stalks leafless and hollow

Distribution: Found throughout Canada and the United States.

Weed Designation
Canada: AB, MB, PQ, SK

A perennial introduced from Europe and Asia.

Also known as: blow ball, faceclock, common dandelion, pee-a-bed, wet-a-bed, lion's-tooth, cankerwort, Irish daisy

French names: pissenlit, dent-de-lion, pissenlit officinal

DESCRIPTION

Seed: Elliptical seeds are olive-green, 3 to 4 mm long and less than 1 mm wide. The surface has 5 to 10 prominent ribs that run length-wise, each with minute teeth. The pappus is composed of fine white-barbed hairs, about 5 mm long. Each flower head produces up to 200 seeds, each plant up to 5,000 seeds. Seeds must be in the top 2 cm of soil to germinate.

Seedling: Cotyledons, 4.5 to 10 mm long and 2 to 3.5 mm wide, are ovate and hairless. The first leaves are highly variable, ranging from wavy to deeply lobed margins. These lobes often point towards the base of the leaf.

Leaves: Leaves are basal, 5 to 40 cm long, with coarse, triangular lobes. The terminal lobe is always largest. Leaves are stalkless. The midrib of the leaf is often hollow and winged near the base.

Flower: Yellow flower heads composed of ray florets rise from the basal leaves on hollow flower stalks, 5 to 75 cm long. Ray florets have 5 tiny lobes at the tip of the corolla. Heads, 2 to 5 cm across and 1.5 to 2.5 cm high, contain 100 to 300 ray florets. The flower head is surrounded by 2 rows of floral bracts. The outer row is often rolled back towards itself. Flower heads open in the morning between 6 and 7 o'clock.

Plant: Dandelion has a fleshy taproot that may reach 2.5 m deep. The whole plant contains a white milky juice. Hollow flowering stalks with a single flower head grow to 75 cm tall. The stem is very short and completely below ground. Reproduction is by seed only. Dandelion is readily eaten by livestock.

Fruit: The fruiting head of dandelion is 3.5 to 5 cm across. A single-seeded fruit, called an achene, is produced by each floret.

REASONS FOR CONCERN

A serious weed of lawns and pastures, dandelion has begun to appear in minimum and zero-till cultivated fields. In all cases, dandelion competes with the crop for moisture and nutrients. It is also an alternate host for aster yellows, beet ring spot, tobacco streak, and raspberry yellow dwarf viruses.

SIMILAR SPECIES

Red-seeded dandelion (*T. laevigatum* (Willd.) DC.) is common in waste areas, roadsides, and lawns. The leaves of red-seeded dandelion are deeply lobed to the midrib, with all the lobes about the same size. The seeds are reddish at maturity. Stems rarely exceed 30 cm tall. Two other introduced species, spotted cat's-ear (*Hypochoeris radicata* L.) and fall hawkbit (*Leontodon autumnalis* L.), are easily confused with dandelion. Spotted cat's-ear is distinguished from dandelion by flower heads that appear in groups of 3 or 4 at the ends of stems. Fall hawkbit has a few scale-like leaves on its flowering stem. All 3 species are found throughout most of Canada and the United States.

rosette

goat's-beard

Tragopogon dubius Scop.

A biennial or perennial introduced from Europe; the first North American report was from Colorado.

Also known as: western salsify, yellow salsify

French names: salsifis majeur

Scientific synonyms: *T. major* Jacq.

QUICK ID
- Milky juice
- Leaves grass-like
- Fruiting head 7 to 10 cm across

Distribution: Found throughout Canada (except the Atlantic provinces) and the United States.

Weed Designation
Canada: MB, ON
USA: TN

DESCRIPTION

Seed: Seeds are spindle-shaped, dull brown, 25 to 35 mm long with 5 to 10 prominent ribs. The pappus is composed of feathery webbed hairs, 2.3 to 3 cm long. Each plant is capable of producing up to 500 seeds.

Seedling: Cotyledons are 4 to 12 cm long and less than 5 mm wide. These grass-like cotyledons are hairless and often arched. The first leaves are similar in appearance. Goat's-beard seedlings are often mistaken for grass seedlings.

Leaves: Leaves are alternate, 5 to 30 cm long, grass-like. These narrow leaves are stalkless and clasp the stem. Leaves are somewhat fleshy, hairless, bluish green.

Flower: Solitary flower heads, 3 to 6 cm across, are composed of yellow ray florets. The flower head is surrounded by a single row of floral bracts. There are 10 to 14 bracts, each 2 to 4 cm long—longer than the flowers. The swollen part below the flower head is often hollow. Flowers remain closed on cloudy days. Flower heads follow the sun in the morning and close mid-afternoon.

Plant: Goat's-beard has a deep, fleshy taproot. All parts of the plant contain a milky white juice. Stems are hairless and often reach 1 m in height. Goat's-beard reproduces by seed only. Young plants are often overlooked as they resemble grass shoots. The previous season's leaves are often found at the base of the plant.

Fruit: The fruiting head of goat's-beard is globe-shaped, 7 to 10 cm across. Each floret produces a single-seeded fruit, called an achene.

REASONS FOR CONCERN

Goat's-beard is a common weed of cultivated crops, roadsides, and waste areas. It is a problem in fall-seeded crops where the biennial phase produces a basal rosette of leaves.

SIMILAR SPECIES

Another goat's-beard (*T. pratensis* L.) is often found alongside *T. dubius*. *T. pratensis* does not have a swollen stem below the flower head and has 8 or 9 floral bracts below the flower. These bracts are about the same length as the flowers. Seeds are 15 to 25 mm long with a feathery pappus. It is found throughout Canada.

cocklebur

Xanthium strumarium L.

An annual, biennial, or short-lived perennial native to North America.

Also known as: broad-leaved cocklebur, clotbur, sheep-bur, ditch-bur, button-bur, noogoora bur

French names: lampourde glouteron, glouteron

QUICK ID
- Plant with a sandpapery texture
- Fruit are bur-like and 2-seeded
- Leaves alternate, ovate to triangular

Distribution: Found throughout Canada (except the Atlantic provinces) and the United States.

Weed Designation
Canada: MB
USA: DE, HI, IA, IN, KS, LA, MD, MI, MS, NC, OK, SC, TN, TX

DESCRIPTION

Seed: Seeds are elliptical with a single pointed tip, light brown to black, 8 to 15 mm long and 5 to 7 mm wide. The seed may be covered with a silver-black, papery membrane. There is no pappus. Each plant is capable of producing over 10,800 seeds. Seeds of 2 types are produced: 1 type germinates readily, while the other has a delayed germination period.

Seedling: Cotyledons, 6 to 7.5 mm long, are lance-shaped, hairless, and somewhat fleshy. The stem below the cotyledons is purplish green. The first pair of leaves is triangular and toothed; the leaves appear opposite.

Three prominent veins can be found on the first leaves. Later leaves are alternate. Cotyledons are photosynthetically active and enable quick growth of young plants. Cotyledons are usually present when the plant has reached maturity.

Leaves: Upper leaves are alternate, ovate to triangular, 2 to 12 cm long. The leaves have a sandpapery texture, with wavy to toothed edges. Leaf stalks, 2 to 8 cm long, emerge from the heart-shaped base of the leaf. Lower leaves are often opposite.

Flower: Small green flower heads appear in clusters in the axils of the upper leaves. Male flower heads are 5 to 8 mm across and have 1 to 3 rows of floral bracts; they are found near the tips of the branches. Female heads have 2 florets surrounded by 2 involucral bracts that eventually become the wall of the spiny bur; they are found in the axils of leaves.

Plant: Coarsely branched stems, 30 to 150 cm tall, are purplish green and rough-haired. The ridged stem often has purplish black spots. If crushed, the plant gives off a distinctive odour. Roots up to 1.2 m deep allow the plant to overwinter in warmer climates.

Fruit: An ovate woody bur, 22 to 28 mm long and less than 17 mm wide, contains 2 seeds. The light-brown bur is covered with numerous hooked spines, 2 to 5 mm long. Large plants may have as many as 5,400 burs.

female flower

REASONS FOR CONCERN

Cocklebur, a weed of cultivated land, pastures, and waste areas, has been reported to reduce crop yields drastically. Cocklebur seeds and seedlings are POISONOUS to livestock and man, but the seeds are rarely eaten because of the spiny bur that surrounds them. Young pigs are often poisoned because they seek out and eat the succulent seedlings. A lethal dose is reported to be 0.75 to 1.5% of body weight. Mature plants are not poisonous.

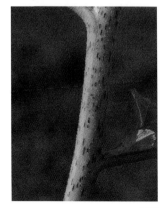

stem

flower

twig with spines

The barberry family is a relatively small family of 600 species of herbs and shrubs. The alternate leaves are simple to compound and have no stipules. Flowers are composed of 4 to many sepals appearing in whorls of 3, 4 to many petals also in whorls of 3, 3 to 6 stamens, and a single style. When an insect lands on the flower, the stamens, which are attached to the petals, spring free and dust the insect with pollen. The fruit is a berry or follicle.

Members of the barberry family are economically important in both positive and negative ways. Some species are grown for their ornamental value, while others provide food for wildlife. Common barberry (*Berberis vulgaris* L.), once widely planted as an ornamental, is a host for wheat rust, a fungal disease of cultivated grains and grasses.

Barberry Family

common barberry,
Berberis vulgaris L.

Berberidaceae

common barberry

Berberis vulgaris L.

A perennial introduced from Asia into Europe as an ornamental plant, common barberry was introduced into North America in the 1600s and proclaimed a weed by Massachusetts in 1754.

Also known as: European barberry, wood-sour, jaundice-tree, pepperidge-bush

French names: épine-vinette commune, épine-vinette, vinettier

QUICK ID
- Shrub up to 3 m tall
- Flowers yellow, in drooping clusters
- Berries red, oblong-shaped

Distribution: Found throughout Canada (except Saskatchewan and Alberta) with infestations primarily in Ontario and Quebec. Once a widespread pest throughout the United States, common barberry is now virtually exterminated.

Weed Designation
Canada: MB, ON, PQ, SK

DESCRIPTION
Seed: Seeds are oblong, dark brown, about 6 mm long. Seed surface is shiny and wrinkled.

Leaves: Leaves are alternate, ovate to elliptical, 2 to 5 cm long. The leaves may appear clustered on the stem. At the base of each leaf is a spine with 3 branches. Leaf margins are finely toothed.

Flower: A drooping cluster, 3 to 6 cm long, of 10 to 20 yellow flowers appears in May and June in the axils of leaves. Flowers, about 6 mm across, are composed of 6 yellowish green sepals, 6 yellow petals with 2 glandular spots near the base, 6 stamens, and a single pistil. Sepals and petals fall off soon after the flower opens.

Plant: Common barberry is a bushy shrub, 1 to 3 m tall, with several stems from the base. The bark is light grey to yellowish grey; the wood is yellowish.

Fruit: Red oblong berries, about 8 mm long, are sour and remain on the branches through winter. Berries usually contain 1 to 3 seeds.

REASONS FOR CONCERN

Common barberry is an alternate host for wheat rust, which affects wheat, oats, barley, and other grasses. The fungus overwinters on the leaves of common barberry and may spread to cereal crops, causing severe reductions in crop yield.

SIMILAR SPECIES

Japanese barberry (*B. thunbergii* DC.), another introduced shrub, is shorter and has smaller leaves with smooth margins. An unbranched spine is located at the base of each leaf. Clusters of 1 to 4 flowers are found in the axils of leaves. This species is not susceptible to rust fungi. It is found throughout eastern North America.

flower

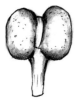

fruit

The bedstraw family is often called the madder family. A large family of more than 6,500 species, it is composed mostly of tropical herbs and shrubs. In temperate North America, members of this family are herbaceous with opposite or whorled leaves. The leaves, usually in whorls of 3 to 8, have stipules similar in shape and size to the leaves. Flowers are composed of 4 or 5 small sepals, 4 or 5 petals fused into a funnel-shaped corolla, 4 to 5 stamens, and a single style. The fruit may be berries, drupes, capsules, or schizocarps.

The bedstraws are economically important, as members of this family include coffee, gardenias, and the quinine-producing genus of *Cinchona*. A few species have a weedy growth habit.

Bedstraw Family

cleavers,
Galium aparine L.

Rubiaceae

cleavers

Galium aparine L.

An annual or winter annual introduced from central Europe and western Asia.

Also known as: bedstraw, white hedge, valiant's cleavers, catchweed, scratch grass, grip grass, goose grass, catchweed bedstraw, spring cleavers

French names: gaillet grateron, gratteron

QUICK ID
- Leaves in whorls of 6 to 8
- Stem square
- Plants cling to clothing by downward-pointing hairs

Distribution: Found throughout Canada and the United States.

Weed Designation
Canada: FEDERAL, AB, BC, MB, SK
USA: CT, MA, NH, NY, PA, VT

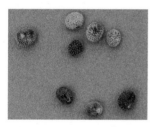

DESCRIPTION
Seed: Seeds are greyish brown, 2 to 3 mm in diameter, round, rough, and bristly. The bristly, hooked hairs, less than 0.6 mm long, often attach themselves to clothing and fur, which assists in seed dispersal. Each plant produces up to 400 seeds. Shallow soil is required for germination, with an optimum depth of 8 to 15 mm; seedlings cannot emerge from more than 4 cm depth. Germination decreases when soil temperatures exceed 20 °C. Seeds are viable for up to 6 years.
Seedling: Cotyledons, 10 to 30 mm long and 5 to 14 mm wide, are ovate with a notch at the tip.

The stem below the cotyledons is often splotched with brown or purple. Roots may be 5 or 6 cm long by the time the first leaves appear. The first leaves appear in a whorl of 4 and are spine-tipped.

Leaves: Leaves, 1 to 8 cm long and 2 to 3 mm wide, appear in whorls of 6 to 8. The leaf margins and midrib have bristly hairs that assist the plant in clinging to surrounding vegetation. The stalkless leaves have a single prominent vein.

Flower: Flowers, about 2 mm across, appear in clusters of 3 to 9 in the axils of the upper leaves. Flowers are often overlooked because of their size. They are composed of 4 minute green sepals, 4 greenish white petals, 4 stamens, and 2 pistils. Plants produce flowers within 8 weeks of germination.

Plant: Weak, trailing stems, square in cross-section, grow up to 150 cm long. The stem has numerous backward-pointing bristly hairs at the base of each leaf. These hairs enable the plant to cling to surrounding vegetation for support. The bristly hairs are found primarily on the corners of the stem.

Fruit: The fruit, 3 to 4 mm long, appear in pairs and are covered with hooked bristles.

REASONS FOR CONCERN

Cleavers is an aggressive weed found in cultivated fields, gardens, and roadsides. It is a weed of particular concern to canola growers. The seeds are similar in size to canola and can be difficult to separate; this results in the downgrading of crop quality. The bristly hairs of cleavers allow the trailing stems to cling to the crop and make harvesting difficult.

northern bedstraw

SIMILAR SPECIES

False cleavers (*G. spurium* L.), another introduced weed, is often confused with cleavers. Its greenish yellow flowers are 1 to 1.5 mm wide and produce fruits that are less than 2.8 mm wide. A related native species, northern bedstraw (*G. boreale* L.), is distinguished from cleavers and false cleavers by erect stems and leaves that appear in whorls of 4.

scorpioid cyme

flower

The borage family is found throughout the world growing in a variety of habitats— ranging from arid deserts to tropical forests. The family, composed of about 2,400 species, is distinguished by the hairy texture of the leaves and stem, and by flowers that usually appear in 1-sided clusters. The simple, entire leaves are alternate and stipulate. The flowers are composed of 5 sepals, 5 fused petals, 5 stamens inserted on the corolla, and a single style. The fruit is a nutlet.

The borage family is horticulturally important and includes borage, bluebells, and forget-me-nots.

fruit (nutlets)

Borage Family

borage,
Borago officinalis L.

Boraginaceae

blueweed

Echium vulgare L.

A biennial introduced from North Africa as a garden plant, blueweed was used as an antidote for snake bites.

Also known as: viper's bugloss, blue thistle, blue devil, snake flower, viper's-grass, cat's-tails

French names: vipérine, vipérine vulgaire, herbe aux vipères

QUICK ID
- Flowers blue
- Plants bristly-hairy throughout
- Hairs with swollen bases

Distribution: Found throughout Canada and the United States.

Weed Designation
Canada: AB, BC, MB, NS, PQ
USA: WA

DESCRIPTION

Seed: Seeds, often referred to as nutlets, are angular, greyish brown, about 3 mm long. Each plant may produce up to 2,800 seeds, which may remain dormant for several years. Seedlings can emerge from 3 cm soil depth.

Seedling: Cotyledons, 9 to 14 mm long and 4.5 to 7 mm wide, are elliptical and covered with fine, needle-like hairs. The stem below the cotyledons is also covered with needle-like hairs. The first leaf is elliptical and bristly-hairy.

Leaves: Leaves are alternate, narrow to lance-shaped, 1 to 15 cm long. The leaves are covered with long, stiff hairs. Each hair has an enlarged red or black base. First-year plants produce a basal rosette of long, narrow, bristly leaves. Stem leaves are reduced in size upwards.

Flower: Blue, funnel-shaped flowers, about 2 cm across, appear on 1 side of the stem. Flowers are reddish purple in bud. They are composed of 5 sepals, 5 petals, 5 long stamens, and 1 hairy pistil. Flower stalks are shorter than the sepals. The flowering stem is bristly haired throughout.

Plant: Blueweed has a stout, black taproot. Several stems rise from a single taproot. The stems are reddish, up to 90 cm tall, and covered with bristly hairs with swollen red or black bases.

Fruit: Each flower produces 4 nutlets.

REASONS FOR CONCERN

Blueweed is not a weed of cultivated crops. An unpalatable plant, blueweed increases in overgrazed pastures, replacing many desirable plants. Blueweed is an alternate host for cabbage black ring spot and tobacco mosaic viruses.

SIMILAR SPECIES

Borage (*Borago officinalis* L.), a common garden plant, has escaped cultivation to become a weed. Borage has cup-shaped blue flowers, 2 to 3 cm across, which distinguishes it from blueweed. The flower stalks of borage are longer than the sepals.

rosette

borage

bluebur

Lappula squarrosa
(Retz.) Dumort.

An annual or winter annual introduced from the eastern Mediterranean region of Europe, bluebur was first reported in North America at Maryland in 1698 and was reported as common in Montreal by 1792.

Also known as: stick-tights, beggar-ticks, stick-seed, sheepbur, European sticktight, bur forget-me-not, European stickweed

French names: bardanette épineuse

Scientific synonyms: *L. echinata* Gilib.

QUICK ID
- Flowers blue
- Seeds with 2 rows of hooked bristles
- Plant has a mousy odour

Distribution: Found throughout Canada and United States, including Alaska.

Weed Designation
Canada: FEDERAL, AB, MB, SK
USA: AK

DESCRIPTION
Seed: Seeds are ovate, greyish brown, and 3.5 to 4 mm long with 2 rows of hooked prickles. Seeds attach to clothing and fur, which assists in dispersal. Winter annual plants may produce as many as 40,000 seeds, while annuals produce up to 2,000. Seeds remain viable in soil for up to 5 years. Germination occurs in the top 2 cm of soil.

Seedling: Cotyledons, 5 to 7 mm long and 2.5 to 4 mm wide, are ovate and hairless. The first leaves, similar in shape and covered with stiff, white hairs, have a distinct crease along the midrib. The first 2 leaves may appear opposite.

Leaves: Leaves are alternate, 2 to 7 cm long, reduced in size upwards. The lower leaves are oblong, stalked, and blunt-tipped. Leaves are covered with stiff, white hairs on both surfaces. The upper leaves are stalkless.

Flower: Flowers are blue with a yellow throat, 3 to 4 mm wide. They appear near the ends of stems in leafy clusters. Flowers are composed of 5 united sepals, 5 united petals, 5 stamens, and a single pistil.

Plant: Bluebur is a profusely branched plant with stems up to 60 cm tall. The entire plant is covered with stiff, white hairs and has a mousy odour. The hairs usually lie flat against the stems and leaves. Plants as short as 3 cm are capable of producing flowers and fruit.

Fruit: Each flower produces 4 nutlets. Each nutlet has 2 rows of hooked prickles that have star-shaped tips. The stalks of the fruit are straight and erect.

REASONS FOR CONCERN

Bluebur is not a major weed in cultivated crops but may increase in overgrazed pastures. It is commonly found on roadsides and waste areas. The hooked bristles on the seed assist in the spread of the weed.

SIMILAR SPECIES

Western bluebur (*L. occidentalis* (S. Wats.) Greene), a weedy native annual of western North America, can be distinguished from bluebur by its seeds. Western bluebur seeds have 1 row of hooked prickles while bluebur seeds have 2. Another native species, stick-seed (*Hackelia floribunda* (Lehm.) I.M. Johnson), resembles both bluebur species. The distinguishing feature between stick-seed and bluebur is the stalk of the fruit: the fruiting stalk of stick-seed is curved or bent downwards. The stems, 50 to 100 cm tall, have leafless flowering clusters, and the flowers, 5 to 8 mm across, are light blue with a yellow throat.

rosette

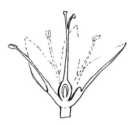

flower

leaf base with ocrea

The buckwheats, a relatively small family of
1,000 species, have their greatest diversity in
western North America. Species are herbs
and shrubs with alternate, opposite, whorled,
or basal leaves. At the base of the simple
leaves, 2 stipules that are fused surround the
stem and form a sheath called an *ocrea*. This
structure is a distinguishing characteristic of
this family. Flowers consist of 2 to 6 petal-like
sepals that appear in 2 whorls, 3 to 9 stamens
and 2 to 4 styles. Petals are absent. The fruit,
an achene, is 3-sided or flattened.

Members of the buckwheat family are of little
economic importance. Some well-known
species are rhubarb and cultivated buckwheat. Many members of this family are
weeds.

fruit

fruit

Buckwheat
Family

marsh smartweed,
Polygonum coccineum
Muhl.

Polygonaceae

tartary buckwheat

Fagopyrum tartaricum
(L.) Gaertn.

An annual introduced from the Himalayan region of Asia as a crop plant.

Also known as: tartarian buckwheat, sarrasin

French names: sarrasin de tartarie

Scientific synonyms: *F. sagittatum* Gilib.

QUICK ID
- Ocrea present
- Leaves triangular
- Plant erect

Distribution: Found throughout Canada and the United States. Tartary buckwheat is a troublesome weed in north-central Alberta and west-central Manitoba.

Weed Designation
Canada: AB, BC, MB, SK

DESCRIPTION

Seed: Seeds are 3-sided and dull grey to brown with a wrinkled surface. The seed is 6 mm long and similar in size to cereal grains, making it difficult to separate. Each plant is capable of producing up to 1,100 seeds.

Seedling: Cotyledons are round, stalked, and notched at the base. The first leaves are triangular with rounded basal lobes. A papery sheath, called an ocrea, is present at the base of the leaves.

Leaves: Leaves, 3 to 10 cm long, are alternate, triangular, and slightly longer than wide. An ocrea is present at the base of the leaf stalks.

Flower: Flowers appear in open terminal and axillary clusters. The greenish white flowers, about 5 mm wide, are composed of 5 petal-like sepals, 8 stamens, and 1 pistil. Petals are absent. Flowering occurs within 4 weeks of germination.

Plant: Tartary buckwheat is an erect plant with stems up to 80 cm tall. The plant is light green and stays green until killed by frost. The plant is hairless throughout.

Fruit: Each flower produces a single-seeded fruit, called an achene.

REASONS FOR CONCERN

Tartary buckwheat has been reported to reduce cereal crop yields by 50%, canola crops by 45%, and flax crops by 70%. Besides competing with the crop for moisture and nutrients, tartary buckwheat can affect the grade and quality of the crop. Harvested crops containing large amounts of tartary buckwheat seed cannot be used for flour, rolled oats, or malting processes.

SIMILAR SPECIES

Cultivated buckwheat (*F. esculentum* Moench) is quite similar to tartary buckwheat. Cultivated buckwheat has stems up to 60 cm tall that turn reddish at maturity. The fruit is smooth, unlike that of tartary buckwheat. Cultivated buckwheat is found throughout Canada and the northern United States.

common knotweed

Polygonum arenastrum
Jord. ex Bor.

An annual (occasionally a perennial) introduced from Europe, common knotweed was first reported in North America in 1809.

Also known as: yard knotweed, knotgrass, doorweed, matgrass, pinkweed, birdgrass, stonegrass, waygrass, goose grass, ninety-knots, bird's-tongue, cowgrass, road-spread

French names: renouée des oiseaux, traînasse, renouée aviculaire

Scientific synonyms: *P. aviculare* L.

QUICK ID

- Prostrate growth habit
- Ocrea present
- Flowers greenish, appearing in leaf axils

Distribution: Found throughout Canada and the United States.

Weed Designation
Canada: MB, PQ

DESCRIPTION

Seed: Seeds are egg-shaped and 3-sided, dark reddish brown, and 2 to 2.5 mm long. The angular seeds have a smooth, shiny surface. Plants produce between 125 and 200 seeds. Germination occurs at or near the soil surface.

Seedling: Cotyledons, 6 to 15 mm long and 1 to 2 mm wide, are united at the base and form a small cup. The first leaves are spatula-shaped and bluish green. A papery white sheath, called an ocrea, is present the base of each leaf.

Leaves: Leaves are alternate, oblong, 6 to 50 mm long and 1 to 8 mm wide. The leaves are bluish green with short stalks. The ocrea, a silvery translucent sheath with jagged edges, can be found at the base of each leaf. The ocrea splits as fruit mature and enlarge.

Flower: Small flowers about 2 mm across appear in groups of 1 to 5 in the axils of leaves. The 5 sepals, 2 to 3 mm long, are green with pinkish white edges. Petals are absent. There are 3 to 9 stamens and 2 or 3 styles.

Plant: A prostrate growing annual, common knotweed has a deep, wiry taproot. The stems, up to 1 m long, usually have swollen leaf nodes. Stems have several branches, giving the plant a mat-like appearance.

Fruit: The single-seeded fruit, called an achene, is 3-sided.

REASONS FOR CONCERN

Common knotweed, a weed of waste areas, has recently appeared in grain fields. It may become a problem because of its prolific seed production and long viability period. It is also an alternate host for aster yellows, beet curly top, and beet ring spot viruses.

SIMILAR SPECIES

Striate knotweed (*P. erectum* L.), a native annual, is often found growing with common knotweed. Striate knotweed has ascending or erect branches and leaves 1 to 3 cm long. The sepals are yellowish green and 3 mm long. Seeds are yellowish brown and 2.5 mm long.

marsh smartweed

Polygonum coccineum
Muhl.

A perennial native to North America

Also known as: water smartweed, tansy mustard, devil's-shoestring, tanweed, shoe-string

French names: renouée écarlate, persicaire des marais

Scientific synonyms: *P. muhlenbergii* (Mesn.) S. Wats.; *P. rigidulum* Sheldon

QUICK ID
- Flowers pink
- Leaves and ocrea hairy
- Plant of moist habitats

Distribution: Found throughout Canada and the northern half of the United States.

Weed Designation
Canada: MB   USA: AK, KS, OK

DESCRIPTION
Seed: Seeds are lens-shaped, flattened on 2 sides, reddish brown to black. The seeds are 2.5 to 3 mm long and less than 0.7 mm across. The seed surface is shiny.

Seedling: Cotyledons, 7 to 18 mm long and 2 to 2.5 mm wide, are dull purplish green. The upper surface of the cotyledons is covered with short, translucent hairs. The first leaf is hairy on the margin and on the midvein below. The sheath at the base of the first leaf is hairless, becoming hairy with age.

Leaves: Leaves are alternate, lance-shaped, 5 to 20 cm long. Floating leaves, if present, are long-stalked and hairless. Leaves rising above the water surface are short-stalked and somewhat hairy. Leaves have pointed tips and rounded bases. The ocrea, a papery sheath at the base of leaves, has numerous stiff, white hairs.

Flower: Dense cylindrical clusters of flowers, 4 to 18 cm long and 7 to 15 mm thick, appear at the ends of stems. The stalk of the flower cluster is hairy. Flowers are of 2 types: 1 with long stamens and short styles, the other with short stamens and long styles. Flowers are composed of 4 to 6 pink sepals, each 4 to 5 mm long, 3 to 9 stamens, and 2 or 3 styles. The sepals are about 7 mm long when the fruit has matured.

Plant: A plant of moist soil or wetland habitats, marsh smartweed has fleshy, whitish tan roots. These creeping rhizomes are tough and woody. Stems, up to 1 m long, are enlarged at nodes. Plants growing in northern climates rarely produce seeds.

Fruit: Each flower produces a single-seeded fruit, called an achene.

REASONS FOR CONCERN

Marsh smartweed is a common weed of moist, low-lying areas of cultivated fields and margins of sloughs.

SIMILAR SPECIES

Water smartweed (*P. amphibium* L.), a native aquatic plant, is similar in appearance to marsh smartweed. The flower cluster of water smartweed is less than 4 cm long, and the stalk of the flower cluster is hairless, as are the leaves and stems.

water smartweed

wild buckwheat

Polygonum convolvulus L.

QUICK ID
- Twining stems
- Leaves arrowhead-shaped
- Ocrea present

Distribution: Found throughout Canada and the United States.

Weed Designation
Canada: AB, MB, PQ, SK

An annual introduced from Europe as a contaminant in seed; the first report in North America was from California in 1860, while the first Canadian report was from Manitoba in 1873.

Also known as: black bindweed, dullseed cornbind, knot bindweed, bear-bind, ivy bindweed, climbing knotweed, cornbind, devil's-bindweed, blackbird bindweed

French names: renouée liseron, faux liseron, sarrasin sauvage

Scientific synonyms: *Bilderdykia convolvulus* (L.) Dumort.; *Tiniaria convolvulus* (L.) Webb. & Moq.

DESCRIPTION

Seed: Seeds are ovate, 3-sided, dull black, 3 to 4 mm long. The seeds are often enclosed in the dried green or brown sepals. Each plant is capable of producing over 30,000 seeds. The hard seed coat allows the seed to remain dormant in the soil for several years. Germination occurs at 0.5 to 5 cm depth, although research has shown emergence from 19 cm depth. Light is not required for germination.

Seedling: Cotyledons are lance-shaped, 7 to 33 mm long and less than 8 mm wide. The cotyledons are attached at 120° to one another. The stem below the cotyledons is often reddish purple. The first leaves are arrowhead-shaped with downward-pointing lobes. A papery sheath, called an ocrea, is found at the base of the first leaves.

Leaves: Leaves are alternate, 2 to 6 cm long, arrowhead-shaped with backward-pointing basal lobes. The tips of the leaves are pointed. The lower leaves are broader than the upper leaves. The leaves are long-stalked and emerge from a papery sheath that surrounds the stem.

Flower: Greenish pink flowers, about 5 mm across, are borne in drooping axillary or terminal clusters of 2 to 6. Flowers are composed of 4 to 6 greenish white, petal-like sepals, 3 to 9 stamens, and 2 or 3 styles.

Plant: A weak-stemmed, twining or trailing plant, wild buckwheat has a deep taproot. Stems and branches are hairless and grow up to 2 m in length. Stems twine on vegetation or structures for support.

Fruit: The fruit, an achene, is 3-sided and contains a single seed.

REASONS FOR CONCERN

Wild buckwheat reduces crop yields by competing for moisture, nutrients, and light. The twining nature of wild buckwheat entangles the crop and makes harvesting difficult. It is also an alternate host for beet yellows, cucumber mosaic, alfalfa mosaic, tobacco rattle, aster yellows, beet ring spot, tobacco mosaic, and tomato spotted wilt.

SIMILAR SPECIES

Field bindweed (*Convolvulus arvensis* L.) is often confused with wild buckwheat. Field bindweed has white or pink trumpet-shaped flowers, 1.5 to 2 cm long. The leaves of field bindweed have a rounded tip, unlike those of wild buckwheat.

field bindweed

green smartweed

Polygonum lapathifolium L.

An annual native to western North America.

Also known as: pale persicaria, pale smartweed, willow-weed, knotweed

French names: persicaire pâle, persicaire à feuilles patience, persicaire élevée

Scientific synonyms: *P. scabrum* Moench

QUICK ID
- Leaves with a black "thumbprint"
- Ocrea present
- Flowers greenish white to pink

Distribution: Found throughout Canada and the United States.

Weed Designation
Canada: MB, PQ

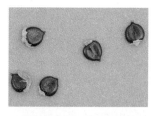

DESCRIPTION

Seed: Seeds are somewhat heart-shaped, shiny black to dark brown, 2.5 to 3.5 mm long and 2.5 mm wide. Seeds are usually concave on both sides. Remnants of the sepals often remain attached after maturity. Each plant may produce between 800 and 1,500 seeds. Germination occurs in the top 4 cm of soil.

Seedling: Cotyledons are ovate, 4 to 15 mm long and less than 5 mm wide. The upper surface of the cotyledons is rough and slightly hairy. The first leaves are alternate and densely hairy on the leaf underside. Leaves after the 5 to 7-leaf stage are hairless. A papery sheath, called an ocrea, surrounds the leaf stalk.

Leaves: Leaves are alternate, stalked, lance-shaped, 5 to 20 cm long. The leaves have a dark blotch or "thumbprint" near the middle of the leaf. The upper leaves have sticky yellow dots or hairs on the underside. The papery sheath at the base of the leaf, called an ocrea, has smooth margins and short hairs.

Flower: Dense terminal and axillary clusters of greenish white to pink flowers are 1 to 10 cm long. Flowers, less than 2.5 mm across, are composed of 5 petal-like sepals, 3 to 9 stamens, and 2 or 3 styles.

Plant: Green smartweed has erect to spreading branched stems, 20 to 150 cm tall. The lower stem nodes of smartweed will often root if they come into contact with soil.

Fruit: The fruit, an achene, is heart-shaped and contains a single seed.

REASONS FOR CONCERN

Green smartweed competes with cultivated crops for moisture and nutrients; it also tends to dry slower than the crop and often delays harvest. Green smartweed is an alternate host for beet curly top virus.

fruit

SIMILAR SPECIES

Lady's-thumb (*P. persicaria* L.), an introduced weed from Europe, is often confused with green smartweed. The flowers of lady's-thumb are pink or purplish and borne in cylindrical terminal and axillary clusters. The leaves, 3 to 15 cm long, have a purplish black spot on the leaf like green smartweed, but lack sticky yellow hairs on the underside. The ocrea has several stiff bristly hairs, each 1 to 2 mm long. Seeds are 3-sided or lens-shaped. Japanese knotweed or fleeceflower (*P. cuspidatum* Sieb & Zucc.), an introduced species from Asia, is found throughout Canada, except for Alberta and Saskatchewan. A large perennial with hollow, reddish purple stems up to 2.5 m tall, it has showy clusters of white flowers. The leaves are 7.5 to 15 cm long and 5 to 13 cm wide.

curled dock

Rumex crispus L.

A perennial introduced from Europe, curled dock was first observed in North America in 1748.

Also known as: yellow dock, curly dock, sour dock

French names: patience crépue, patience rumex crépu

DESCRIPTION

Seed: Seeds are 3-sided, reddish brown, 2 to 2.5 mm long. Each plant is capable of producing over 60,000 seeds. Research has shown that after 50 years, 52% of seeds will germinate, with some seeds still viable after 80 years. Although light is required for germination, seeds will germinate from a depth of 3 cm.

Seedling: Cotyledons, 7 to 16.3 mm long and 1.5 to 5.1 mm wide, are oblong, hairless, dull green. The first leaves, lance-shaped with prominent veins on the underside, are surrounded by a papery sheath at the base.

Leaves: Lance-shaped leaves, 10 to 30 cm long, are alternate with wavy or crinkled leaf margins. The leaf stalk is 2.5 to 5 cm long, with a papery sheath surrounding the stem. Leaves are reduced in size upward. A basal rosette of leaves, 10 to 30 cm long, is produced in the first year of growth. The ocrea, a papery sheath at the base of the leaf, is up to 5 cm long, turning brown and papery with age.

Flower: Greenish red flowers, about 4 mm across, are borne in terminal clusters up to 60 cm long. The flowers are composed of an outer whorl of 3 green sepals and an inner whorl of 3 red sepals, 6 stamens, and 1 pistil. The inner 3 sepals enlarge as the fruit matures. Petals are absent. The stalks of flowers are jointed. The flower cluster turns brown at maturity.

Plant: A robust plant, curled dock has a thick, fleshy taproot with a yellow center. Roots can grow up to 1.5 m deep. The reddish stems are rarely branched and grow up to 1.6 m tall. The stem is enlarged at leaf and branch nodes.

juvenile

Fruit: The fruit, an achene, is 3-sided and enclosed by the inner sepals. Seeds are spread by wind and water.

REASONS FOR CONCERN
Curled dock is common in moist areas and low-lying depressions; it is a troublesome weed in cultivated cropland and pastures. The seeds and vegetation of curled dock are TOXIC to poultry. Curled dock is also an alternate host for beet curly top, cucumber mosaic, rhubarb ring spot, tobacco broad ring spot, tobacco mosaic, tobacco streak, and tobacco ring spot.

cross-section of root

SIMILAR SPECIES
Narrow-leaved dock (*R. triangulivalvis* (Dans.) Rech. f.) is often found growing alongside curled dock. Narrow-leaved dock has small side branches below the flower cluster. The leaves are 10 to 30 cm long with flat to wavy margins. It is found throughout Canada and the United States.

flower

The caltrop family is a small family of 250 species of herbs, shrubs, and trees found in arid tropic and subtropical regions. Leaves are opposite, simple, or compound and stipulate. The flowers are composed of 4 to 5 sepals, 4 to 5 petals, 3 to 15 stamens (commonly 10), and a single style. The fruit may be a capsule, schizocarp, berry, or drupe.

leaf arrangement

fruit

Caltrop
Family

puncture-vine,
Tribulus terrestris L.

Zygophyllaceae

puncture-vine

Tribulus terrestris L.

An annual introduced from the Mediterranean region of southern Europe and the northern fringes of the Sahara Desert in Africa.

Also known as: caltrop, ground burnut, tack-weed

DESCRIPTION

Seed: Seeds are wedge-shaped, tan, 4.7 to 5.7 mm long and 3.5 to 6 mm wide. One or 2 short spines, each 3 to 5 mm long, radiate from the midpoint of the top of the seed. The surface is covered with ridges and prominent white bristles which are easily broken. Each plant can produce up to 10,000 seeds which remain viable for 4 to 5 years.

Seedling: Cotyledons, 8 to 15 mm long and 3 to 4 mm wide, are oblong. Ranging from peach to green, the cotyledons are rough-textured, thick, notched at the tip, and distinctly creased on the upper surface. The stem below the cotyledons is salmon-coloured and covered with short hairs. The first leaf, composed of 6 to 10 leaflets, is bristly with sharp-pointed hairs.

Leaves: Leaves are opposite, about 6 cm long, and composed of 8 to 16 leaflets. The leaflets, 5 to 15 mm long and 5 mm wide, are slightly to densely hairy. Stipules are up to 1 cm long.

Flower: Pale-yellow flowers, about 2 cm across, appear singly in the axils of leaves. Flowers are composed of 5 sepals (3 to 5 mm long), 5 petals (3 to 12 mm long), 10 stamens, and 1 pistil. Flowering occurs within 2 weeks of germination.

Plant: Puncture-vine is a densely hairy, branched annual of semi-arid regions. The woody taproot extends to 2.6 m deep and spreads to 6.6 m in diameter. The green to reddish brown stems are prostrate, and up to 2.4 m long. The whole plant is covered with stiff white hairs giving it a bristly texture.

Fruit: The fruit is pod-like, about 1.2 cm long, and breaks into 5 woody, triangular pieces at maturity. Each section is bristly and contains 1 to 4 seeds; the sections have 2 to 4 sharp spines. Fruits are produced within 5 weeks of germination.

REASONS FOR CONCERN

Puncture-vine is reported to be POISONOUS to livestock. Fair-coloured livestock that eat this plant become highly SENSITIVE TO BRIGHT LIGHT and should be provided shade to escape the rays of the sun. It is also reported to cause bighead in sheep, a condition that causes the head to swell. Puncture-vine may also cause irreversible high quarter stagger in sheep. In late summer, livestock often refuse to graze in areas where this plant is abundant. The spiny fruit can cause injury to livestock and humans, and damage to vehicle tires.

flower

The carpetweeds are often separated into their own family, Molluginaceae. Primarily herbs of tropical and subtropical regions, members of this family have opposite, alternate, or whorled leaves. The simple and entire leaves do not have stipules. Flowers are composed of 5 sepals, 2 to many stamens, and 1 to 5 styles; petals are absent. The fruit is a capsule.

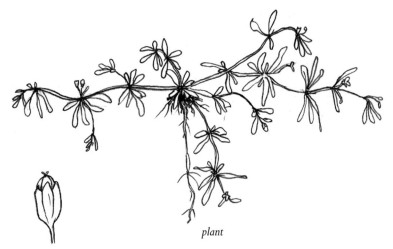

plant

fruit

Carpetweed Family

carpetweed,
Mollugo verticillata L.

Aizoaceae

carpetweed

Mollugo verticillata L.

An annual introduced from tropical North America.

Also known as: Indian chickweed, whorled chickweed, devil's-grip

French names: mollugine verticillée, mollugo verticillé

QUICK ID
- Plants with prostrate stems
- Leaves in whorls of 3 to 8
- Flowers white

Distribution: Found throughout Canada (except the prairie provinces, Prince Edward Island and Newfoundland) and the United States, except for the north-central plains.

Weed Designation
None

DESCRIPTION
Seed: Seeds are kidney-shaped, dark orange to brown, 0.5 mm long and 0.5 mm wide. Under high magnification, the seed is shiny and has several ridges.

Seedling: Cotyledons, 1.5 to 3.5 mm long and less than 1.3 mm wide, are oblong and thick. The seed leaves are hairless and remain attached to the stem. The stem below the cotyledons is often brown. The first leaf is spatula-shaped, dull green above and pale below.

Leaves: Leaves are whorled, spatula-shaped, and 1 to 2.5 cm long. The leaves are dull green with a pale underside and appear in whorls of 3 to 8. The lower part of the leaf margin has a few hairs.

Flower: Clusters of 2 to 5 white flowers appear in the axils of leaves. The stalks of these small flowers are 3 to 14 mm long. Flowers are composed of 5 sepals (1.5 to 2.5 mm long), 3 to 4 stamens, and 1 pistil. The sepals are green on the outside and white on the inside. Petals are absent.

Plant: A prostrate annual of sandy areas, carpetweed has numerous branches that form large, circular mats. The taproot is short and has very few branches. Yellowish green stems, up to 30 cm long, are hairless and branched at the base. Carpetweed germinates in late spring or early summer, but grows quickly.

Fruit: The fruit is an ovate capsule, 3 mm long, with 3 compartments, each containing numerous seeds. The thin-walled fruit opens by 3 valves, releasing small orange to brown seeds.

REASONS FOR CONCERN

Carpetweed is a serious weed in gardens and row crops. It is also found on roadsides, railways, and waste areas. It is reported to be an alternate host for cucumber mosaic, tobacco etch, and tobacco mosaic viruses.

SIMILAR SPECIES

Other common names for carpetweed, Indian or whorled chickweed, imply that it resembles common chickweed (*Stellaria media* (L.) Cyrill.). Common chickweed is distinguished from carpetweed by its ovate opposite leaves and 5 deeply lobed petals. Carpetweed may also be confused with cleavers (*Galium aparine* L.). Cleavers has bristly stems and leaves in whorls of 6 to 8 (see pp 72-73).

common chickweed

flower

fruit (schizocarp)

Another scientific name for this family is Umbelliferae, which means "bearer of umbels." This name refers to the common flower cluster of this large, mostly north-temperate, family. There are more than 3,000 species in this family; most are strongly scented. The carrots have hollow stems and alternate or basal compound leaves with petioles that are sheathed near the base. Some members of this family occasionally have simple leaves. Flowers, composed of 5 sepals, 5 petals, 5 stamens, and 2 styles, are found in simple or compound umbels. The primary umbels are frequently bractless, while secondary umbels (often called umbelets) have bracts. The fruit is a schizocarp that breaks into 2 mericarps at maturity.

The carrot family is very important economically, boasting several food crops such as carrot, dill, parsley, celery, parsnips, and caraway. The family also contains several poisonous plants, such as fool's parsley, water hemlock, and poison hemlock.

Carrot Family

cow parsnip,
Heracleum lanatum L.

Apiaceae

water hemlock

Cicuta maculata L.

A perennial native to North America.

Also known as: musquash-root, beaver poison, spotted cowbane, muskratweed, children's-bane, poison parsnip, snakeroot, snakeweed, false parsley, poison hemlock

French names: carotte à Moreau, cicutaire maculée

Scientific synonyms: *C. douglasii* (DC.) Coult. & Rose

QUICK ID

- Flowers in umbrella-shaped clusters
- Leaves compound with 1 to several leaflets
- Roots with horizontal chambers

Distribution: Found throughout Canada and the eastern half of the United States, except the Gulf Coast states.

Weed Designation
Canada: MB, PQ
USA: ID

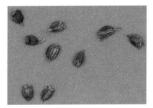

DESCRIPTION

Seed: Seeds are elliptical with 1 flat side; they are light brown, with 5 yellowish to orange-brown ribs, 2.7 to 3.3 mm long and 1.7 to 2.0 mm wide. The ribs are smooth but the areas between are wrinkled.

Seedling: Cotyledons are needle-shaped, 16 to 23 mm long and 1 to 2 mm wide, with a distinct parsnip odour when bruised. First leaves are compound with 3 toothed leaflets.

Leaves: Leaves are alternate and compound with several leaflets. Each leaflet is 3 to 20 cm long and 0.5 to 3.5 cm wide. The leaflets are divided twice into narrow segments and have coarsely toothed margins.

Flower: White to greenish white flowers are borne in terminal umbrella-shaped clusters called umbels. The primary umbel, 3 to 10 cm across, has 18 to 28 rays. These rays support smaller umbels with 12 to 25 rays. Each ray ends in a single flower, about 2 mm across. Flowers are composed of 5 small green sepals, 5 white petals, 5 stamens, and 2 styles. Below each umbel are a few narrow bracts.

Plant: Water hemlock is THE MOST TOXIC PLANT IN NORTH AMERICA. It is a stout perennial of wet habitats. The hollow stem up to 2.2 m tall, often has purplish spots and streaks. The short rootstalk, 3 to 10 cm long, is tuber-like with numerous horizontal chambers.

Fruit: The fruit, called a schizocarp, splits into 2 seeds. Fruit are about 2 to 4 mm long.

REASONS FOR CONCERN

The roots and stems of water hemlock contain cicutoxin, and are EXTREMELY POISONOUS to man and livestock. One root is sufficient to kill a cow or horse. Animals are usually poisoned in spring when the plants are easily uprooted and eaten. A violent death occurs 15 minutes to 3 hours after ingesting a lethal dose.

longitudinal section of root

SIMILAR SPECIES

There are several native species of water hemlock in North America. Water hemlock is easily confused with water parsnip (*Sium suave* Walt.), an edible native plant that grows in similar habitats. The distinguishing characteristic between these 2 species is the leaves. The leaves of water parsnip are divided once into narrow segments, while those of water hemlock are divided 2 or 3 times. The white flowers of water parsnip are borne in compound umbels. The primary umbel has 6 to many rays. Another VERY POISONOUS introduced species, hemlock (*Conium maculatum* L.), is often mistaken for water hemlock. A foul-smelling perennial herb of marshy areas, hemlock has stems up to 2 m tall that are blotched with purple. It is found throughout Canada and the northern United States.

leaf of water parsnip

wild carrot

Daucus carota L.

A biennial (occasionally an annual) introduced from Europe, southwest Asia, and north Africa into the United States in 1739; the first Canadian reports are from Ontario and Quebec in 1883.

Also known as: Queen Anne's lace, bird's-nest, devil's-plague, lace-flower

French names: carotte sauvage, carotte

QUICK ID
- Flowers in umbrella-shaped clusters
- Flowers white with 1 black central flower
- Leaves compound with 1 to several leaflets

Distribution: Found throughout Canada (except Newfoundland and the prairie provinces) and the United States (except the north-central plains).

Weed Designation

Canada: FEDERAL, MB, ON, PQ USA: IA, ID, IL, KS, MI, SD, TX, WV

DESCRIPTION

Seed: Elliptical seeds with 1 flat side are yellowish to greyish brown, 3.2 mm to 4.2 mm long and 1.7 to 2.6 mm wide. The surface has 4 rows of short curved spines and 5 lengthwise rows of white hairs. Each plant produces up to 40,000 seeds. Seeds require less than 6 months dormancy before germination. Light is not required for germination.

Seedling: Cotyledons, about 20 mm long and 1 mm wide, are hairless. The first leaves are compound and composed of 3 leaflets. Later leaves are compound with numerous divisions. When crushed, the seedling has a characteristic carrot odour.

Leaves: Leaves, alternate, are divided 2 to 4 times into narrow segments, giving a lacy appearance. Basal leaves are 5 to 40 cm long and long-stalked. Upper leaves are stalkless with white papery sheaths at the base.

Flower: Small white flowers are borne in flat-topped, umbrella-shaped clusters called umbels. The primary umbel is 6 to 15 cm across and composed of numerous small umbels, called umbelets. An average plant may have as many as 100 umbels. The main umbel may contain more than 1,000 white flowers with a single purplish black flower in the centre. Flowers are composed of 5 small green sepals, 5 white petals, 5 stamens, and 2 styles. Below each umbel is a whorl of finely divided green bracts with 3 to 5 branches. As the fruit mature, the umbel becomes concave and resembles a bird's nest. When the seeds reach maturity, the "bird's nest" flattens and releases the seeds.

Plant: The taproot of wild carrot is less than 5 cm in diameter, white, and somewhat woody. The whole plant has a characteristic carrot odour. The hollow stem, up to 1.6 m tall, is reddish purple near the base. Stems are bristly-hairy and branched near the top. The range of wild carrot is climatically controlled, as it requires at least 120 frost-free days and 80 to 100 cm of precipitation.

Fruit: The fruit, called a schizocarp, breaks into 2 seeds. Fruit are about 2 to 4 mm long.

REASONS FOR CONCERN

Controlling wild carrot in cultivated carrot crops is very difficult as the 2 species are closely related. Wild carrot is common on roadsides, pastures, and waste areas. The carrot rust fly affects both wild and cultivated carrot.

SIMILAR SPECIES

Several varieties of cultivated carrot (*D. carota* L.) have been developed. Wild carrot can be distinguished from cultivated carrot by its white taproot.

root

fruit

The cattail family contains 10 to 15 species with worldwide distribution. Cattails are erect, semi-aquatic herbs with creeping roots and flat, upright leaves. The terminal flower clusters are differentiated into male and female, with the uppermost being composed of male flowers. Two large spathes surrounding each flower cluster fall off soon after opening. The sepals of both flowers are reduced to small scales or bristles. Petals are absent. Male flowers have 1 to 7 stamens, and females have a single style. The wind-dispersed fruit is an achene-like follicle.

The cattail family is of limited economic importance. A few species are grown for their ornamental value. Cattails provide food and shelter for a number of wildlife species.

Cattail Family

cattail,
Typha latifolia L.

Typhaceae

cattail
Typha latifolia L.

A perennial native to North America.

Also known as: broad-leaved cattail, cat-o-nine-tails, cooper's reeds, reed mace, cattail flag, black-sap, blackamoor, candlewick, water-torch, flax-tail

French names: quenouille à feuilles larges

- ⌀ Flowers borne in club-shaped terminal clusters
- ⌀ Leaves basal and spongy
- ⌀ Extensive creeping rhizome

Distribution: Found throughout Canada and the United States.

Weed Designation
Canada: MB

cross-section of inflorescence

DESCRIPTION
Seed: Seeds are ovate, dark brown, less than 1 mm long. The seed is elevated on a long stalk. Numerous white hairs, up to 1 cm long, are connected at the base of the stalk. These soft hairs assist in seed dispersal. Each plant can produce up to 70,000 seeds, which do not require a dormant period prior to germination. Research in laboratories has shown that high amounts of moisture, light, and temperature increase germination. In nature, existing vegetation usually inhibits germination.

Seedling: Seedlings are rarely produced. Cattail spreads by long, creeping rhizomes.

Leaves: Leaves are basal, flat, up to 100 cm long and 1 to 3 cm wide. The upright, sheathing leaves are parallel-veined and spongy. A cross-section of the leaves will show numerous hollow chambers.

Flower: Flowers and their clusters are of 2 types, male and female. The terminal flower cluster is 7 to 13 cm long, dark brown and composed of male flowers. Male flowers are composed of bristle-like sepals and 1 to 7 (usually 3) stamens. The larger female spike is located below the male. It is 2.5 to 20 cm long and up to 3.5 cm thick at maturity. Female flowers are composed of bristle-like sepals and a single pistil. The male and female spikes are connected. A deciduous green sheath surrounds the spikes before flowering occurs.

Plant: An erect perennial, cattail is a common plant of marshes, ditches, and lakeshores. The stems, up to 2.7 m tall, rise from an extensive creeping rhizome.

Fruit: Each flower produces a single-seeded fruit, called an achene.

rhizome

REASONS FOR CONCERN

Cattail is a problem in ditches and irrigation canals where large colonies may impede the flow of water.

SIMILAR SPECIES

Narrow-leaved cattail (*T. angustifolia* L.), a closely related species, has leaves 4 to 10 mm wide and 3 m long. The male and female flower clusters are 25 to 40 cm long and separated by 3 to 5 cm. It is common in eastern North America and the Pacific coast states.

narrow-leaved cattail

fruit

The crowfoot family, often called the buttercup family, has more than 2,000 species worldwide. It is composed of herbs, shrubs, and climbing vines with simple to compound leaves that may be alternate, opposite, or whorled. The flowers may be extremely variable within this family. Flowers are composed of 3 to 15 often petal-like sepals, 0 to 5 petals, 5 to many stamens, and 5 to many styles. The fruit is a cluster of achenes or follicles.

Several members of this family are grown as ornamentals, including anemones, clematis, columbines, and buttercups. Some species, while beautiful, are POISONOUS to livestock.

Crowfoot Family

Clockwise from top:
blue columbine,
Aquilegia brevistyla Hook.;
northern buttercup,
Ranunculus hyperboreus
Rottb.;
windflower,
Anemone multifida Poir.

Ranunculaceae

low larkspur

Delphinium bicolor Nutt.

A perennial native to North America.

Also known as: plains delphinium

French names: pied d'alouette bicolore

QUICK ID
- Flowers purple to light blue
- Leaves deeply lobed
- Stem and leaves somewhat hairy

Distribution: Found from Saskatchewan to British Columbia and Montana to Wyoming and Washington.

Weed Designation
Canada: MB

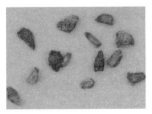

DESCRIPTION

Seed: Seeds are ovate, brown, 2 mm long with small greyish wings on the edges.

Seedling: Cotyledons are ovate and hairless. The first leaf is kidney-shaped with rounded teeth.

Leaves: Basal leaves are long-stalked, circular in outline, 3 to 6 cm wide. The leaves are deeply divided into several narrow lobes. Stem leaves are alternate, stalkless, and divided into a few narrow segments.

Flower: The flowering stalk, up to 20 cm long, has less than 15 flowers. Each flower has a stalk 10 to 30 mm long. Flowers, 15 to 35 mm across, are composed of 5 dark blue sepals, 4 petals (upper 2 light blue, lower 2 dark blue), several stamens and 3 pistils. The hairy sepals have spurs 12 to 35 mm long.

Plant: A perennial of grassland habitats, low larkspur has thick, fibrous roots. The unbranched stems are solid and up to 50 cm tall. The stems are hairless to slightly hairy. Where present, the yellowish hairs are somewhat sticky.

Fruit: The fruit, a capsule 15 to 25 mm long, is slightly hairy. Each capsule has several seeds.

REASONS FOR CONCERN

Low larkspur is VERY POISONOUS. Under normal pasture conditions, horses and sheep are not affected by larkspurs. Cattle are often poisoned because they find larkspur very palatable—especially the new growth in spring. It has been reported that a lethal dose is 0.7% of body weight.

SIMILAR SPECIES

Tall larkspur (*D. glaucum* S. Wats.) is closely related to low larkspur. The stems, up to 2m tall, are hollow and leafy. The flower stalk is more than 15 cm long. It is also VERY POISONOUS to livestock. Tall larkspur is found throughout western North America.

tall larkspur

tall buttercup

Ranunculus acris L.

A perennial introduced from Europe.

Also known as: meadow buttercup, tall crowfoot, blister plant, gold cup, butter-rose, butter-daisy, horsegold, bachelor's-buttons

French names: renoncule âcre, bouton-d'or

- Flowers yellow
- Stem leaves with 3 lobes
- Plant with soft hairs

Distribution: Found throughout Canada and the United States, except for the north-central region.

Weed Designation
Canada: MB, PQ

DESCRIPTION

Seed: Seeds are disc-shaped, reddish brown, about 3 mm long with a short hook. Each plant is capable of producing up to 250 seeds.

Seedling: Cotyledons, 4 to 11 mm long and 1.5 to 3 mm wide, have 3 or 5 visible veins. The young taproot is often zig-zagged with several lateral white roots. The first leaves are kidney-shaped and somewhat hairy below. The margin of the first leaf has rounded teeth.

Leaves: Basal leaves are long-stalked and deeply divided into 3 to 7 coarsely lobed segments. Stem leaves are alternate, short-stalked, and 3-lobed. Stem and basal leaves are soft-haired on both sides.

Flower: Golden-yellow flowers, 2 to 3.5 cm across, are borne on long stalks. They are composed of 5 hairy sepals (4 to 8 mm long), 5 shiny yellow petals (8 to 16 mm long), and numerous stamens and pistils.

Plant: Tall buttercup has several stems that rise from a thick and fibrous rootstalk. Stems, up to 100 cm tall, are leafy below and branched above. The plant is somewhat hairy.

Fruit: Each flower produces a globe-shaped cluster of sharp-pointed achenes.

REASONS FOR CONCERN

Tall buttercup is often found in overgrazed pastures because livestock find it unpalatable. Tall buttercup contains a bitter juice that causes INFLAMMATION of the mouth and intestinal tract when ingested. Hay containing tall buttercup does not cause these symptoms as the poisonous property is destroyed when the hay is cured. Tall buttercup is an alternate host for anemone mosaic and tomato spotted wilt viruses.

SIMILAR SPECIES

Creeping buttercup (*R. repens* L.), a native buttercup of eastern North America, is found throughout Canada and the northern half of the United States. It is distinguished from tall buttercup by its growth habit. Creeping buttercup, as the common name implies, has low stems that often root at nodes. Leaves are 3-lobed. The terminal lobe is stalked while the 2 lateral lobes are stalkless. Another species, white water crowfoot (*R. aquatilis* L.), often forms large mats in still water. The leaves of white water crowfoot, composed of numerous thread-like segments, collapse when removed from water.

white water crowfoot

plant

A large plant family of more than 2,000 species, the dogbanes reach their greatest diversity in tropical regions. Species may be herbs, shrubs, vines, or trees, and many contain milky sap. The simple, entire leaves are opposite or whorled. The flowers are composed of 5 sepals, 5 fused petals forming a bell-shaped corolla, 5 stamens, and a single style. The fruit may be berries, drupes, schizocarps, or follicles. The follicles contain numerous seeds with long, silky hairs. Despite its wide distribution and diversity, the dogbane family is of little economic importance.

flower

Dogbane Family

Indian hemp,
Apocynum cannabinum L.

Apocynaceae

spreading dogbane

Apocynum androsaemifolium L.

A perennial native to North America.

Also known as: wandering milkweed, honey-bloom, milk ipecac, rheumatism-weed, western wallflower

French names: apocyn à feuilles d'androsème, fausse herbe à la puce

QUICK ID
- Milky juice
- Leaves opposite
- Flowers white and bell-shaped

Distribution: Found throughout Canada and the United States.

Weed Designation
Canada: MB

mature plant in autumn

DESCRIPTION

Seed: Seeds are ovate, light brown, 2.5 to 3 mm long, with long, white silky hairs attached at 1 end.

Seedling: Cotyledons are 3 to 8 mm long and 1 to 2 mm wide. Milky juice is present at the 4-leaf stage.

Leaves: Leaves are opposite, ovate to oblong, 2 to 7 cm long. These dark-green leaves on short stalks droop from the stems. The midvein on the lower surface of the leaf is slightly hairy. Young leaves at the ends of branches are often whitish green. The leaves turn bright yellow or red in autumn.

Flower: Clusters of fragrant white to pink-striped flowers appear at the end of stems. Flowers are composed of 5 united sepals, 5 united petals (6 to 10 mm long), 5 stamens, and 1 style. The corolla is bell-shaped with the lobes curled back.

Plant: A native perennial reproducing by seeds and underground rhizomes, spreading dogbane has smooth reddish stems that contain milky juice. Erect stems, up to 150 cm tall, are branched near the top. Spreading dogbane prefers dry, sandy areas. Because of dogbane's high latex content, there have been several attempts to grow this plant commercially for rubber production.

Fruit: Each flower produces 2 slender pods, 7 to 20 cm long. These pods split lengthwise, releasing numerous seeds.

REASONS FOR CONCERN

Spreading dogbane is a common weed of pastures, roadsides, orchards, and waste areas. It is now recognized as a problem in minimum to zero-till cultivated fields. Some reports indicate that spreading dogbane MAY BE POISONOUS to livestock. It is also an alternate host for several *Prunus* viruses.

root

SIMILAR SPECIES

Indian hemp (*A. cannabinum* L.), a native perennial, has whitish green flowers less than 5 mm long. Erect reddish stems, up to 1.5 m tall, have numerous spreading leaves, 3 to 10 cm long. The leaves do not droop as in spreading dogbane. Seeds, 4 to 6 mm long, have white, silky hairs 2.5 to 3 cm long. Seed pods are 6 to 12 cm long (pp 122-23).

Indian hemp

Indian hemp

Apocynum cannabinum L.

A perennial native to North America.

Also known as: Indian physic, choctaw-root, bowman's-root, rheumatism-weed, hemp dogbane, American hemp, wild cotton, amy-root

French names: apocyn chanvrin, chanvre du Canada

Scientific synonyms: *A. sibiricum* Jacq.

- Milky juice
- Flowers greenish white
- Fruit a pod, 6 to 20 cm long

Distribution: Found throughout Canada (except Prince Edward Island) and the United States.

Weed Designation
Canada: MB

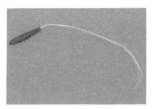

DESCRIPTION

Seed: Seeds are flat, reddish brown, and 4 to 6 mm long. Silky hairs, 2.5 to 3 cm long, are attached at 1 end of the seed.

Seedling: Cotyledons, 4 to 11 mm long and about 1.5 mm wide, have smooth margins. The stem below the cotyledons is often reddish purple. The seedling has milky juice by the time the second pair of leaves has emerged.

Leaves: Leaves are opposite, ovate to lance-shaped, and 5 to 12 cm long. Leaves on the main stem have stalks, 2 to 7 mm long, while those on side branches are nearly stalkless.

Flower: Greenish white tube-shaped flowers, 2 to 4 mm long, appear in clusters at the ends of branches. Flowers are composed of a 5 lobed calyx, 5 lobed corolla, 5 stamens and 2 pistils. Bracts below each flower are greenish white and papery.

Plant: A perennial of moist habitats, Indian hemp reproduces by seed and spreading horizontal rhizome. The stems, 30 to 80 cm tall, rise from a woody base. Stems and leaves exude a milky juice when broken.

Fruit: The fruit, a pod 6 to 20 cm long, contains numerous, silky haired seeds.

REASONS FOR CONCERN

Indian hemp is a weed of pastures, orchards, and roadsides. Recently, it has been recognized as a weed in minimum to zero-till cultivated fields. Indian hemp is POISONOUS to livestock, especially horses; between 15 and 30 g is reported to be TOXIC.

SIMILAR SPECIES

Spreading dogbane (*A. androsaemifolium* L.) is closely related to Indian hemp. It is distinguished from Indian hemp by drooping leaves, pinkish white flowers and smaller seeds. Spreading dogbane, as the common name implies, spreads by underground rhizomes (see pp 120-21). The stems, up to 75 cm tall, are often reddish. A hybrid between Indian hemp and spreading dogbane, *A. medium* Greene, is found wherever their ranges overlap. It has features common to both species.

spreading dogbane

flowers

plant

A small family with 30 species worldwide, the duckweeds are floating or submersed aquatic herbs. The plant bodies, often referred to as *thalli*, are not differentiated into stem and leaves. Plants are male or female and may have 0 to several roots, depending on the species. Flowers are rarely observed because of their size and colour. Male flowers are composed of a single stamen, while females have a single pistil. Flowers may or may not have a floral bract called a *spathe*. The fruit is a *utricle* containing 1 to 7 seeds.

Duckweeds reproduce by budding, a type of vegetative reproduction. Colonies expand when new plants are formed on the edges of the parent thallus.

Duckweed Family

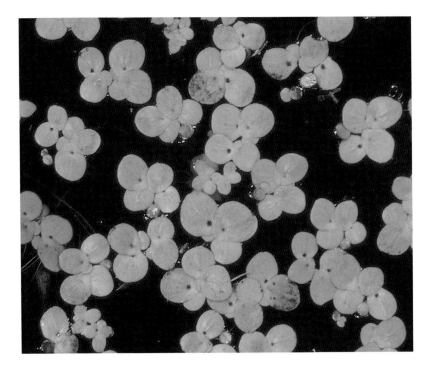

larger duckweed,
Spirodela polyrhiza (L.)
Schleiden

Lemnaceae

star duckweed

Lemna trisulca L.

A perennial native to North America.

Also known as: ivy duckweed, ivy-leaved duckweed

French names: lenticule trisulquée

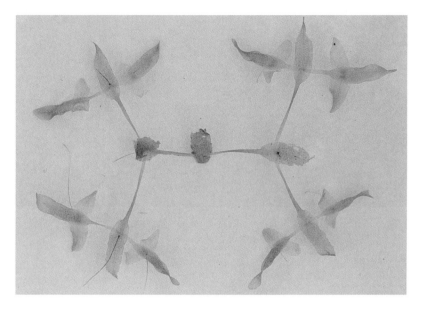

QUICK ID
- Floating aquatic plant
- Leaves absent
- Flowers small and inconspicuous

Distribution: Found throughout Canada (except the Atlantic provinces) and the United States.

Weed Designation
Canada: MB

DESCRIPTION

Seed/Seedling: Seeds are ovate, black, and less than 0.5 mm long. Seeds and seedlings are rarely produced by members of this family.

Leaves: Leaves are absent.

Flower: Flowers are rarely seen because of their small size. Flowers are of 2 types: male and female. Male flowers consist of a single stamen. Female flowers have a single pistil. Sepals and petals are absent.

Plant: A submersed aquatic plant, star duck-weed is 6 to 10 mm long and not differentiated into stem and leaves. Plant bodies, often referred to as a thallus, are joined together to form T-shaped colonies. A single root can be found on the underside of the thallus. Thalli have 3 faint nerves. Reproduction is by a process called budding. New plants are formed on the edges of the parent plant. These buds increase in numbers and form large colonies. In the fall, buds produced on the edge of parent bodies sink to the bottom. These buds overwinter on the bottom of the pond or lake and in the spring, rise to form new colonies.

Fruit: The fruit is a capsule containing 1 to 7 seeds.

REASONS FOR CONCERN

Duckweeds affect water quality for recreational purposes.

SIMILAR SPECIES

Common duckweed (*L. minor* L.) has an ovate thallus, 2 to 5 mm long, and a single root. These plants float on the surface of quiet waters. Another species, larger duckweed (*Spirodela polyrhiza* (L.) Schleiden), has a floating, round thallus, 3 to 8 mm across, and several roots. Both species are found throughout North America.

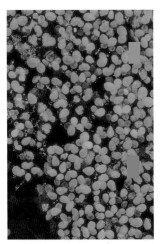

common duckweed

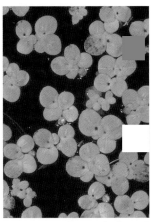

larger duckweed

With more than 600 species, the evening primrose family displays its greatest diversity in western North America. The simple and entire leaves are either alternate or opposite. In North American species, flowers parts (sepals, petals, stamens, and pistils) occur in multiples of 2 or 4. The plants in this family produce capsules, berries, nutlets, or achenes. The name evening primrose refers to the flowers of some species that open in late afternoon or early evening.

The evening primrose family has limited economic importance. Most species are grown for ornamental value, including evening primrose, clarkia, and fuchsia.

Evening Primrose Family

yellow evening
primrose,
Oenothera biennis L.

Onagraceae

yellow evening primrose

Oenothera biennis L.

A biennial native to North America.

Also known as: evening primrose

French names: onagre bisannuelle, onagre commune, herbe aux ânes

DESCRIPTION

Seed: Seeds are oblong to triangular, reddish brown, 1 to 1.7 mm long and 0.6 to 1.4 mm wide. The surface of the seed is dull and roughened with ridges that run lengthwise.

Seedling: Cotyledons, 6 to 11 mm long and 4 to 6 mm long, are spatula-shaped with a few short hairs near the base. The seed leaves are dull green above with shiny veins. The stem at the base of the cotyledons is bright red. The first leaves are alternate, although they appear opposite.

Leaves: A basal rosette of elliptical to oblong leaves are produced in the first year of growth. These stalked leaves have a pinkish midrib and wavy margins. Stem leaves are alternate, oblong to lance-shaped, and 2.5 to 12 cm long. Leaves are reduced in size upwards. Upper leaves are stalkless with wavy to toothed margins.

Flower: Bright-yellow flowers, 2 to 5 cm across, are borne in leafy terminal clusters. Flowers open in the evening and are composed of 4 sepals, 4 petals, 8 stamens, and a single pistil. The sepals are fused when the flower is in bud, and split apart and turn backward as the flower opens. The petals are yellow, 12 to 25 mm long. The stamens are 3 to 11 mm long.

Plant: A biennial with a thick, deep taproot, yellow evening primrose has greyish to reddish green stems. A leafy rosette is produced in the first year of growth. In the second year, an erect stem up to 2 m tall, with a few branches is produced. Yellow evening primrose is often cultivated in gardens for use as a vegetable or medicinal herb.

Fruit: The fruit is an erect capsule, 1 to 3.5 cm long. The hairy capsule is 4-valved and splits from the top at maturity.

REASONS FOR CONCERN

Yellow evening primrose is a weed of roadsides and waste areas. It is serious problem in cultivated fields of winter wheat or fall rye.

SIMILAR SPECIES

Fireweed (*Epilobium angustifolium* L.), a native plant found throughout Canada and the United States, is related to yellow evening primrose. Fireweed is distinguished by its pink flowers composed of 4 pinkish green sepals, 4 pink petals, 8 stamens, and 4 lobed stigma. Stems, up to 3 m tall, have numerous alternate leaves that are prominently 3-veined.

fireweed

flower

A large family with over 4,000 species worldwide, the figwort family is often referred to as the snapdragon family. Plants in this family are herbs or shrubs and have alternate, opposite, or whorled leaves. The flowers are composed of 5 sepals, 5 petals, 2, 4 or 5 stamens, and a single style. The petals are fused into a 2-lipped corolla with 2 upper petals and 3 lower. A sterile stamen is often present. The fruit, a capsule, has 2 compartments.

Scrophulariaceae is of limited economic importance. The extract of 1 species, foxglove (*Digitalis purpurea* L.), is an important drug used in cardiac care. Some ornamental species include snapdragons, beard's-tongues, Indian paintbrushes, and monkeyflowers. Genera such as *Striga* and *Linaria* are serious weeds and can cause significant reductions in crop yield.

Figwort Family

lilac-flowered
beard-tongue,
Penstemon gracilis Nutt.

Scrophulariaceae

small snapdragon

Chaenorrhinum minus
(L.) Lange

An annual introduced from the Mediterranean region of Europe.

Also known as: dwarf snapdragon

French names: chénorhinum mineur, linaire mineure

Scientific synonyms: *Linaria minor* L.

QUICK ID
- Lower leaves opposite, upper leaves alternate
- Flowers light blue with a yellow throat
- Plants less than 40 cm tall

Distribution: Found throughout Canada (except Newfoundland) and the United States.

Weed Designation
USA: WA

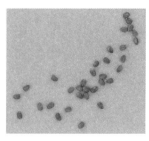

DESCRIPTION

Seed: Seeds are elliptical to ovate, brown, and 0.8 to 1.2 mm wide. The surface is rough with several ridges running lengthwise.

Seedling: Cotyledons, 2.5 to 10 mm long and less than 4 mm wide, are lance-shaped and wither soon after the first leaves appear. The first pair of leaves is spatula-shaped and slightly hairy. The midvein is only visible in the first pair of leaves.

Leaves: Lower leaves are opposite and upper leaves are alternate. Leaves are lance to club-shaped, stalkless, 1 to 2.5 cm long. The margins are smooth.

Flower: Light-blue to purplish flowers with a yellow throat are borne singly in the axils of the upper leaves. Flowers, 6 to 8 mm long, appear on stalks, 10 to 15 mm long. Flowers are composed of 5 united sepals, 5 united petals, 4 stamens, and a single pistil. A spur, 1.5 to 2 mm long, can be found at the base of the fused petals.

Plant: A bushy annual of gravelly or sandy soils, small snapdragon is often found on railway grades. The stems, 5 to 40 cm tall, are covered with short sticky hairs. Small snapdragon reproduces by seed only.

Fruit: The fruit is a round capsule, about 5 mm in diameter. The hairy capsule releases seeds through 2 small pores.

REASONS FOR CONCERN

Small snapdragon is a weed in cultivated fields, gardens, waste areas, roadsides, and railway grades. Recently, it has been recognized as a serious weed problem in strawberry fields.

SIMILAR SPECIES

Blue-eyed mary (*Collinsia parviflora* Lindl.), a native species of western North America, may be mistaken for small snapdragon. Blue-eyed mary is distinguished from small snapdragon by opposite or whorled stem leaves. The light-blue flower does not have a spur, another distinguishing characteristic. The stems, up to 30 cm tall, are often hairy.

blue-eyed mary

Dalmatian toadflax

Linaria dalmatica (L.) Mill.

A perennial introduced from southeastern Europe around 1900.

Also known as: smooth toadflax

French names: linaire à feuilles larges, linaire de Dalmatie

Scientific synonyms: *L. genistifolia* (L.) Mill.

QUICK ID

- Flowers yellow
- Leaves alternate
- Leaves bluish green and hairless

Distribution: Found throughout Canada (except Newfoundland and Prince Edward Island) and scattered locations throughout the western United States.

Weed Designation

  Canada: FEDERAL, AB, BC, MB, SK

  USA: CO, ID, MT, NV, OR, WA, WY

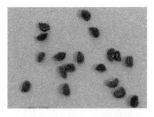

DESCRIPTION

Seed: Seeds are ovate to somewhat angular, black, and 1.3 to 1.9 mm long. Each plant is capable of producing up to 500,000 seeds, which remain viable for up to 10 years. No dormancy is required for germination.

Seedling: Cotyledons are ovate with a distinct point. They are hairless, 3 to 9 mm long and 1 to 3 mm wide. The first pair of leaves are opposite, but later leaves are alternate.

Leaves: Leaves are alternate, ovate to lance-shaped, 3 to 8 cm long and 1 to 2 cm wide. Stem leaves are stalkless and clasp the stem with heart-shaped bases. The leaves appear opposite because they are crowded on the stem. All leaves are bluish green and hairless.

Flower: Large yellow flowers are borne in long terminal clusters. The flowers are nearly stalkless. The buds of unopened flowers are often purplish red. Flowers are composed of 5 united sepals (6 to 8 mm long), 5 united petals (1.7 to 3.5 cm long), 4 short stamens, and a single style. A prominent spur, 1.3 to 2 cm long, is projected from the back of the petals.

Plant: A stout plant, Dalmatian toadflax rises from a woody rootstalk. The stems, up to 120 cm tall, are often branched. The stem and leaves of the plant are smooth and bluish green.

Fruit: The fruit is a cylindrical capsule, 7 to 8 mm long.

REASONS FOR CONCERN

Dalmatian toadflax is an aggressive weed of pastures, rangeland, and roadsides. It is a deep-rooted perennial that is difficult to eradicate once established.

SIMILAR SPECIES

Toadflax (*L. vulgaris* Hill.) is closely related to Dalmatian toadflax. It has numerous narrow leaves, 2 to 10 cm long, and smaller yellow flowers. These yellow flowers, 2 to 3 cm long, have an orange throat (see pp 138-39).

fruit

toadflax

Linaria vulgaris Hill.

A perennial introduced from Europe in the mid-1800s as a garden plant.

Also known as: butter-and-eggs, wild snapdragon, yellow toadflax, flaxweed, ramsted, eggs-and-bacon, perennial snapdragon, Jacob's-ladder, rabbit-flower, impudent lawyer

French names: linaire vulgaire, linaire commune

QUICK ID

- Flowers yellow with a spur
- Leaves alternate
- Stems with numerous narrow leaves

Distribution: Found throughout Canada and the United States. Toadflax has been found as far north as Fort Smith, Northwest Territories and Fairbanks, Alaska.

Weed Designation

Canada: Federal, AB, BC, MB, SK
USA: AK, CO, ID, MT, WA, WY

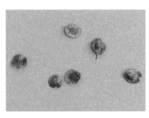

DESCRIPTION

Seed: Seeds are flattened, dull black, ovate, 1.5 to 2 mm in diameter. A papery wing surrounds the seed. Each plant is capable of producing up to 8,700 seeds. Germination occurs in the top 2 cm of soil.

Seedling: Cotyledons, 1.3 to 10 mm long and 1 to 4 mm wide, are ovate with a distinct point and hairless. The first leaves are opposite and ovate. Later leaves are alternate and lance-shaped.

Leaves: Leaves are alternate, 2 to 10 cm long and 1 to 5 mm wide. Toadflax has numerous short-stalked, pale-green leaves that are lance-shaped and hairless. Leaf margins are smooth. Stem leaves are crowded and may appear opposite.

Flower: Flowers, resembling snapdragons, appear in dense terminal clusters. They are yellow with an orange throat and 2 to 3.5 cm long. Flowers are composed of 5 united sepals, 5 united petals, 4 stamens, and 1 pistil. A long spur, 2 to 3 cm long, at the base of the corolla points backward. Flowering stalks are about 5 mm long.

Plant: Toadflax reproduces by seed and extensive creeping rhizomes. This root system allows the plant to form large colonies. The hairless stems can reach a height of 1.3 m and are rarely branched. Buds on the creeping rhizome develop into new shoots and stems.

Fruit: The fruit is an ovate to egg-shaped capsule, 8 to 12 mm long. Numerous seeds are found in the 2 compartments.

REASONS FOR CONCERN

Toadflax is a potential weed problem in zero and minimum-till areas because of its prolific seed production and creeping rhizome. It is an aggressive weed in rangeland where it quickly replaces grasses and herbs. Toadflax is an alternate host for tobacco mosaic virus. Some sources report that toadflax is POISONOUS to cattle.

SIMILAR SPECIES

Dalmatian toadflax (*L. dalmatica* (L.) Mill.), a closely related species, is more robust than toadflax. Stems, up to 1 m tall, have numerous ovate to lance-shaped leaves that clasp the stem. Flowers are yellow and 3 to 4 cm long (see pp 136-37).

fruit

common mullein

Verbascum thapsus L.

QUICK ID
- Flowers yellow
- Leaves covered with soft felt-like hairs
- Flowering stems with small stem leaves

Distribution: Found throughout Canada (except Saskatchewan) and the United States, except eastern Montana and western North Dakota.

Weed Designation

Canada: MB
USA: HI

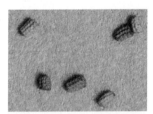

A biennial introduced from Greece into North America as a medicinal plant, common mullein was also used as a fish control agent in the mid 1700s in Virginia, and had spread to the Pacific Coast by 1876.

Also known as: velvet dock, big taper, candle-wick, flannel-leaf, torches, Jacob's-staff, blanket-leaf, iceleaf, velvet-leaf, hedge taper, Aaron's-rod, devil's-tobacco

French names: grande molène, bouillon-blanc, tabac de diable

DESCRIPTION
Seed: Seeds are oblong, dark grey to brown, less than 1 mm long and 0.5 mm in diameter. The surface is wrinkled with several intersecting ridges. Each plant is capable of producing over 180,000 seeds. Seeds require light and temperatures above 10°C for germination. Seeds may remain viable for at least 100 years.

Seedling: Cotyledons are egg-shaped, 1 to 6 mm long and 1 to 3.5 mm wide, and slightly hairy. The first 2 leaves appear opposite and are slightly hairy. Leaves appearing after the third leaf stage are densely woolly. Seedlings are established more readily on bare soil than vegetated areas.

Leaves: Leaves of the first-year rosette are 15 to 45 cm long, up to 10 cm wide and covered with thick, woolly branched hairs. Stem leaves are alternate, 10 to 40 cm long, and reduced in size upwards with their bases running down the stem. Rosettes less than 15 cm diameter at the arrival of winter have a small chance of surviving the winter.

Flower: A dense compact spike, 20 to 50 cm long and 3 cm across, has numerous yellow flowers, 2.5 cm across. The flowers are stalkless and saucer-shaped. They are composed of 5 united sepals, 5 united petals, 5 stamens (3 short and 2 long), and a single pistil. Stamens are covered with white or yellow hairs.

Plant: Common mullein produces a basal rosette of leaves in its first season of growth. In the second year, a flowering stem, up to 2.5 m, rises from the deep taproot. The flowering stem may have a few short branches near the top. The whole plant is covered with woolly hairs. The range of common mullein is climatically controlled as this species requires a growing season of at least 140 days.

rosette

Fruit: The fruit is a woolly ovate capsule, 3 to 10 mm long. The capsule splits to release an average of 600 seeds.

REASONS FOR CONCERN

Common mullein increases on overgrazed pastures as livestock find the woolly leaves unpalatable. The large number of seeds and their longevity make control of this weed difficult. It is often found growing in gravelly soils.

SIMILAR SPECIES

Black mullein or black torch (*V. nigrum* L.) is distinguished from common mullein by stamens that are covered with purple hairs. Another species, woolly mullein (*V. phlomoides* L.), is similar to common mullein. The leaf bases of woolly mullein do not continue down the stem as they do in common mullein.

fruit

fruit

The geranium family has more than 700 species worldwide. Species are herbs and shrubs with alternate or opposite leaves. The leaves are simple to compound and have stipules. The flowers are composed of 5 sepals, 5 petals, 5 or 10 stamens, and a pistil of 5 carpels with the styles fused to form a central column. This central column appears as a single style. The fruit is a capsule or schizocarp that breaks into 5 long-tailed mericarps at maturity. The schizocarp splits from the bottom upwards. The seed tails coil and uncoil depending on their moisture content, enabling it to work its way into the soil.

Members of this family include wild and garden geraniums as well as stork's-bill. The wild geraniums are represented by the genus *Geranium*, and garden geraniums by *Pelargonium*.

flower

Geranium Family

Left: wild white
geranium,
Geranium richardsonii,
Fisch. & Trautv.
Right: Bicknell's
geranium,
Geranium bicknellii Britt.

Geraniaceae

stork's-bill

Erodium cicutarium
(L.) L'Her.

An annual, winter annual, or biennial introduced from the Mediterranean region of southern Europe.

Also known as: pin clover, alfileria, red stem filaree, heron's-bill, pinweed, pingrass, wild musk, pink needle, thunder flower, crane's-bill

French names: érodium cicutaire, érodium à feuilles de ciguë

QUICK ID

- Leaves opposite, compound, hairy
- Flowers pink with 5 petals
- Fruit resemble a stork's bill

Distribution: Found throughout Canada (except Prince Edward Island and Newfoundland) and the United States.

Weed Designation

Canada: AB, MB

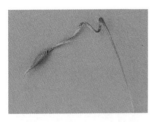

DESCRIPTION

Seed: Seeds are club-shaped, brown, 5 mm long. The attached tail is 2 to 3 cm long and becomes spiralled when dry. Each plant can produce up to 250 seeds.

Seedling: Cotyledons, oblong in outline, have 3 unequal lobes and a hairy stalk. The first leaves are densely hairy, long-stalked, and divided into toothed segments.

Leaves: Leaves are compound, primarily basal, with some opposite stem leaves present. These compound leaves have irregularly shaped stalkless leaflets, 1 to 2.5 cm long. The leaves are covered with short, stiff hairs.

Flower: Umbrella-shaped clusters of 2 to 12 pink to purple flowers appear about 12 weeks after germination. Flowers are 1.5 cm across and composed of 5 bristle-tipped hairy sepals, 5 petals, 10 stamens (5 fertile and 5 sterile,) and a single 5-parted style (2 to 4 cm long). Flower stalks are 1 to 2 cm long.

Plant: Stork's-bill is a low-spreading plant with stems up to 40 cm long. The plant is densely haired throughout. Plants produce flowers within 12 weeks of germination.

Fruit: A long-tailed capsule, 2 to 4 cm long, splits from the bottom to the top. Each flower produces 5 capsules.

REASONS FOR CONCERN

Stork's-bill is often found in large populations and competes with crops for moisture and nutrients, adversely affecting the yield. Stork's-bill is reported to accumulate nitrates, which MAY CAUSE LIVESTOCK POISONING. Stork's-bill is an alternate host for aster yellows, beet curly top, peach yellow bud mosaic, strawberry green petal, tobacco yellow dwarf, and vaccinium false bottom.

SIMILAR SPECIES

Bicknell's geranium (*Geranium bicknellii* Britt.) is a native geranium with a weedy growth habit (see pp 146-47). It has hand or palm-shaped compound leaves. The pink flowers have 10 stamens, unlike the 5 in stork's-bill.

fruit

Bicknell's geranium

Geranium bicknellii Britt.

An annual or biennial native to North America.

French names: géranium de Bicknell

QUICK ID
- Leaves opposite
- Flowers pink with 10 stamens
- Plant with prostrate stems

Distribution: Found throughout Canada (except Prince Edward Island) and the northern half of the United States.

Weed Designation

Canada: MB

DESCRIPTION
Seed: Seeds are cylindrical, about 8 mm long, with a coiled, black tail; the tail of the seed is up to 15 mm long. The surface of the seed is a network of intersecting ridges.

Seedling: Cotyledons are round with a granular texture. The first leaf is kidney-shaped with round-toothed margins. Scattered short hairs can be found on the leaves and their stalks.

Leaves: Leaves are opposite, palmately 5-lobed, 2 to 7 cm across. The leaf lobes are wedge-shaped with shallow lobes or toothed margins. The leaf stalks are covered with sticky hairs.

Flower: Flowers are borne singly or in pairs in the axils of leaves. Sharp-pointed sepals, 4 to 6 mm long, have sticky hairs on the edges and veins. Five petals, 5 to 7 mm long, are pink to rosy purple. There are 10 stamens in 2 sets of unequal length. There is 1 pistil.

Plant: A sticky-haired plant, Bicknell's geranium has spreading branched stems, up to 60 cm long.

Fruit: The fruit is a capsule that splits into 5 seeds. The capsule splits from the bottom to the top.

REASONS FOR CONCERN
Bicknell's geranium is a weed of row crops, gardens, and roadsides.

SIMILAR SPECIES
Stork's-bill (*Erodium cicutarium* (L.) L'Her.) is closely related to Bicknell's geranium. Stork's-bill has deeply lobed and densely hairy leaves (see pp 144-45). Flowers are pink and have 5 stamens, unlike Bicknell's geranium which has 10. Field geranium (*G. pratense* L.) is found on roadsides and waste areas throughout eastern Canada and the United States. A rhizome-producing perennial, it has pinkish purple flowers, 2 to 3 cm across. Its leaves have 5 to 7 lobes.

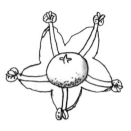

flower

The goosefoot family has over 1,500 species of herbs and shrubs worldwide. Many species of this family are capable of growing soils with high alkalinity. The simple leaves are usually alternate and succulent. Stipules are absent. The small flowers are green and inconspicuous; they may be perfect or imperfect. They are composed of 0 to 5 sepals, 1 to 5 stamens, and 2 or 3 styles. Petals are absent. The fruit, an achene or utricle, is often surrounded by the calyx.

Economically important members of this family include spinach, beets, chard, and quinoa. Many species are considered noxious weeds and compete with agricultural crops for light, moisture, and nutrients.

Goosefoot Family

lamb's-quarters,
Chenopodium album L.

Chenopodiaceae

garden orache

Atriplex hortensis L.

An annual introduced from Asia as a garden vegetable.

Also known as: halberleaf orach, fat-hen, lamb's-quarters, saltbrush, Hungarian spinach

French names: arroche des jardins, arroche-épinard

QUICK ID

- Leaves alternate
- Flowers borne in dense clusters
- Plant reddish purple in late summer

Distribution: Found throughout Canada (except the Atlantic provinces) and the United States, except the New England states.

Weed Designation

Canada: MB

DESCRIPTION

Seed: Two types of seeds are produced. Small, shiny, black seeds, about 2 mm in diameter, are produced in female flowers with a small calyx and lacking a bracteole. Large, flat, brown seeds, 3 to 10 mm long, are produced in female flowers with no calyx and 2 large bracteoles. Large seeds germinate a few days after being planted. Small seeds remain dormant for several months. Each plant is capable of producing over 6,000 seeds.

Seedling: Cotyledons, 7 to 20 mm long and 1.2 to 2.5 mm wide, are oblong to lance-shaped. The stem below the cotyledons is often tinged with purple. The first leaves are alternate, but appear opposite.

Leaves: Leaves are alternate and vary from lance-shaped to triangular with heart to arrowhead-shaped bases. The leaves are green above and whitish green below, 5 to 25 cm long and 15 cm wide. Lower leaves may be opposite. Both basal and stem leaves are stalked.

Flower: Flowers are borne in large terminal clusters, up to 30 cm long. Flowers are of 3 types. Male flowers are composed of 3 to 5 sepals and 3 to 5 stamens. There are 2 kinds of female flowers: 1 with no sepals and 2 bracts (up to 12 mm long at maturity), the other with no bracts and 3 to 5 sepals.

Plant: Garden orache has yellowish green to reddish purple stems. These erect branched stems are up to 2 m tall and hairless.

Fruit: The single-seeded fruit is called an achene. The small seeds, also achenes, do not have 2 large bracts.

REASONS FOR CONCERN

Garden orache is a common weed of roadsides and waste areas. It is an alternate host for beet mosaic, beet yellows, and beet curly top viruses.

SIMILAR SPECIES

At maturity, garden orache could be easily mistaken for curled dock (*Rumex crispus* L.; see pp 92-93). Both species have a large, reddish fruiting stem and lance-shaped leaves. The distinguishing characteristic between the 2 species is the shape of the fruit. The fruit of curled dock is 3-sided, while those of garden orache are flat. A closely related species, salt sage (*A. nuttallii* S. Wats.), is found on badland slopes throughout western North America. It is distinguished from garden orache by its growth habit and leaves. Salt sage is some-what woody and has stems up to 60 cm tall. The oblong leaves are 1 to 5 cm long. The plant is greyish green throughout.

salt sage

Russian pigweed

Axyris amaranthoides L.

An annual introduced from Siberia; the first Canadian report was from Headingly, Manitoba in 1886.

Also known as: axyris

French names: ansérine de Russie

⌀ Leaves alternate

⌀ Flowers in dense clusters

⌀ Stems whitish green

Distribution: Found throughout Canada (except Newfoundland) and the northern third of the United States.

Weed Designation

Canada: MB

DESCRIPTION

Seed: Seeds are of 2 types: ovate, dark brown 2.5 to 3 mm long, or round, greyish brown, 1.5 to 2 mm across. The dark-brown seeds have a 2-lobed papery wing at 1 end of the seed. The round, greyish brown seeds are wingless. Winged seeds germinate readily, while wingless seeds remain dormant for a longer period of time.

Seedling: Cotyledons, 7 to 15 mm long and 2 to 5 mm wide, are slightly hairy. The first leaves are alternate and dull green; these ovate leaves are prominently veined.

Leaves: Leaves are alternate, ovate to lance-shaped, up to 6 cm long. The upper surface of the leaves is hairless while the lower has numerous star-shaped hairs. Leaves are short-stalked and reduced in size upwards.

Flower: Flowers are of 2 types, male and female. Male flowers are yellowish and appear at the ends of branches. Male flowers are composed of 3 to 5 papery sepals and 2 to 5 stamens. Female flowers are green and found in leaf axils or intermixed with the male flowers. They are composed of 3 to 5 papery sepals and a single style with a 2-lobed stigma.

Plant: An erect, bushy annual, Russian pigweed has stems up to 120 cm tall. The stems are light green to white and turn straw-coloured at maturity.

Fruit: A single-seeded fruit, called an achene, is enclosed by a papery membrane.

REASONS FOR CONCERN

Russian pigweed is a serious weed of cultivated crops, forages, and pastures. It is commonly found on roadsides, waste areas, and gardens.

male flowers

female flowers

lamb's-quarters

Chenopodium album L.

QUICK ID
- Leaves with a mealy texture
- Stems and leaves often have purple blotches
- Dense clusters of flowers at the ends of branches

Distribution: Found throughout Canada and the United States.

Weed Designation

Canada: MB, PQ
USA: FL

An annual introduced from Europe and possibly native to North America, lamb's-quarters was first reported in Canada in 1858.

Also known as: pigweed, fat-hen, white goosefoot, lamb's-quarters goosefoot, netseed lamb's- quarters, mealweed, frost-blite, bacon-weed, wild spinach

French names: chénopode blanc, chou gras, poulette grasse, ansérine blanche

Scientific synonyms: *C. lanceolatum* Muhl.; *C. dacoticum* Standl.

DESCRIPTION
Seed: Disc-shaped, shiny black seeds are 1.1 to 1.6 mm long and 1 mm wide. Seeds remain viable in the soil for up to 40 years. Each plant can produce over 500,000 seeds. Seeds must be in the top 3 cm of soil to germinate.

Seedling: Cotyledons, up to 15 mm long and 2 mm wide, are oblong to ovate and fleshy. The underside of the cotyledons and the stem below are often pink to purple. The first 2 sets of leaves are opposite and egg-shaped, and have a mealy appearance. Later leaves are alternate.

Leaves: Leaves are alternate, green above and mealy-white below. Stalked leaves, up to 12

cm long and 8 cm wide, have wavy margins. Leaf shape is highly variable and may be triangular, diamond-shaped, or lance-shaped. The leaves often have reddish purple blotches.

Flower: Dense terminal and axillary clusters of small flowers (less than 3 mm wide) have a bluish tinge. The 5-lobed calyx has a mealy texture. There are no petals. There are 2 to 5 stamens and 2 to 5 styles. Lamb's-quarters blooms from June to September. Flowers are wind-pollinated.

Plant: An extremely variable plant, lamb's-quarters can grow up to 2.5 m tall. Bluish green stems are branched, grooved, and blotched with red or purple. The taproot is short with several branches.

Fruit: The single-seeded fruit, called an achene, is surrounded by a papery sac.

inflorescence

REASONS FOR CONCERN

Lamb's-quarters, a rapid-growing plant that uses large amounts of water, is capable of crowding out cultivated crops and adversely affecting crop yield. Lamb's-quarters is an alternate host for a number of viral diseases: barley stripe mosaic, beet curly top virus, beet mosaic, beet yellows virus, potato mosaic, turnip crinkle, turnip mosaic, and tobacco streak. Plants are reported to be POISONOUS to sheep and pigs if eaten in large quantities.

juvenile

SIMILAR SPECIES

Several species of goosefoot grow throughout North America. Two species of note are strawberry blite (*C. capitatum* (L.) Aschers.) and Berlandier's goosefoot (*C. berlandieri* Moq.). Strawberry blite is distinguished from lamb's-quarter's by the juicy, red fruit that appear in late summer. Berlandier's goosefoot, a closely related species to lamb's-quarters, is an intermediate host for the beet leafhopper which transmits curly top virus to sugarbeets. It is less mealy than lamb's-quarters and has a leafy flower cluster.

strawberry blite

maple-leaved goosefoot

Chenopodium gigantospermum Aellen

An annual native to North America.

Also known as: sowbane

French names: chénopode hybride

Scientific synonyms: *C. hybridum* L.

- Leaves with 1 to 4 large teeth on each side
- Plants bright green
- Dense clusters of flowers at the ends of branches

Distribution: Found throughout Canada (except Newfoundland and Prince Edward Island) and the United States.

Weed Designation

Canada: MB

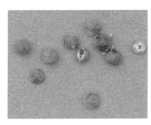

DESCRIPTION

Seed: Seeds are nearly round, dull brown to black, 2.1 to 2.4 mm across. Under low magnification, the surface of the seed is smooth and shiny. Each plant is capable of producing up to 15,000 seeds.

Seedling: Cotyledons, up to 18 mm long and 5 mm wide, are lance-shaped and reddish magenta below. The stem below the cotyledons is often pink to purple. The first 2 leaves are opposite and have wavy margins. Later leaves are alternate. Leaves with toothed margins appear by the third leaf stage.

Leaves: Leaves are alternate, bright green above and pale green below. Leaves are long-stalked, broadly ovate to triangular in shape, 5 to 20 cm long. The margins have 1 to 4 large teeth on each side. The veins of the leaf are prominent.

Flower: Small green flowers less than 2 mm wide appear in loose spike-like clusters at the ends of stems. Flowers are composed of a 5-lobed calyx, 2 to 5 stamens, and 2 to 5 styles. Petals are absent. Flowers are wind-pollinated.

Plant: A bright-green plant, maple-leaved goosefoot has erect grooved stems up to 1.5 m tall. An annual with an unpleasant smell, this goosefoot is found on roadsides, cropland, and waste areas.

Fruit: The single-seeded fruit, called an achene, is surrounded by a papery sac.

REASONS FOR CONCERN

Maple-leaved goosefoot is a common weed of gardens, waste areas, roadsides, and edges of cultivated fields.

SIMILAR SPECIES

Oak-leaved goosefoot (*C. salinum* Standl.) is closely related to maple-leaved goosefoot. An introduced species from Europe and Asia, it is a low-growing, somewhat fleshy plant with reddish stems up to 40 cm long. The leaves, as the common name implies, are shaped like oak leaves, with wavy to toothed margins.

oak-leaved goosefoot

kochia

Kochia scoparia
(L.) Schrad.

An annual introduced from Europe and Asia as an ornamental garden plant.

Also known as: summer cypress, burning bush, mock cypress, red belvedere, Mexican fire-weed, fireball, broom-cypress

French names: kochia à balais

QUICK ID
- Plants pyramid-shaped
- Plants turn reddish green in late summer
- Leaves alternate and hairy

Distribution: Found throughout Canada except Newfoundland, Prince Edward Island, New Brunswick, and coastal British Columbia. It is found throughout the northern half of the United States, except for the west coast region.

Weed Designation
    Canada: BC, MB   USA: OR, WA

DESCRIPTION
Seed: Seeds are egg-shaped, dark reddish brown to black, 1 to 2 mm long and 1 to 1.5 mm wide. The surface of the seed is dull and somewhat granular.

Seedling: Cotyledons, about 4.5 mm long and 1.5 mm wide, are elliptical, dull green above and bright pink below. The first and later leaves are lance-shaped and have numerous soft hairs. A basal rosette of leaves is produced when the seedling is not in competition with other vegetation.

Leaves: Leaves are alternate, linear to lance-shaped, 6 cm long and 2 to 5 mm wide. Numerous short-stalked leaves, 6 cm long and 2 to 5 mm wide, are reduced in size upwards. The leaf underside and edges are usually hairy.

Flower: Small green flowers, about 3 mm across, are borne in groups of 2 to 6 in leaf axils. Flowers are composed of a 5-lobed calyx with long hairs, 3 to 5 stamens, and 2 styles. Some flowers may be lacking stamens. Petals are absent.

Plant: Kochia is a bushy, pyramid-shaped plant capable of reaching 2 m in height. The stem and branches are somewhat hairy. The whole plant turns reddish purple in autumn. When the plant has dried, the stem breaks off at ground level and acts as a tumbleweed, scattering seeds in its path.

Fruit: The single-seeded fruit is called an achene; it is often enclosed by the calyx.

REASONS FOR CONCERN

In severe infestations, kochia has been reported to reduce crop yields up to 100%. Seeds germinate in early spring and seedlings are controlled by late-spring cultivation. Kochia, once planted as a hay crop on alkaline soils, is readily grazed by livestock. The nutritional value of kochia is equal to that of alfalfa. Kochia is an alternate host for beet yellows and tobacco mosaic viruses.

SIMILAR SPECIES

Bassia (*Bassia hyssopifolia* (Pall.) Ktze.), an introduced annual native to the Caspian Sea region, is often confused with kochia. Bassia is distinguished from kochia by the hooked spines on the sepals; the sepals of kochia are spineless. The leaves of bassia are alternate, fleshy, lance to oblong-shaped, 1 to 2 cm long.

stem of tumbleweed

spear-leaved goosefoot
Monolepis nuttalliana (Schultes) Greene

An annual native to western North America.

Also known as: poverty-weed, monolepis, patota, patata

French names: ansérine hastée

QUICK ID
- Leaves spear-shaped
- Leaves alternate
- Flowers in dense clusters

Distribution: Found throughout Canada (except New Brunswick, Prince Edward Island and Newfoundland) and the western states of the United States.

Weed Designation
Canada: MB

DESCRIPTION
Seed: Seeds are round, dark orangish brown, 1 to 1.3 mm in diameter. A thin, pale-green covering may surround the seed.

Seedling: Cotyledons are narrow, 8 to 19 mm long and 1 to 2 mm wide, and bright purplish red. The stem below the cotyledons is usually tinged with pink or purple. The first pair of leaves is opposite and mealy in appearance.

Leaves: Leaves are alternate and lance-shaped with a pair of lobes near the base. The reddish or purplish green leaves are thick and fleshy, 1 to 5 cm long.

Flower: Clusters of small green flowers are found in the axils of leaves. Flowers, less than 2 mm across, are composed of 1 sepal, 1 stamen, and 1 pistil. Petals are absent.

Plant: A low-spreading annual, spear-leaved goosefoot has stems up to 50 cm long. The fleshy red stems have numerous branches and form large, circular mats.

Fruit: The single-seeded fruit, called an achene, is surrounded by a papery membrane.

REASONS FOR CONCERN

Spear-leaved goosefoot is a common weed of waste areas, roadsides and moist, low-lying areas of cultivated fields. It has been reported that livestock that ingest large amounts of spear-leaved goosefoot are at risk of NITRATE POISONING. It is an alternate host for beet curly top and beet yellows viruses.

SIMILAR SPECIES

Oak-leaved goosefoot (*C. salinum* Standl.) closely resembles spear-leaved goosefoot. The prostrate, reddish stems of oak-leaved goosefoot are up to 40 cm long. The leaves, 2 to 3 cm long, are ovate with wavy-toothed margins and often resemble oak leaves as the common name implies. The shape of the leaf is the most distinguishing characteristic between these 2 species.

oak-leaved goosefoot

Russian thistle

Salsola kali L.

QUICK ID
- Stems with red stripes
- Plants bristly at maturity
- Leaves spine-tipped

Distribution: Found throughout Canada (except Newfoundland) and the United States (except states between the Mississippi River and the Atlantic coast).

Weed Designation
Canada: AB, BC, MB, ON, SK
USA: AZ, HI, MO

An annual introduced from Russia into South Dakota in 1874 as a contaminant in flax seed, Russian thistle was first observed in Ontario, Canada in 1894.

Also known as: Russian tumbleweed, Russian cactus, tumbling Russian thistle, glasswort, burning bush, saltwort, prickly glasswort, wind witch

French names: soude roulante, chardon de Russie, herbe roulante de Russie

Scientific synonyms: *S. pestifer* A. Nels.; *S. iberica* Sennen & Pau; *S. tragus* L. subsp. *iberica* Sennen and Pau

DESCRIPTION

Seed: Seeds are cone-shaped, dull brown to grey, about 2 mm long. Each plant is capable of producing up to 200,000 seeds. If soil moisture is adequate, seeds germinate at temperatures ranging from below freezing to very hot. Research has shown that no seeds will germinate from 8 cm soil depth.

Seedling: Cotyledons are narrow, fleshy, 10 to 50 mm long and less than 3 mm wide. The first pair of leaves is opposite and resembles the cotyledons except for a soft spine at the tip of the leaf. The stem is often tinged with purple.

Leaves: Leaves are alternate, 2 to 6 cm long and 1 mm wide. The lower leaves are thread-like and the upper leaves are awl-shaped and spine-tipped. The upper leaves become stiff with age.

Flower: Small, inconspicuous flowers, less than 2 mm wide, are borne singly in leaf axils. Flowers are of 2 types, male and female. Male flowers are composed of 5 sepals and 5 stamens. Female flowers have 5 sepals and 1 style with a 2-lobed stigma. Petals are absent in both male and female flowers. There are 2 spine-tipped bracts, about 6 mm long, below each flower.

Plant: Russian thistle has spiny stems, up to 120 cm tall, with numerous branches. Stems and branches are often striped with red. The pyramid-shaped plant turns red in late summer. At maturity, the dried stem breaks off at ground level and becomes a tumble-weed, scattering seeds in its path.

Fruit: A coiled, top-shaped fruit, about 2 mm long, contains a single seed.

REASONS FOR CONCERN

Russian thistle is a common weed of roadsides, railways, and dry open areas. It establishes itself in areas where there is reduced competition from other plants. The wide temperature range for germination and the mechanism of seed dispersal have assisted in the spread of this plant. It is an alternate host for beet yellows, beet curly top, and beet mosaic viruses.

SIMILAR SPECIES

The seedling of corn spurry (*Spergula arvensis* L.; see pp 330-31) is often mistaken for the seedling of Russian thistle. The leaf tips of corn spurry are blunt while those of Russian thistle are spine-tipped. The tumbleweed of kochia (*Kochia scoparia* (L.) Schrad.; see pp 158-59) may also be mistaken for Russian thistle. The tumbleweed of kochia is slightly hairy, unlike that of Russian thistle, which is spiny.

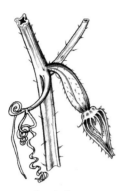

female flower

male flower

With over 700 species worldwide, the gourd family is found primarily in tropical regions with a few species in temperate regions of North America. Gourds are herbaceous plants with alternate palmately veined leaves and tendrils. Flowers are of 2 types, male and female. Male flowers are composed of 4 to 6 sepals, 4 to 6 petals, and 1 to 5 stamens. Female flowers have similar sepals and petals and a single style. The fruit may be a berry, pepo, capsule, or achene.

The gourd family has several economically important members which include cucumbers, melons, squash, and luffa. A few species are considered weedy.

Gourd Family

wild cucumber,
Echinocystis lobata
(Michx.) T. & G.

Cucurbitaceae

wild cucumber

Echinocystis lobata
(Michx.) T. & G.

An annual introduced from Europe.

Also known as: balsam-apple, mock-apple, creeping jenny, four-seeded bur cucumber

French names: concombre grimpant, concombre sauvage, échinocystis lobé

DESCRIPTION

Seed: Elliptical and flattened, seeds are 16 to 20 mm long, 8 to 10 mm wide, and less than 4 mm thick. The seed surface is dull brown marbled with patches of dark brown. Each plant is capable of producing over 400 seeds. A cold period of at least 4 months is required to break dormancy. Seeds germinate readily when soil temperatures reach 25 °C.

Seedling: Cotyledons are ovate, 3 to 7 cm long and 1 to 3 cm wide, dark green above and pale beneath. Seed leaves are thick and prominently veined. The stem below the cotyledons is pale green and hollow until the second leaf stage. The first leaves are kidney-shaped with 3 to 7 prominent lobes. The leaves are rough-textured on both sides.

Leaves: Leaves are alternate, palmately 3 to 7-lobed with toothed margins, 5 to 13 cm across. Leaves are bright green and sandpapery on both surfaces. They are long-stalked with a heart-shaped base. A long, curly, branched tendril is opposite the leaf. Tendrils are modified leaves that help the plant cling to other vegetation or structures for support.

Flower: Flowers are of 2 types, male and female. Male flowers appear in showy branched clusters from leaf axils. These white to greenish yellow flowers are composed of 6 sepals, 6 petals, and 2 or 3 yellow stamens. Single female flowers can be found in the axil of the tendrils. Female flowers are composed of 6 sepals, 6 yellowish green, and a single short pistil.

Plant: A creeping or climbing annual vine with stems to 8 m in length, wild cucumber reproduces by seeds only. The twining stems are often grooved and angled. The bright-green plants climb on surrounding vegetation or structures for support.

Fruit: The fleshy fruit, called a pepo, is oblong-shaped, 2.5 to 5 cm long. The thick, mottled, pale-green skin is covered with weak prickles. When the seeds have matured, the fruit opens at the apex, releasing 4 seeds. The inside of the fruit is fibrous and mesh-like.

REASONS FOR CONCERN

Wild cucumber is a weed of fencelines, waste areas, and meadows. It is an alternate host for cucumber mosaic, cucurbit mosaic, and several *Prunus* viruses.

SIMILAR SPECIES

Bur-cucumber (*Sicyos angulatus* L.), an introduced annual also with twining stems, is closely related to wild cucumber. Bur-cucumber is distinguished from wild cucumber by its fruit. The spiny fruit, up to 23 mm long, appear in groups of 3 to 10 in the axils of the tendrils. The leaves have 3 to 5-pointed lobes and a deep, heart-shaped base. Bur-cucumber is found in southern Ontario and Quebec and in states east of the Mississippi River.

inflorescence

spikelet

The grass family is often referred to by its old
scientific name, Gramineae. It is a large,
diverse family of over 10,000 species ranging
from small herbs to shrubs and trees. The
grass family is often divided into several
subfamilies and tribes based on morpholog-
ical characteristics. The stems, also called
culms, are round and hollow except at the
leaf nodes, where they are solid. The alternate or basal leaves are 2-ranked. The base of
the leaf that surrounds the stem is referred
to as a sheath. At the junction of the sheath
and the blade is a papery structure called a
ligule. Ear-like projections called *auricles* may
also be present at this junction. Grass flowers
are borne in clusters called spikelets. Each
spikelet has 2 bracts at its base which are
referred to as the first and second glume.
Each floret in the spikelet consists of 2
bractlets and a small flower. The bractlets,
called the *lemma* and *palea*, enclose a small
flower composed of 2 *lodicules* (evolutionary
remnants of the perianth), 3 stamens, and a
single ovary with 2 feathery styles. Glumes,
lemmas, and palea are important structures
used in identification of grasses. The fruit is
called a caryopsis or grain.

Grass
Family

floret

Economically, the grasses are the most important plant family in the world. Some
important species include wheat, rice, corn,
sorghum, sugar cane, and bamboo. Several
species are weedy, however, and can drastically reduce cultivated crop yields.

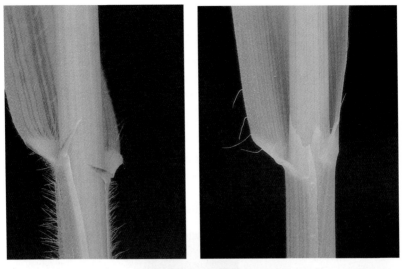

Clockwise from top left:
quackgrass, *Agropyron repens* (L.) Beauv.;
wild oat, *Avena fatua* L.;
wild oat, *Avena fatua* L.

Poaceae

quackgrass

Agropyron repens
(L.) Beauv.

QUICK ID
- Extensive creeping rhizome
- Auricles and ligules present
- Sheath hairy at base and open with overlapping margins

Distribution: Found throughout Canada and the northern two-thirds of the United States.

Weed Designation
Canada: FEDERAL, AB, BC, MB, PQ, SK
USA: ALL EXCEPT AR

A perennial introduced from Europe as a contaminant in hay or straw, quackgrass was first reported in North America in 1672.

Also known as: couch grass, twitch grass, quitch grass, scutch grass, quick grass, shellygrass, knotgrass, devil's-grass, witchgrass, bluejoint, pondgrass, Colorado bluegrass, false wheat, dog grass, seargrass, quickens, stroil, wickens

French names: chiendent, chiendent rampant, agropyron rampant

Scientific synonyms: *Elytrigia repens* (L.) Nevski; *Elymus repens* (L.) Gould

DESCRIPTION
Seed: Seeds are elliptical, pale yellow to brown, 10 mm long and less than 1.7 mm wide. Awns are 1 to 10 mm long. About 2% of all seeds are viable after 10 years. Each stem can produce up to 400 seeds, although 20 to 40 is common.

Seedling: First leaves are slightly hairy and bright green. Roots are fibrous. The lower part of the

stem is often pinkish brown and hairy. Tillers are produced at the 4 to 6-leaf stage. Rhizomes begin to form at the 6 to 8-leaf stage.

Leaves: Blades are flat, 6 to 20 cm long and 4 to 10 mm wide, sparsely hairy above and hairless below. The open sheath has overlapping margins and has soft hairs. Lower leaf sheaths have several downward-pointing hairs. Auricles are about 3 mm long and pointed. The ligule is short (less than 1 mm long) and papery.

Flower: Flower clusters, called spikes, are 5 to 25 cm long and composed of several spikelets, 10 to 15 mm long. Spikelets have 2 to 9 flowers. These short-awned spikelets are set edgewise on the stem. The stamens, 3 to 7 mm long, protrude from the flower. A feathery white stigma can also be seen when the plant is flowering. Glumes have 5 to 7 prominent nerves. The lemmas have short awns.

rhizome

Plant: Stems, with 3 to 6 joints, are up to 1.2 m tall and often form clumps. The root system is an extensive creeping network of yellowish white rhizomes, about 3 mm thick. Rhizomes, up to 150 cm long, usually grow between 5 and 20 cm depth. Fibrous roots rise at each node of the underground stem. A plant may spread up to 3 m per year and can give rise to more than 200 new shoots.

Fruit: The fruit is called a caryopsis or grain. Three to 7 seeds are produced per spikelet.

REASONS FOR CONCERN

In severely infested fields, quackgrass rhizomes can weigh as much as 7 to 9 tonnes/acre. The rhizomes produce a chemical that can suppress the growth of other plants. Quackgrass adversely affects the yield of all cultivated crops. It is often a contaminant of cultivated seed, which results in grade reduction.

SIMILAR SPECIES

Northern wheat grass (*A. dasystachyum* (Hook.) Scribn.) is distiguished by leaf edges that are rolled inward.

wild oat

Avena fatua L.

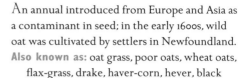

An annual introduced from Europe and Asia as a contaminant in seed; in the early 1600s, wild oat was cultivated by settlers in Newfoundland.

Also known as: oat grass, poor oats, wheat oats, flax-grass, drake, haver-corn, hever, black oats

French names: folle avoine, avoine folle, avoine sauvage

QUICK ID
- Ligule present
- Auricles absent
- Hairy on base of leaf blade

Distribution: Found throughout Canada and the United States, except the southeastern states.

Weed Designation
Canada: FEDERAL, AB, BC, MB, PQ, SK
USA: AK, AZ, CO, ID, KS, MO, MI, MT, NM, ND, OK, SC, SD, TX, WA, WI, WY

DESCRIPTION
Seed: Seeds are elliptical, light yellow to black, 1 cm long, with numerous brown hairs at the base. The dark-brown to black awn is 2 to 5 cm long, twisted, and bent at a 90° angle. A scar, often referred to as a "suckermouth," is located on the end of the seed where numerous hairs are found. Each plant is capable of producing up to 500 seeds. Research shows that seeds may be viable after 75 years, although 4 to 10 years is more common. Seeds require a dormant period and will not germinate when exposed to light.

Seedling: Seedling leaves are twisted counter-clockwise. Leaves are slightly hairy. The seed is retained on the root of the seedling. Seedlings grow slowly for the first 2 weeks, but soon surpass cultivated crops in height.

Leaves: Leaf blades are flat, up to 60 cm long and 4 to 18 mm wide, and twisted counter-clockwise. The open sheath has transparent, slightly hairy edges. A few long white hairs can be found at the base of the blade. The papery ligule is irregularly torn and 2 to 5 mm long. Auricles are absent.

Flower: The open panicle, 10 to 40 cm long, has large spikelets, each composed of 2 to 3 flowers. Spikelets, 2 to 2.5 cm long, occur singly at the end of branches and produce a drooping inflorescence. Glumes are smooth with fine lines. Lemmas have awns that are twisted and slightly bent.

Plant: A tufted plant with an extensive fibrous root system, wild oat has stems with dark-coloured nodes. Three to 5 hairless stems, up to 1.5 m tall, rise from the plant base. Seeds are shed at maturity, usually before the crop is harvested. The straw of wild oat is somewhat allelopathic and may cause damage to sensitive plants. Plants require a growing season of 2 to 3 months to reach seed maturity.

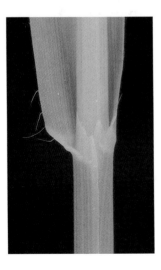

Fruit: The single-seeded fruit is called a caryopsis or grain.

REASONS FOR CONCERN

Wild oat is one of the most serious weeds in North America. It has the potential to reduce crop yields by 50%, due to dockage losses, lower crop grade and quality, and the ability to produce chemicals that inhibit germination of other plants. Wild oat is an alternate host for barley yellow dwarf, lucerne dwarf, ryegrass mosaic, and wheat streak mosaic viruses.

SIMILAR SPECIES

Cultivated oat (*A. sativa* L.) is distinguished from wild oat by its short straight awn. The seeds of cultivated oat are not shed at maturity.

smooth brome

Bromus inermis Leyss.

An introduced perennial; native subspecies occur. Introduced subspecies from Eurasia were grown for forage as early as 1875.

Also known as: awnless brome, Hungarian brome, Russian brome, Austrian brome

French names: brome inerme

Scientific synonyms: *B. pumpellianus* (Scribn.) Wagon.

QUICK ID
- Ligule present
- Auricles absent
- Sheath closed

Distribution: Found throughout Canada and the United States, except in the southeastern states.

Weed Designation
USA: TN

DESCRIPTION

Seed: Elliptical, pale-yellow to dark-brown seeds are about 10 mm long and 2 mm wide. A short awn, less than 3 mm long, may be present. Each plant is capable of producing up to 200 seeds.

Seedling: First leaves are covered with fine, silky hairs. The base of the young stem is often pink to pale red. Rhizomes begin to form about 3 weeks after germination.

Leaves: Leaf blades are flat, 15 to 40 cm long and 5 to 15 mm wide, and nearly hairless. Leaf sheaths are closed, with a small V-shaped notch. A few hairs may be found on the sheath. The ligule, 1 to 2 mm long, is brownish at the base. Auricles are absent.

Flower: A nodding, open panicle, 5 to 20 cm long, has 1 to 4 branches per node. Each branch has several spikelets, each 1.5 to 3 cm long. Spikelets are purplish brown and 7 to 10-flowered. Glumes have 1 to 5 prominent nerves. Lemmas, 7 to 16 mm long, are 5 to 9-nerved and have short awns (less than 3 mm long).

Plant: Smooth brome is common in hay fields and roadsides throughout most of North America. Erect, hairless stems, up to 1.5 m tall, rise from an extensive creeping rhizome that is dark-coloured and jointed. The internodes are covered with large, scaly, brown to black sheaths. Roots and shoots are produced at each node.

Fruit: The single-seeded fruit is called a caryopsis or grain. 7 to 10 seeds are produced per spikelet.

REASONS FOR CONCERN
Smooth brome, often planted as a forage crop, persists after cultivation and infests later crops. Smooth brome is an alternate host for the viral diseases barley stripe mosaic, barley yellow dwarf, brome mosaic, and oat pseudo-rosette.

SIMILAR SPECIES
Nodding brome (*B. anomalus* Rupr. ex Fourn.), another native brome grass, is distinguished from smooth brome by a drooping panicle and fibrous roots. Rhizomes are not present. It is found in moist grassland areas of western North America.

downy brome

Bromus tectorum L.

An annual or winter annual introduced from the Mediterranean Region of Europe, downy brome was first observed near Denver, Colorado in the 1890s.

Also known as: downy chess, early chess, cheatgrass, cheatgrass brome, slender brome, drooping brome grass, thatch grass

French names: brome des toits

QUICK ID
- Ligule present
- Auricles absent
- Leaves covered with soft hairs

Distribution: Found throughout Canada (except Newfoundland) and the United States (except Florida).

Weed Designation
Canada: AB, MB
USA: WI

DESCRIPTION
Seed: Elliptical seeds are pale brown with a red tinge, about 11 mm long and 1.5 mm wide. The awn is straight, 12 to 17 mm long. Seeds may remain dormant for several years. Optimal germination occurs in the top 2.5 cm of soil with no seedlings emerging from 10 cm depth.

Seedling: First leaf is tall and narrow. Leaves are soft-haired and twisted, with a prominent midrib.

Leaves: Leaf blades are flat, 5 to 12 cm long and 2 to 4 mm wide, and covered with long, soft, white hairs. Sheaths are soft-haired and closed at the bottom. The thin, somewhat transparent ligule is 1 to 3 mm long and irregularly toothed. Auricles are absent.

Flower: The nodding panicle, 7 to 20 cm long, has several drooping branches. The panicle, often purple, is covered with soft, white hairs. Spikelets are 2 to 4 cm long, including the awn, and contain 3 to 10 flowers. Glumes are woolly and 1-nerved. Lemmas are lance-shaped, woolly, and long-awned.

Plant: Downy brome is a prolific seed producer. A tufted grass, 2.5 to 60 cm tall, it is covered with silky hairs. Downy brome flowers early in the spring and has dried by midsummer. Roots are fibrous and often root at lower nodes.

Fruit: The single-seeded fruit is called a cary-opsis or grain. Each spikelet produces between 5 and 10 seeds.

REASONS FOR CONCERN

Downy brome has been reported to reduce wheat yields by 92%. It is an aggressive species that invades pastures and rangeland. Early spring growth is readily eaten by live-stock. By midsummer, the sharp spikelets and rough awns may injure the eyes and mouths of livestock. Downy brome is an alternate host for barley stripe mosaic, barley yellow dwarf, ryegrass mosaic, and wheat streak mosaic viruses.

SIMILAR SPECIES

Japanese chess (*B. japonicus* Thunb.), another introduced brome grass, is distinguished from downy brome by the number of nerves on the first glume. Japanese chess has 3 nerves; downy brome has 1. Japanese chess grows from 20 to 60 cm tall and is covered with soft, white hairs.

large crabgrass

Digitaria sanguinalis
(L.) Scop.

An annual introduced from Europe.

Also known as: purple crabgrass, finger-grass, Polish millet, crowfoot-grass, pigeon-grass, hairy finger grass

French names: digitaire sanguine, digitaire poupre, panic sanguin

QUICK ID
- 3 to 13 finger-like terminal spikes
- Auricles absent
- Ligules present

Distribution: Found throughout Canada (except Newfoundland and Saskatchewan) and the United States, except for the north-central plains.

Weed Designation
Canada: FEDERAL, MB, PQ   USA: NV, NH

DESCRIPTION
Seed: Elliptical to lance-shaped seeds are dull olive to brown, 2.7 to 3.0 mm long and less than 1 mm wide. Each plant is capable of producing up to 150,000 seeds.

Seedling: The first leaf is short and wide with a blunt tip.

Leaves: Leaf blades are 5 to 20 cm long and 4 to 10 mm wide. The split sheath has overlapping hairy margins. Numerous long, white hairs are found at the junction of the leaf blade and sheath. The ligule is membranous and less than 2 mm long. Auricles are absent.

Flower: A panicle of 3 to 13 finger-like branches, 5 to 15 cm long, whorled at the top of the stem. Spikelets, about 3 mm long, are single-flowered and arranged alternately on 1 side of the stem. The second glume is about half the length of the spikelet. The lemmas are 5-nerved and pale brown.

Plant: Large crabgrass is often killed by the first frost. The ascending to prostrate stems are 30 to 120 cm long and often root at lower nodes. The fibrous roots may extend to a depth of 2 m. The base of the plant is quite leafy. Each plant may produce up to 700 tillers.

Fruit: The single-seeded fruit is called a caryopsis or grain.

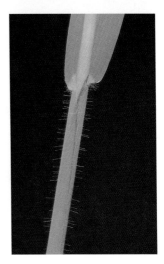

REASONS FOR CONCERN

Large crabgrass is a serious weed in row crops, cultivated fields, and lawns. It is an alternate host for barley stripe, wheat streak mosaic, sugar cane mosaic, and lucerne dwarf viruses.

SIMILAR SPECIES

Small crabgrass (*D. ischaemum* Schreb. ex Muhl.) is closely related to large crabgrass. Small crabgrass has hairless leaves with a few long hairs at the junction of the blade and sheath. The membranous ligule is 2 to 3 mm long. Small crabgrass has 2 to 6 finger-like terminal spikes.

barnyard grass

Echinochloa crusgalli
(L.) Beauv.

An annual introduced from Europe and India, barnyard grass was first reported from California in 1825 and from Nova Scotia in 1829.

Also known as: cockspur grass, Japanese millet, cocksfoot panicum, barn-grass, water-grass, summer grass, billion dollar grass

French names: échinochloa pied-de-coq, pied-de-coq

Scientific synonyms: *E. pungens* (Poir.) Rydb.

QUICK ID
- Auricles and ligules absent
- Sheath open
- Stems reddish at base

Distribution: Found throughout Canada and the United States, except Florida.

Weed Designation
   Canada: MB, PQ   USA: AR

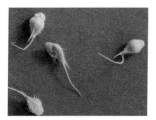

DESCRIPTION
Seed: Elliptical seeds with a long tip are whitish to greyish brown, rounded on 1 side and flat on the other. Seeds are 3.5 to 4.2 mm long and 1.6 to 2.0 mm wide. A short awn, 1 to 2 cm long, is attached to the narrow end of the seed. The seed has numerous short, stiff hairs. Seeds are viable for up to 9 years. Each plant is capable of producing as many as 40,000 seeds.

Germination is shallow, as soil temperatures must be over 30 °C for seedlings to emerge.

Seedling: Leaves with pointed tips are hairless and may be slightly red at the base. The stem of barnyard grass is somewhat flattened up to the 3-leaf stage. The first tillers appear about 10 days after germination.

Leaves: Leaf blades are flat or V-shaped, 5 to 50 cm long and 0.5 to 2 cm wide, and hairless. Sheaths are flattened, open with overlapping margins, and slightly hairy. The edges of the base may have a few soft hairs present. Ligules and auricles are absent.

Flower: The erect panicle is 5 to 20 cm long and composed of numerous spikelets, each about 3 mm long. The panicle is greenish red or purplish, due to the flower's feathery red stigmas. Glumes are prominently 3-nerved. Lemmas are prominently nerved and awned.

Plant: Barnyard grass is a vigorously growing plant with several branches from its base. A prolific seed producer, it has stems that can grow to 1.5 m long. The base of the stem is often reddish purple and can be either erect or prostrate. Stems often root from lower nodes when in contact with soil. Roots are fibrous. Barnyard grass usually produces about 15 tillers.

Fruit: The single-seeded fruit is called a caryopsis or grain.

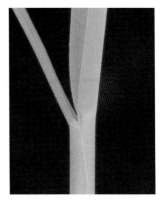

REASONS FOR CONCERN

Barnyard grass is a common weed of gardens and shelterbelts. Ranked third among the world's worst weeds, it has the potential to be a serious weed in row crops such as beets, potatoes, and corn. Barnyard grass may consume 60 to 80% of available soil nitrogen in a single growing season. It can accumulate high levels of nitrates in plant tissues, which may be TOXIC to livestock. Barnyard grass is an alternate host for maize dwarf disease, barley stripe mosaic, wheat streak mosaic, and sugar cane mosaic viruses.

foxtail barley

Hordeum jubatum L.

A perennial native to western North America.

Also known as: wild barley, foxtail, squirrel-tail barley, skunktail grass, flicker-tail grass, tickle grass, foxtail grass

French names: orgequeue d'écureuil, orge agréable, queue-d'écureuil, orge sauvage

QUICK ID
- Bluish green bunchgrass
- Ligule present
- Auricles absent

Distribution: Found throughout Canada and the northern two-thirds of the United States.

Weed Designation
Canada: MB, PQ

DESCRIPTION
Seed: Elliptic, yellowish brown seeds are 3 to 4 mm long with 4 to 8 awns. Awns are 1.5 to 6 cm long. Seeds have sharp, backward-pointing barbs that catch on the hair of animals. Each plant is capable of producing more than 180 seeds. Seeds require extended

hours of darkness for germination, which usually occurs in late August or early September. Seeds are viable up to 7 years.

Seedling: The first leaf is tall and narrow. Leaves are usually bluish green because of the short white hairs. Seedlings cannot emerge from a depth of 7.5 cm of soil.

Leaves: Leaf blades are flat or V-shaped, 5 to 15 cm long and 2 to 9 mm wide. Leaves are greyish green and have a sandpapery texture. The sheaths are split with overlapping margins. The sheath margin has numerous soft hairs. Auricles are very small or absent. The ligule is transparent and about 1 mm long.

Flower: Foxtail barley has a nodding panicle, 5 to 12 cm long. There are 3 spikelets per node, each 1-flowered. The awns, up to 8 cm long, are purplish green and fade to white as the seeds mature. The spike breaks into several pieces at maturity. Each piece, consisting of 3 florets, has 7 awns. Glumes and lemmas have long awns.

Plant: A bunchgrass with stems up to 1 m tall, foxtail barley is a prolific seed producer. The bluish green stems often have swollen nodes. Foxtail barley is common on roadsides, waste ground, and open fields.

Fruit: The single-seeded fruit is called a caryopsis or grain.

REASONS FOR CONCERN

Foxtail barley is palatable to livestock in early summer, prior to flowering. In late summer, the sharp-pointed awns may cause damage to the mouth, eyes, and skin of livestock that feed on this plant. Foxtail barley is an alternate host for wheat rust and barley stripe mosaic viruses.

SIMILAR SPECIES

Cultivated barley (*H. vulgare* L.) is distinguished from foxtail barley by shorter awns, 6 to 15 mm long, and the presence of auricles.

Persian darnel

Lolium persicum
Boiss. & Hohen.

An annual introduced from southwestern Asia, Persian darnel was first reported in Canada in 1923.

Also known as: darnel

French names: ivraie de Perse

QUICK ID
- Auricles and ligules present
- Sheaths closed
- Leaves shiny

Distribution: Found in all provinces west of and including Ontario, and throughout the western United States.

Weed Designation
Canada: AB, MB, SK
USA: MT, TX

DESCRIPTION

Seed: Seeds are light brown, 8 to 10 mm long, with a slightly bent awn, 5 to 12 mm in length. Seeds are similar in size to wheat grains, which makes them difficult to separate.

Seedling: The first leaf is long, narrow, and folded. It is dark green and shiny on the upper surface. The base of the first leaves is often reddish brown or purple.

Leaves: Leaf blades are flat, twisted, 5 to 15 cm long and 2 to 6 mm wide. The upper surface of the leaf is sandpapery. The sheaths are hairless and round with prominently veined overlapping margins. Auricles are present at the fifth leaf stage. The ligule is short, 1 mm long, and papery.

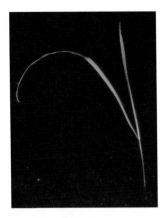

Flower: The panicle, 3 to 10 cm long, is composed of several stalkless spikelets set edgewise to the stem. The spikelets are 5 to 7-flowered, 10 to 20 mm long. The second glume is 5 to 9-nerved. Lemmas are 5-nerved, 9 to 10 mm long.

Plant: Persian darnel is a bright-green grass that branches from the lower nodes. Stems, 15 to 75 cm tall, are similar in colour to wheat. The base of the stem is usually reddish purple. Roots are fibrous.

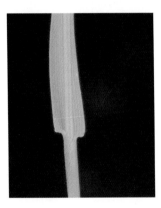

Fruit: The single-seeded fruit is called a caryopsis or grain.

REASONS FOR CONCERN

Large populations of Persian darnel have been reported to cause significant decreases in crop yield. A problem pest in wheat, the seeds of Persian darnel lower the quality and grade of the crop.

SIMILAR SPECIES

Perennial rye grass (*L. perenne* L.) is an introduced grass cultivated in pastures, hayland, and lawns. Stems are usually 20 to 80 cm tall. The panicle, 5 to 25 cm long, is composed of 5 to 10 flowered spikelets. Another species, poison darnel (*L. temulentum* L.), is an annual grass with stems up to 1 m tall. It is distinguished from Persian darnel by its wider leaves (3 to 10 mm wide).

witch grass

Panicum capillare L.

An annual native to North America.

Also known as: old witch grass, tickle grass, witches'-hair, tumbleweed grass, fool hay, tumble panic grass

French names: panic capillaire

QUICK ID
- Ligule present
- Auricles absent
- Sheath open with hairy, overlapping margins

Distribution: Found throughout Canada (except Newfoundland) and the United States. A troublesome weed in Ontario and Quebec.

Weed Designation
Canada: FEDERAL, MB, PQ

DESCRIPTION
Seed: Seeds are elliptical, dull brown to dark grey, 1.3 mm long and 0.8 mm wide. Seeds germinate late in the spring, and the plant is well developed by July.

Seedling: The first leaf is 1 to 1.5 cm long and 3 to 4 mm wide. The young stem is often bent.

Leaves: Leaf blades, 10 to 25 cm long and 5 to 15 mm wide, have a prominent white midrib. Leaves are densely hairy on both sides and reduced in size upwards. The open sheath has overlapping margins with hairs, 2 to 3 mm long. The sheath is strongly ribbed. The ligule is a fringe of hairs, 1 to 2 mm long. Auricles are absent.

Flower: The open panicle, 20 to 25 cm long, has numerous fine branches. The panicle breaks off at maturity and becomes a tumbleweed. Spikelets are 2 to 3 mm long. The first glume is 1 to 2 mm long, while the second is 2 to 3 mm long. Lemmas are 2 to 3 mm long and 7-nerved.

Plant: An annual grass with a fibrous root system, witch grass has simple or branched stems, 20 to 90 cm tall. As the plant matures, the hairs become stiff and prickly.

Fruit: The single-seeded fruit is called a caryopsis or grain.

REASONS FOR CONCERN

A problem pest of cultivated fields, gardens, roadsides, and waste areas, witch grass does not compete with other grasses in well-maintained pastures. Livestock that ingest large amounts of witch grass are PRONE TO PHOTOSENSITIZATION AND NITRATE POISONING. Witch grass is an alternate host for barley stripe mosaic, barley yellow dwarf, wheat streak mosaic, and wheat striate mosaic.

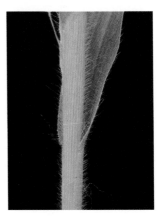

SIMILAR SPECIES

Fall panicum (*P. dichotomiflorum* Michx.), a native grass of eastern North America, is closely related to witch grass. It is distinguished from witch grass by the zigzag appearance of the stem, the absence of hairs on the sheath, and a coarser panicle, 15 to 50 cm long. Another species, wild proso millet (*P. miliaceum* L.), is a coarse annual that has escaped from cultivation. It is distinguished from witch grass by larger spikelets (more than 4 mm long) and larger seeds (about 3 mm long); see pp 188-89.

wild proso millet

wild proso millet

Panicum miliaceum L.

An annual introduced from Europe as a cultivated crop; the cultivated form of wild proso millet is a common constituent of bird seed.

Also known as: proso millet, broom-corn millet

French names: panic millet

QUICK ID
- Ligule a fringe of hairs
- Auricles absent
- Panicle arched and nodding

Distribution: Found throughout Canada and the northern two-thirds of the United States.

Weed Designation
USA: WY

DESCRIPTION

Seed: Seeds are elliptical, pale orange to black, 2.9 to 3.2 mm long and 2 to 2.2 mm wide. The surface of the seed is shiny and has several faint nerves.

Seedling: The seed of wild proso millet remains attached to the primary root. Seedlings resemble young corn plants, but are hairy.

Leaves: Blades, up to 30 cm long and 5 to 25 mm wide, are smooth to somewhat hairy. The open sheath is covered with stiff hairs that are often perpendicular to the stem. The sheath margins overlap just above the node below. The ligule is composed of a fringe of hairs 2 to 5 mm long; the hairs are fused at the base. Auricles are absent.

Flower: The open panicle, 8 to 30 cm long, can be erect, arched, or nodding. The spikelets, 4 to 5.5 mm long, are composed of 2 florets. The first glume is distinctly 5-nerved, while the second glume and lemma are 7 to 9-nerved.

Plant: A coarse annual, wild proso millet has stems up to 1 m tall. The erect to reclining stems rise from a shallow fibrous root system.

Fruit: The single-seeded fruit is called a grain or caryopsis.

REASONS FOR CONCERN

Wild proso millet is a serious weed of cultivated crops, especially corn. It is also common in forage crops, gardens, and farmyards. Wild proso millet is an alternate host for barley stripe mosaic, oat pseudo-rosette, panicum mosaic, rice dwarf mosaic, and wheat streak mosaic.

SIMILAR SPECIES

Wild proso millet is closely related to witch grass (*P. capillare* L.), but witch grass may be distinguished by its erect panicle and smaller seeds (see pp 186-87). Fall panicum (*P. dichotomiflorum* (L.) Michx.) is distinguished from wild proso millet by its hairless leaf sheaths and larger spikelets.

witch grass

annual bluegrass

Poa annua L.

An annual or winter annual introduced from Europe and Asia.

Also known as: dwarf meadow grass, causeway grass, speargrass, six-weeks grass

French names: pâturin annuel

QUICK ID
- Sheath loose
- Leaf tips boat-shaped
- Plants less than 30 cm tall

Distribution: Found throughout Canada and the United States.

Weed Designation
USA: AK, CT, DC, DE, FL, KY, MA, MD, NJ, NY, PA, SD, TN, TX, VA

DESCRIPTION

Seed: Seeds are straw-coloured and ovate with 1 pointed end, 2 to 3 mm long and 1 to 1.3 mm wide.

Seedling: The first leaf is 5 to 9 mm long and 1 to 3 mm wide. Young leaves have scattered soft hairs.

Leaves: Leaf blades are soft-haired and 1 to 4 mm wide. The flattened sheaths are loose and hairless. Leaves are light green with boat-shaped tips.

Flower: The panicle, 2 to 10 cm long, is pyramid-shaped. The open panicle has spikelets with 3 to 6 flowers, each 3 to 5 mm long. Glumes are lance-shaped. Lemmas are elliptical with 5 distinct nerves.

Plant: A tufted grass, often rooting at lower nodes, annual bluegrass forms large mats. The stems, 3 to 30 cm long, are bright green. It is a common weed in lawns, parks, and golf courses. As the common name six-weeks grass implies, a full life-cycle may be completed within 6 weeks.

Fruit: The single-seeded fruit is called a caryopsis or grain.

REASONS FOR CONCERN
Annual bluegrass is a serious weed in lawns, golf courses, and waste areas. In early summer, plants mature and die, leaving brown patches of dead grass in turf. It is an alternate host for barley yellow dwarf and lucerne dwarf viruses.

SIMILAR SPECIES
Canada bluegrass (*P. compressa* L.), another introduced species, is common in meadows and waste ground. It is distinguished from annual bluegrass by its creeping rhizomes and flattened stems. The panicle, 2 to 8 cm long, has several paired branches.

Canada bluegrass

giant foxtail

Setaria faberi Herrm.

An annual introduced from China in 1931 as a contaminant in Chinese millet, giant foxtail was first reported in Ontario in 1978.

Also known as: Faber's foxtail

French names: sétaire géante, sétaire de faber

- Ligule a fringe of hairs
- Auricles absent
- Sheath open with hairy margins

Distribution: Found in southern Ontario and throughout the east-central United States.

Weed Designation
USA: AL, AR, CO, DE, GA, IA, IL, IN, KS, KY, MD, MI, MN, MO, MS, NC, OK, SC, SD, TN, TX, VA, WI

DESCRIPTION

Seed: Seeds are elliptical, 2.5 to 2.8 mm long and 1.4 to 1.6 mm wide. They are grey-brown to pale green, with wrinkled surface.

Seedling: The first leaf is 1.2 to 2.5 cm long and 2 to 4 mm wide.

Leaves: Blades, 30 to 50 cm long and 8 to 17 mm wide, are rough-haired on the upper surface. The open sheath has hairy margins. The ligule is composed of a dense fringe of hairs, about 1 mm long. Auricles are absent.

Flower: The nodding panicle, 4 to 20 cm long and up to 3 cm thick, is composed of spikelets, 2.5 to 3 mm long; the panicle often nods. Each spikelet has 3 to 6 yellowish green bristles.

Plant: A large annual grass reproducing by seed, giant foxtail is a serious weed in the east-central United States. The stems, 80 to 200 cm tall, often fall over if not supported by other plants.

Fruit: The single-seeded fruit is called a grain or caryopsis.

REASONS FOR CONCERN

Giant foxtail is an aggressive weed in cultivated fields and waste areas. It has been reported to reduce crop yields drastically.

SIMILAR SPECIES

Green foxtail (*S. viridis* (L.) Beauv.) is distinguished from giant foxtail by its erect panicle, the absence of hairs on the upper surface of the leaves, and seeds that are not wrinkled. Green foxtail has shorter stems that rarely exceed 1 m in height (see pp 198-99).

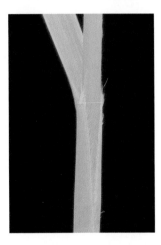

green foxtail

yellow foxtail

Setaria glauca
(L.) Beauv.

An annual introduced from Europe or Asia, yellow foxtail was first reported in Canada from Montreal in 1821, and had spread to British Columbia by 1889.

Also known as: summer grass, golden foxtail, wild millet, pigeon grass, glaucous bristly foxtail, yellow bristle grass

French names: sétaire glauque, sétaire jaune, foin sauvage, mil sauvage

Scientific synonyms: *S. lutescens* (Weigel) Hubb.

QUICK ID
- Ligule composed of a fringe of hairs
- Auricles absent
- Long, fine hairs on base of leaf

Distribution: Found throughout Canada and the United States.

Weed Designation
Canada: MB, PQ

DESCRIPTION
Seed: Elliptical, dark-greyish brown seeds are 2.3 to 2.5 mm long and 1 to 1.2 mm wide. The surface is dull, but may appear somewhat shiny under low magnification. Each panicle is capable of producing about 180 seeds, and each plant may produce over 8,400 seeds.

About 3% of seeds are viable after 13 years. Light is not required for germination.

Seedling: Early leaves are arched and hairless. The sheath is ridged and slightly flattened. The base of the seedling is often reddish.

Leaves: Leaf blades are flat or V-shaped, up to 30 cm long and 0.5 to 1.2 cm wide. Leaf blades are loosely twisted. Blades are hairless except for long, silky, white hairs, 3 to 10 mm long, at the base. Sheaths are open, hairless, and flat by the third leaf stage. The sheath is distinctly nerved with overlapping margins. The ligule is composed of a fringe of hairs, about 3 mm long. Auricles are absent.

Flower: The flower head or panicle is cylindrical, 5 to 10 cm long and about 1 cm wide. The spikelets, 2 to 3 mm long, are 1-flowered and have 5 to 20 yellowish brown bristles. The bristles, 4 to 9 mm long, turn yellow at maturity. The glumes and lemmas are 1 to 3 mm long.

Plant: Yellow foxtail has erect solitary or tufted stems that can reach a height of 130 cm. Stems are often reddish at the base.

Fruit: The single-seeded fruit is called a caryopsis or grain.

REASONS FOR CONCERN

Yellow foxtail is a highly competitive weed that can drastically reduce crop yield and increase seed-cleaning costs. Yellow foxtail is an alternate host for ergot, browning root rot, downy mildew, and smut.

SIMILAR SPECIES

Green foxtail (*S. viridis* (L.) Beauv.) another introduced annual grass, can be distinguished from yellow foxtail by the presence of 1 to 3 greenish purple bristles below each spikelet. Spikelets, 1.5 to 2 mm long, are smaller than those of yellow foxtail. Green foxtail does not have long white hairs at the base of the leaf blade (see pp 198-99).

panicle

bristly foxtail

Setaria verticillata
(L.) Beauv.

An annual introduced from Europe, bristly foxtail was first reported from Montreal in 1882.

Also known as: bristle grass, catch grass, garden grass, bur bristlegrass

French names: sétaire verticillée

QUICK ID
- Ligule present
- Auricles absent
- Bristles with backward-pointing barbs

Distribution: Found in British Columbia, Manitoba, Ontario, Quebec, and Nova Scotia, and throughout the United States.

Weed Designation None

DESCRIPTION

Seed: Elliptical, straw-coloured seeds are 2.3 to 2.5 mm long and 1 to 1.2 mm wide. The bristle, 2 to 8 mm long, has numerous backward-pointing barbs. These barbs cause the seeds to stick to each other.

Seedling: The first leaf is 9 to 18 mm long and 3 to 5 mm wide.

Leaves: Blades, 10 to 20 cm long and 5 to 10 mm wide, are bluish green and thin. The ligule is composed of a fringe of hairs, about 1 mm long. Auricles are absent.

Flower: The panicle is composed of numerous interrupted spikelets. The spike, 5 to 15 cm long and 7 to 15 mm wide, is tapered upwards. One bristle, 2 to 8 mm long, can be found below each spikelet. The greenish bristle has numerous backward-pointing barbs that may attach to skin, clothing, or fur.

Plant: Bristly foxtail has several stems from the base of the plant. The stems, 60 to 100 cm tall, are weak and often fall over when not supported by other vegetation. Stems blown around by the wind are often tangled because of the barbed bristles.

Fruit: The single-seeded fruit is called a caryopsis or grain.

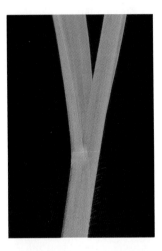

REASONS FOR CONCERN

Bristly foxtail is a serious weed in orchards, cereals, corn, and cotton. The stems often become entangled with the crop, making harvest difficult. It is an alternate host for barley stripe mosaic, wheat spot mosaic, and wheat streak mosaic viruses.

SIMILAR SPECIES

Green foxtail (*S. viridis* (L.) Beauv.) is closely related to bristly foxtail, but can be distinguished by its smooth panicle that does not cling to clothing, fur, or other plants (see pp 198-99). The inflorescence of green foxtail is compact, unlike the interrupted spike of bristly foxtail.

green foxtail

green foxtail

Setaria viridis
(L.) Beauv.

An annual introduced from Europe, green foxtail was first reported in Montreal in 1821 and had spread to Alberta by 1931.

Also known as: bottle grass, green brittle grass, wild millet, pigeon grass, pussy grass

French names: sétaire verte, mil sauvage

QUICK ID
- Ligule present
- Auricles absent
- Sheath open with over-lapping margins

Distribution: Found throughout Canada and the United States.

Weed Designation
Canada: AB, BC, MB, PQ, SK
USA: TN

DESCRIPTION

Seed: Elliptical, pale green to greyish brown seeds are 1.5 to 1.9 mm long and 1 mm wide. The surface appears shiny under low magnification. Seeds germinate at an optimum depth of 1.5 to 2.5 cm; research shows that seeds will not germinate from depths below 12 cm. Seeds germinate late in spring, often after the crop has emerged.

Seedling: The first leaves are arched and hairless. The margins of the leaf sheath are hairy after emergence of the second leaf.

Leaves: Leaf blades are flat, 5 to 15 mm wide and up to 25 cm long. Leaves are usually light green. The open sheath is slightly compressed with hairs along the overlapping margins. The ligule is a fringe of hairs, 1.5 to 2 mm long. Auricles are absent.

Flower: The purplish green panicle, 3 to 11 cm long and 1 to 2.3 cm wide, is cylindrical. The panicle is composed of several 1-flowered spikelets, each 1.5 to 2 mm long. Each spikelet has 1 to 3 purplish green bristles that are 6 to 12 mm long. Glumes and lemmas are about as long as the spikelet.

Plant: A tufted grass, green foxtail has stems to 100 cm tall. A prolific seed producer, this species is capable of producing seed within 6 weeks of germination. Several generations of green foxtail can be produced in a single growing season. The root system is fibrous.

Fruit: The single-seeded fruit is called a cary-opsis or grain.

REASONS FOR CONCERN

Green foxtail is a serious weed of cultivated crops, gardens, and roadsides. Besides competing with crops for nutrients and mois-ture, green foxtail causes dockage losses in wheat, barley, canola, and flax. The seeds of green foxtail germinate throughout the growing season whenever conditions are favourable. This factor allows many plants to survive or miss cultivation or herbicide appli-cation. The roots of green foxtail produce a chemical that is toxic to cabbage seedlings. Green foxtail is also an alternate host for barley stripe mosaic, corn new mosaic, and wheat streak mosaic.

yellow foxtail

SIMILAR SPECIES

Yellow foxtail (*S. glauca* (L.) Beauv.), another introduced annual grass, is distinguished by 5 to 12 yellowish brown bristles below each spikelet and a ligule composed of several long hairs (see pp 194-95).

Johnson grass
Sorghum halapense (L.) Pers.

A perennial introduced from the Mediterranean region of Europe into South Carolina as a forage crop in 1830, Johnson grass was deemed a weed by the United States Department of Agriculture in the early 1900s; the first Canadian report was from Ontario in 1959, and by 1980, 60 sites had been reported in 13 counties of southern Ontario.

Also known as: means grass, Egyptian grass, false Guinea grass, millet grass, Morocco millet, Cuba grass, St. Mary's grass, evergreen millet, maiden-cane

French names: sorgho d'Alep, sorgho de Johnson

- Ligule present
- Auricles absent
- Sheath open with overlapping margins

Distribution: Found in southwestern Ontario and the southern two-thirds of the United States.

Weed Designation
Canada: FEDERAL, ON
USA: FEDERAL, AL, AR, AZ, CA, CO, DE, FL, GA, HI, ID, IL, IN, KS, KY, LA, MD, MI, MO, MS, NC, NE, NJ, NM, OH, OK, OR, PA, SC, TN, TX, UT, VA, WA, WV

DESCRIPTION

Seed: Seeds are elliptical, 4.5 to 4.8 mm long and 1.5 to 2 mm wide, pale yellow to purplish brown or mottled purple and yellow. The surface is smooth and shiny. Seeds are viable for up to 7 years. Seeds are capable of germination at 7 to 15 cm depth. Each plant can produce up to 28,000 seeds. Seeds are similar in size to maize and sorghum, making them difficult to separate.

Seedling: The first leaf of Johnson grass is 1.6 to 2.5 cm long and 4 to 6 mm wide. The leaves are hairless. Seedlings reach the 7-leaf stage 50 days after germination. Young Johnson grass plants resemble young corn or grain sorghum.

Leaves: Leaf blades have a prominent white midrib and are 20 to 60 cm long and 0.5 to 5 cm wide. Leaf margins are finely toothed. The open sheath has overlapping hairless margins that are conspicuously ribbed. The ligule is papery and 2 to 5 mm long. Auricles are absent.

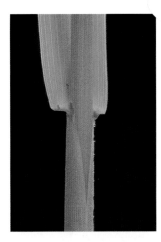

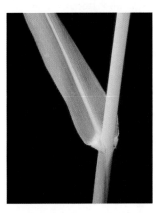

Flower: The purplish panicle is pyramid-shaped, 15 to 50 cm long, and hairy. Branches, up to 25 cm long, are whorled at the nodes and further branched. Spikelets, 4.5 to 5.5 mm long, have a deciduous awn, 1 to 1.5 cm long, that is bent and twisted.

Plant: Johnson grass is a large perennial grass that spreads by seeds and long creeping rhizomes. The rhizomes, 2 cm in diameter and up to 2 m long, are white with red and purple areas. The nodes of the rhizomes are covered with brown, scale-like sheaths. The rhizomes are easily killed by frost and rarely overwinter in southern Ontario. Stems are 90 to 300 cm tall and 2 cm in diameter. Fresh or decaying leaves, rhizomes, and roots release a chemical that affects the growth of other plants. This effect, combined with the invasive root system, allows large colonies to form. Seeds are shed at maturity.

Fruit: The single-seeded fruit is called a caryopsis or grain.

REASONS FOR CONCERN

Johnson grass is one of the world's 10 worst weeds. It is extremely competitive and is a serious weed of corn crops. It has been reported that livestock grazing on large amounts of young Johnson grass are at risk of HYDROGEN CYANIDE POISONING. Johnson grass is an alternate host for corn leaf gall, maize dwarf mosaic, wheat streak mosaic, and beet yellows viruses; it also harbours sorghum midge, an insect pest of cultivated sorghum.

root system

flower

fruit

Also called the bellflower family, the harebells feature more than 2,000 species worldwide. Species growing in the tropics are palm-like, while those of temperate regions are small herbs with milky juice. The simple, entire leaves are alternate and lack stipules. The flowers, often blue or violet, are bell or funnel-shaped. They are composed of 5 united sepals, 5 united petals, 5 stamens, and a single style. The fruit is a capsule that releases seeds through pores on its side.

The harebell family is of limited economic importance, but several species are grown for their ornamental value.

Harebell Family

creeping bellflower,
Campanula rapunculoides L.

Campanulaceae

creeping bellflower

Campanula rapunculoides L.

A perennial introduced from Europe and Asia as a garden flower.

Also known as: purple-bell, garden harebell, rover bellflower, creeping campanula, creeping bluebell

French names: campanule fausse raiponce, campanule raiponce

QUICK ID
- Flowers purple, bell-shaped
- Leaves alternate
- Root white

Distribution: Found throughout Canada and the northeastern United States.

Weed Designation
Canada: AB, MB

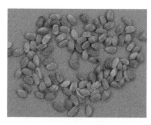

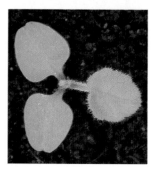

DESCRIPTION

Seed: Seeds are elliptical, light brown, glossy, 1.5 mm long and 1 mm wide. Each plant may produce up to 3,000 seeds. Germination occurs in the top 2 cm of the soil.

Seedling: Cotyledons, 2 to 5 mm long and 1 to 3 mm wide, are ovate and have upward-curled margins. The first leaves are heart-shaped and hairy on the upper surface and margin.

Leaves: Leaves are alternate, 3 to 7 cm long. Lower leaves are long-stalked and heart-shaped with coarsely toothed margins. Upper leaves are sessile and lance-shaped with some hairs on the lower surface. Leaves are reduced in size upwards, changing from heart to lance-shaped.

Flower: Solitary, nodding blue to light-purple flowers are borne in the axils of the upper leaves. Flowers are composed of 5 united sepals, 5 united petals (2 to 3 cm long), 5 stamens, and a single pistil. The bell-shaped flowers usually appear on 1 side of the stem.

Plant: Creeping bellflower reproduces by a white, creeping root and by seeds. The rhizome is thick and somewhat tuber-like, making the plant difficult to eradicate. Erect stems, reaching up to 1 m, are unbranched and form dense clumps; the stems are often hairy.

Fruit: The fruit is a round capsule that opens at 3 to 5 pores, releasing numerous small seeds.

root system

REASONS FOR CONCERN

Creeping bellflower is a weed of gardens, fence-lines, and occasionally cultivated fields. It is shade tolerant and able to survive in crops. Creeping bellflower is a serious weed in lawns, where it competes with the turf, robbing it of moisture and nutrients.

SIMILAR SPECIES

Harebell (*C. rotundifolia* L.), a native plant found throughout North America, is closely related to creeping bellflower. Harebell is distinguished by smaller flowers (1 to 2 cm long) and stem leaves less than 1 cm across. The round basal leaves of harebell are rarely present when the plant is flowering.

harebell

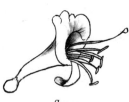

flower

The honeysuckle family contains more than 400 species worldwide, found primarily in northern temperate regions. Species may be herbs, shrubs, or woody vines. The simple leaves are opposite and lack stipules. (Genus *Sambucus* (elderberry) has compound leaves.) The flowers, composed of 5 sepals, 5 united petals, 4 or 5 stamens, and 1 style, are wheel to tube-shaped. The fruit may be a berry, drupe, capsule, or achene.

The honeysuckle family is of limited economic importance. Species such as honeysuckles and bush cranberries are grown for their ornamental value.

Honeysuckle Family

Clockwise from top left: high-bush cranberry, *Viburnum opulus* L.; snowberry, *Symphoricarpos albus* (L.) Blake; elderberry, *Sambucus racemosa* L.

Caprifoliaceae

buckbrush

Symphoricarpos occidentalis Hook.

A perennial native to western North America.

Also known as: wolfberry

French names: symphorine de l'ouest

QUICK ID
- Shrub with copper-coloured bark
- Flowers white
- Fruit a greenish white berry

Distribution: Found in all provinces west of Ontario and the western half of the United States.

Weed Designation
  Canada: MB

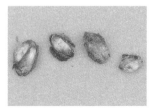

DESCRIPTION
Seed: Seeds are elliptical, light brown, 3 to 4 mm long, and bony.

Leaves: Leaves are alternate, ovate to oblong, 3 to 5 cm long. The leaf margins have rounded teeth. Leaves are thick, with a leathery texture.

Flower: White to pinkish flowers are borne in terminal or axillary clusters. Flowers are composed of 4 or 5 united sepals, 4 or 5 united petals, 4 or 5 stamens, and 1 pistil. The corolla, 5 to 9 mm long, is densely hairy inside. The stamens and pistil are longer than the corolla.

Plant: A robust shrub with stems to 1 m tall, buckbrush spreads by underground suckers. Large colonies of this shrub can be found on prairie slopes and margins of fields. The hollow stems are golden-brown. Young stems are often hairy.

Fruit: The fruit is a globe-shaped berry called a drupe. The berry is greenish white and waxy, and contains 2 seeds. The berry turns brown as it dries.

REASONS FOR CONCERN

Although cattle and sheep graze on buckbrush, it often increases on overgrazed pastures, where it crowds out desirable vegetation. Buckbrush is also found on the edge of fields. Recently, it has been reported in minimum and zero-till fields.

SIMILAR SPECIES

Snowberry (*S. albus* (L.) Blake), a slender native shrub found throughout North America, is closely related to buckbrush. It is distinguished from buckbrush by stamens and style that are shorter than the petals. The round, white berry is 6 to 12 mm across.

snowberry

snowberry

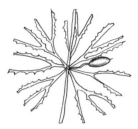

leaf arrangement

fruit

flower

A small family with 6 species worldwide, the hornworts are free-floating aquatic herbs that rarely have roots. Leaves appear in whorls of 5 to 12 and are divided 2 to 3 times into forked linear segments. These segments are often spiny-toothed. Small, inconspicuous flowers of 2 types—male and female—are borne in leaf axils. Male flowers are composed of 8 to 12 sepals and 12 to 16 stamens. Female flowers have similar sepals and a single style. The fruit is an achene with 2 basal spines.

The hornwort family is of limited economic importance.

Hornwort Family

coontail,
Ceratophyllum demersum L.

Ceratophyllaceae

coontail

*Ceratophyllum
demersum* L.

A perennial native to North America.

Also known as: hornwort

French names: cornifle nageant

QUICK ID
- Free-floating aquatic plant
- Leaves in whorls of 5 to 12
- Roots usually absent

Distribution: Found throughout Canada and the United States.

Weed Designation
Canada: MB

DESCRIPTION
Seed: Seeds are elliptical, black, 4 to 6 mm long. Each seed has 2 basal spines, each 10 to 12 mm long.

Seedling: Seedlings germinate in bottom substrate and rise to the surface when the stems are about 8 cm long.

Leaves: Leaves, 1 to 4 cm long, appear in a whorl of 5 to 12 leaves; they collapse when removed from water. Whorls are widely spaced on the stem and crowded near the tip, giving a "coontail" appearance. Each leaf is forked into 2 to 4 narrow segments; the segments are less than 0.5 mm wide. Leaf margins are conspicuously toothed.

Flower: Small, stalkless flowers appear in the axils of leaves. Flowers are of 2 types: male and female. Sepals and petals are absent. Flowers are enclosed by 8 to 12 transparent floral bracts. Male flowers consist of 12 to 16 short-stalked stamens. The anthers or pollen sacs are white. Female flowers are composed of a single pistil.

winter buds

Plant: A free-floating aquatic plant, coontail has branched stems, 30 to 150 cm long, and often forms large colonies. Plants prefer slightly alkaline waters with a pH of between 7.1 and 9.2. Roots are usually absent. Reproduction is by seeds and winter buds. Winter buds, produced when daylength shortens and water temperatures begin to drop, are clusters of tightly held leaves near the tip of the stem. These buds break off and sink to the bottom, where they overwinter. When water temperatures and daylight hours increase in the spring, these bud rise and elongate to form new plants.

Fruit: The single-seeded fruit, called an achene, is black and 4 to 6 mm long. The achene has 3 prominent spines, 1 apical and 2 basal. The spines are 10 to 12 mm long.

REASONS FOR CONCERN

Coontail is a concern in irrigation canals, where large colonies may impede the flow of water. It also reduces water quality for recreational use.

SIMILAR SPECIES

Northern water milfoil (*Myriophyllum exalbescens* Fern.) is often confused with coontail. It is distinguished from coontail by its feather-like leaves that appear in whorls of 4. Small, whitish red flowers appear in terminal spikes in midsummer (see pp 386-87). Spiny hornwort (*C. echinatum* Grey.), a closely related species, is found in still waters east of the Mississippi River. It is distinguished from coontail by its smooth leaflet margins.

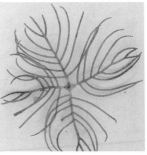

northern water milfoil

habit

strobilus

The horsetail or scouring-rush family contains a single genus with 35 species. Horsetails are found throughout the world in moist to wet soil. Horsetails, one of the most primitive living plant families, were huge trees that dominated the landscape during the Carboniferous period, 300 to 400 million years ago.

Today, species are herbaceous and less than 5 m tall. The characteristic feature of the family is hollow, jointed stems. The leaves are scale-like and whorled at stem nodes. In some species, branches appear from the axils of the leaves. Horsetails reproduce by spores and creeping rhizomes. The minute green spores are produced in terminal, cone-shaped structures called *strobili*.

Horsetails are of little economic importance. They are TOXIC to livestock, especially horses.

Horsetail Family

longitudinal section of strobilus

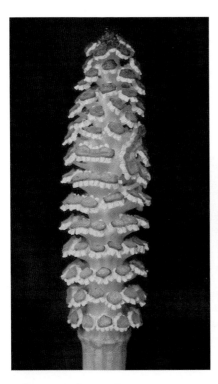

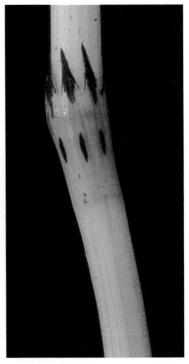

Left: common horsetail,
Equisetum arvense L.
Right: common horse-
tail, *Equisetum arvense* L.

Equisetaceae

common horsetail

Equisetum arvense L.

A perennial native to North America.

Also known as: field horsetail, mare's-tail, pipe-weed, paddy's-pipe, scouring-rush, horsetail fern, meadow pine, pine-grass, foxtail-rush, bottle-brush, horse-pipes, snake-grass, corn-field horsetail, toad-pipes

French names: prèle des champs, queue-de-renard, prèle commune

vegetative stem

QUICK ID
- Stems jointed
- Leaves in whorls of 8 to 12
- Rhizome black, felt-like

Distribution: Found throughout Canada and the United States except for the southeastern states.

Weed Designation
Canada: MB, PQ USA: OR

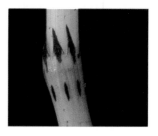

DESCRIPTION
Seed: Horsetails do not produce seeds. Reproduction is by spores: pale green to yellow, globe-shaped, and very small (less than 0.1 mm). Spores are viable for about 48 hours.

Seedling: Horsetails do not produce seedlings. Young plants are often called sporelings. Spores will germinate only in damp soil. A small (less than 1 mm across), flat, green structure, called a *prothallus*, will grow into a new plant. Male prothalli are 2 to 3 mm across, while female prothalli are 4 to 5 mm.

Leaves: Leaves appear in whorls of 8 to 12. The leaves are small, scale-like, and brown. Whorls of branches appear from the leaf axils; the branches are 3 to 5-sided.

Flower: Horsetails do not produce flowers. A cone-like structure, 1 to 3 cm long, called a *strobilus*, is borne at the top of reproductive stems.

Plant: Horsetail has 2 types of stems, reproductive and vegetative. Both types are jointed and can grow up to 30 cm tall. The extensive creeping rhizome, up to 100 m long, is dark brown with a texture similar to felt. The rhizome produces small tubers, which store food energy. Roots may extend to 2 m in depth. The plant is highly variable in appearance, depending on habitat and climatic conditions. Reproductive stems appear in April and early May and are flesh-coloured. These stems have 8 to 12 leaves, 5 to 9 mm long, per node and lack branches. These cone-tipped stems wither soon after producing the spores. Vegetative stems are green, with 12 leaves per node. Stem internodes are 1.5 to 6 cm long and up to 5 mm thick. Stems have 6 to 8 branches, 10 to 15 cm long, appearing in a whorl around the stem. These branches have 3 or 4 teeth at each joint. The role of these stems is food production.

Fruit: Millions of spores are produced in small, tube-like appendages inside the cone-like structure at the top of the reproductive stem.

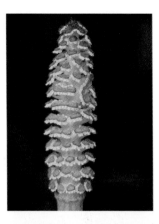

reproductive stem

REASONS FOR CONCERN

Common horsetail is an aggressive weed capable of reducing crop yields by 50%. In 1910, it was determined that horsetails are POISONOUS, especially to young horses. Ingestion of the plant causes vitamin B deficiency in animals feeding on it. Hay containing horsetails can be MORE TOXIC than plants found in pastures.

The lily family has worldwide distribution with more than 4,000 species. The family contains herbs, shrubs, and woody vines with alternate, whorled, or basal leaves. The simple leaves of various shapes and sizes are parallel-veined. Flowers are composed of 3 sepals and 3 petals, all similar in appearance, 6 stamens, and a single 3-lobed style. The fruit may be a capsule or berry.

The lily family is an important family in the horticultural industry. It includes lilies, tulips, hostas, daffodils, agave, yucca, and lily-of-the-valley. Other species—such as onion, garlic, and asparagus—are grown for their food value.

Lily Family

Clockwise from top left: white camas, *Zigadenus elegans* Pursh; white camas, *Zigadenus elegans* Pursh; fairy-bells, *Disporum trachycarpum* (S. Wats.) B. & H.

Liliaceae

death camas

Zigadenus venenosus
S. Wats.

A perennial native to western North America.

Also known as: soap plant, alkali-grass

French names: zigadène vénéneux

Scientific synonyms: *Zygadenus gramineus* Rydb.

QUICK ID
- Leaves grass-like
- Flowers white
- Roots bulb-like

Distribution: Found in Saskatchewan, Alberta, and British Columbia, and in states west of the Mississippi River.

Weed Designation
Canada: MB

DESCRIPTION

Seed: Seeds are ovate, light brown, 5 to 6 mm long and 1.5 mm wide.

Seedling: Death camas has 1 grass-like cotyledon. As the seedling matures, the lower part of the leaf becomes bulbous.

Leaves: Leaves are grass-like, primarily basal, 10 to 30 cm long and 2 to 3 mm wide. The leaves are whitish green and V-shaped. The veins of the leaves run parallel along the length of the leaf.

Flower: Creamy-white flowers, about 1 cm across, appear in terminal clusters. Flower stalks, rising from small, papery bracts, are 5 to 25 mm long. Flowers are composed of 3 sepals and 3 petals, all similar in size and appearance, 6 stamens, and 1 style. Sepals and petals are 4 to 5 mm long.

Plant: A grass-like plant of dry prairies and hillsides, death camas has hairless stems up to 50 cm tall. An onion-like bulb can be found 6 to 15 cm below the ground surface.

Fruit: The fruit is a papery capsule with 3 compartments, each containing several angular seeds.

REASONS FOR CONCERN

Death camas, as the name implies, is VERY POISONOUS to livestock. The bulb is the most poisonous part of the plant and is easily pulled from the soft ground in spring—which is when most poisonings occur. Due to its early spring growth, livestock are at risk until better grazing conditions develop. The lethal dose in sheep is estimated to be 0.6 to 2% of body weight in plant material.

SIMILAR SPECIES

White camas (*Z. elegans* Pursh) is closely related to death camas. It is distinguished by larger, greenish to yellowish white sepals and petals 7 to 10 mm long. A native plant of western North America, white camas is not as POISONOUS as death camas, although poisonings have occurred. A lethal dose is estimated to be 2 to 6% of body weight.

white camas

white camas

flower

The loosestrife family has over 500 species worldwide, with the majority of the species occurring in tropical regions. A few herbaceous species are found in temperate zones of North America. The simple leaves are opposite or whorled and lack stipules. Flowers are composed of 3 to 16 sepals, 3 to 16 petals, 6 to 32 stamens, and a single style. The fruit is a capsule.

One species, purple loosestrife, is a serious weed of wetlands and marshes. Although it was once widely planted for its ornamental value, many jurisdictions have now designated purple loosestrife a noxious weed.

Loosestrife Family

purple loosestrife,
Lythrum salicaria L.

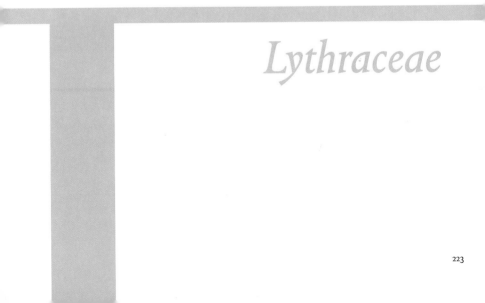

Lythraceae

purple loosestrife

Lythrum salicaria L.

A perennial introduced from Europe as an ornamental plant in the late 1800s.

Also known as: purple lythrum, spiked loosestrife

French names: salicaire, salicaire commune, lythrum salicaire, bouquet-violet

QUICK ID
- Leaves opposite
- Flowers pink in dense terminal spikes
- Plant of moist habitats

Distribution: Found throughout Canada and the northeastern United States.

Weed Designation
Canada: AB, MB
USA: CO, ID, NE, NH, UT, VT, WY

DESCRIPTION

Seed: Seeds are brown to black, less than 1 mm across.

Seedling: Cotyledons, 3 to 6 mm long and 2 to 3 mm wide, are ovate and hairless. The first pair of leaves are opposite and similar in shape to the cotyledons.

Leaves: Leaves are opposite or in whorls of 3. The stalkless, lance-shaped leaves are 3 to 10 cm long and slightly hairy. Leaves in the inflorescence may be alternate.

Flower: The flowering stalk of purple loosestrife is leafy, 10 to 40 cm long. The showy axillary flowers are 15 to 20 mm across. Flowers are composed of 4 to 8 green sepals, 4 to 8 pinkish purple petals 7 to 10 mm long, 8 to 16 stamens, and 1 pistil. Flowers are whorled in the axils of upper leaves. The sepals have 8, 10, or 12 prominent green veins.

Plant: Purple loosestrife, a perennial plant of marshy areas, has square stems, 50 to 150 cm tall. These branching stems are soft-haired and rise from an extensive root system. Reproduction is by seed, root fragments, and pieces of the stem. Once believed to be sterile and incapable of producing seeds, purple loosestrife was widely planted in gardens. It has now been determined that the following varieties thought to be sterile are capable of producing fertile seed: Morden Pink, Dropmore Purple, Morden Gleam, and Morden Rose.

Fruit: The fruit, a 2-chambered capsule about 6 mm long, contains numerous seeds.

root system

REASONS FOR CONCERN

Purple loosestrife spreads rapidly and replaces all native vegetation, destroying wetland areas. It is a concern along canals and rivers, where it slows the flow of water. Purple loosestrife is also an alternate host for cucumber mosaic virus.

SIMILAR SPECIES

Purple loosestrife may be confused with fireweed (*Epilobium angustifolium* L.; see p 131). Fireweed, like purple loosestrife, has pink flowers borne in long, terminal clusters. The flowers of fireweed are composed of 4 pinkish green sepals, 4 pink petals, 8 stamens, and a 4-lobed style. Another distinguishing characteristic between the species is the leaf arrangement: fireweed has alternate stem leaves. Fireweed is found throughout North America.

fruit

The mallow family is found throughout the world and has over 1,500 species. Its greatest diversity is found in the tropical regions of North and South America. Several species are found in temperate North America. These plants may be herbs, shrubs, or trees. The simple alternate leaves have stipules that often fall off. The flowers are composed of a calyx of 5 united sepals, 5 petals, numerous stamens, and a single style. The stamens are fused and form a tube around the style, an important characteristic of the mallow family. The fruit may be a capsule or a schizo-carp that breaks into several sections, called mericarps.

The mallow family is very important economically. Cotton and okra are important crop species, while hollyhock and hibiscus are grown for ornamental value. The family also contains weedy species such as mallow and velvetleaf.

Mallow Family

Left: round-leaved mallow,
Malva rotundifolia L.
Right: velvetleaf,
Abutilon theophrasti Medic.

Malvaceae

velvetleaf
Abutilon theophrasti
Medic.

An annual introduced from India.

Also known as: Indian mallow, butter print, velvet-weed, Indian hemp, cotton-weed, button-weed, pie-maker, elephant-ear

French names: abutilon, abutilon feuille de velours

QUICK ID
- Flowers orangish yellow
- Leaves alternate, heart-shaped
- Leaves covered with soft hairs

Distribution: Found throughout Canada (except New Brunswick and Newfoundland) and throughout the United States (except the north-central plains and the extreme south).

Weed Designation
Canada: FEDERAL, BC
USA: CO, IA, KS, MI, NC, NH, RI, VT, WA

DESCRIPTION

Seed: Seeds are kidney-shaped, flattened, dull greyish brown, 2.9 to 3.4 mm long and 2.6 to 2.9 mm wide. Seeds are less than 1.6 mm thick. Seeds may remain viable in the soil for at least 50 years. Each flower is capable of producing over 200 seeds.

Seedling: Cotyledons are round and 6 to 10 mm across. The stalk of the cotyledon is up to 10 mm long. The cotyledons are covered with short hairs. The stem below the cotyledons is covered with short hairs and is often purplish near the soil level. The first leaves have prominent veins beneath. Leaves are covered with short, velvety hairs.

Leaves: Heart-shaped alternate leaves are 5 to 20 cm wide. As the common name implies, the leaves are covered with soft, velvety hairs. The margins are irregularly toothed and hairy.

Flower: Orangish yellow flowers, 15 to 20 mm across, appear singly or in clusters in the axils of leaves. Flowers are composed of 5 sepals, 5 petals, and numerous stamens that are united to form a column around the style.

Plant: A robust annual, velvetleaf has hairy stems up to 2.3 m tall, although 30 to 60 cm tall is more common. The taproot is white.

Fruit: The fruit, a circular cluster of 12 to 15 seed pods, is 2 to 2.5 cm across. Seed pods are green and turn black at maturity. Each pod contains 5 to 15 seeds.

fruit

REASONS FOR CONCERN

Velvetleaf is a serious weed in corn and soy beans. It is commonly found in cultivated fields, gardens, fence rows, and waste areas. It is an alternate host for tobacco streak and turnip mosaic viruses.

SIMILAR SPECIES

Scarlet mallow (*Sphaeralcea coccinea* (Pursh) Rydb.), a native perennial plant of prairie grasslands and roadsides, has orange to red flowers. The stems, 5 to 20 cm tall, rise from a woody black rootstalk. The leaves are deeply 3 to 5-lobed and are covered with short grey hairs.

scarlet mallow

flower-of-an-hour

Hibiscus trionum L.

An annual introduced from southern Europe; the first Canadian report was from Prince Edward Island in 1952.

Also known as: Venice mallow, bladder ketmia, shoo-fly, rosemallow

French names: ketmie trilobée, fleur d'une heure, ketmie enflée

QUICK ID
- Calyx inflated and surrounding the capsule
- Leaves alternate, 3-lobed
- Flowers pale yellow with purple centres

Distribution: Found throughout Canada (except Alberta and British Columbia) and the eastern United States.

Weed Designation
USA: WA

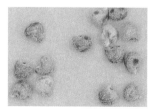

DESCRIPTION
Seed: Round to triangular seeds are purplish brown to black, 2 to 2.2 mm long and wide. The surface of the seed is rough and dull; under high magnification, it is covered with small, rounded bumps.

Seedling: Cotyledons, 4 to 17 mm long and 4 to 9 mm wide, are heart to kidney-shaped; they are yellowish green when they first emerge. The stem below the cotyledons is covered with gland-tipped hairs. The first leaf is round. By the third leaf stage, leaves are 3-lobed. Stipules also appear at the third leaf stage.

Leaves: Leaves are alternate, 3-lobed, and coarsely toothed. The upper leaves are deeply 3-lobed. The hairy stalks of the leaves are usually as long as the leaf blade.

Flower: Pale-yellow flowers with a purplish brown eye are borne in the axils of leaves. Flowers are composed of 5 sepals, 5 petals, numerous stamens, and a single pistil. The papery sepals are hairy on the prominent purple veins. Below each flower is a ring of narrow papery bracts. As the common name implies, the flowers of this plant open for only a few hours.

Plant: Flower-of-an-hour, a weed of row crops, fields, and waste places, has bristly haired stems, 30 to 50 cm tall. The main stem has numerous branches near the base of the plant.

Fruit: The fruit, a globe-shaped capsule, opens at the top to release numerous seeds. The inflated calyx surrounding the bristly haired capsule is papery and purple-veined.

REASONS FOR CONCERN

Flower-of-an-hour is a common weed of cultivated fields, row crops, orchards, and rangeland.

SIMILAR SPECIES

Several species of *Hibiscus* are found throughout North America. Flower-of-an-hour is the only North American *Hibiscus* species with lobed leaves.

fruit enclosed by papery calyx

round-leaved mallow

Malva rotundifolia L.

An annual, winter annual, or biennial introduced from Europe.

Also known as: cheeses, low mallow, running mallow, blue mallow

French names: mauve à feuilles rondes

Scientific synonyms: *M. pusilla* Sm.

QUICK ID
- Leaves round to kidney-shaped
- Flowers pale blue to white
- Plants with low, spreading stems

Distribution: Found throughout Canada (except the Atlantic provinces) and the United States (except the New England states).

Weed Designation
Canada: AB, MB, SK

DESCRIPTION

Seed: Seeds are kidney-shaped, 1.7 to 2 mm across and less than 1 mm thick. Seeds are dark brown and have a wrinkled surface. The seeds may remain dormant in soil for up to 100 years. Each plant produces as many as 500 seeds.

Seedling: Cotyledons, 4.5 to 7 mm long and 3 to 3.5 mm wide, are heart-shaped, with 3 prominent veins. The upper surface of the cotyledon is shiny. The stem below the cotyledons has a few short, soft hairs. The first leaves are kidney-shaped, with irregular lobes and rounded teeth.

Leaves: Leaves are alternate, round to kidney-shaped, shallowly 5-lobed, 2 to 5 cm across. Stalks are 10 to 15 cm long. Leaf margins have rounded teeth.

Flower: Small, pale-blue to white flowers, 5 mm across, appear in groups of 2 to 5 in leaf axils. Three small bracts appear below each flower. Flowers are composed of a 5-lobed calyx, 5 petals, many stamens, and a single pistil. Petals are about 6 mm long.

Plant: Round-leaved mallow has a prostrate to ascending growth habit, with stems up to 1.25 m long. The branched stems often form large mats.

Fruit: Each flower produces a fruit with 8 to 15 segments around a central axis. Each segment is 1-seeded and separates from the others much as do the segments of an orange. The calyx becomes enlarged and prominently veined as the fruit matures.

REASONS FOR CONCERN

Round-leaved mallow is a strong competitor of cultivated crops. It is also a weed of gardens, waste areas, and farmyards. Round-leaved mallow is an alternate host for several viral diseases: aster yellows, beet curly top, tobacco streak, tomato spotted wilt, and hollyhock mosaic.

SIMILAR SPECIES

High mallow (*M. sylvestris* L.), an introduced annual or biennial weed, has dark bluish purple flowers and leaves with 3 to 7 lobes. High mallow is found in Alberta, British Columbia, Ontario, and Quebec. Another introduced species, whorled mallow (*M. verticillata* L.), has white to pale-purple flowers and stems up to 2 m tall. The leaves are round to kidney-shaped, with 5 to 9 lobes. It is found throughout Canada, except for British Columbia and Newfoundland.

fruit

prickly sida

Sida spinosa L.

An annual introduced from tropical North America.

Also known as: spiny sida, prickly mallow

French names: sida épineuse

QUICK ID
- Flowers pale yellow
- Leaves alternate, yellowish green
- Pod splits into 5 sections

Distribution: Found in southern Ontario and throughout the eastern United States, except the northern New England states.

Weed Designation
None

DESCRIPTION

Seed: Seeds are egg-shaped with 1 flat side, reddish brown, 2.1 to 2.2 mm long and 1.3 to 1.5 mm wide. The surface is smooth and dull.

Seedling: Cotyledons, 6.5 to 14 mm long and 5 to 8 mm wide, have hairy margins. The stem below the cotyledons is covered with short, velvety hairs. The root is brown and corky by the time the first leaf appears. Awl-shaped stipules appear at the third leaf stage.

Leaves: Leaves are alternate and ovate to egg-shaped. The toothed leaves, 2 to 4 cm long, are yellowish green and long-stalked. The surface of the leaves and stalks are covered with soft hairs.

Flower: Pale-yellow flowers in clusters of 1 to many are borne in the axil of leaves. The flower stalks are 2 to 12 mm long. Flowers are composed of a star-shaped calyx, 5 petals, numerous stamens, and 5 styles. The petals are 4 to 6 mm long.

Plant: An annual with a long, slender taproot, prickly sida reproduces only by seed. The stems, 20 to 100 cm tall, have several branches. There are 2 or 3 short, blunt spines below each leaf. The whole plant is covered with soft hairs.

Fruit: The fruit is a pod that splits into 5 sections. Each section is 1-seeded and topped with 2 spines.

flower

REASONS FOR CONCERN

Prickly sida is a serious weed of cultivated fields and row crops. It is an alternate host for cotton leaf curl virus.

SIMILAR SPECIES

Virginia mallow (*S. hermaphrodita* (L.) Rusby) is closely related to prickly mallow. A perennial with stems to 3 m tall, Virginia mallow has white flowers and leaves with 3 to 7 lobes. It is native to the east-central United States.

fruit

flower

plant

The mare's-tail family contains 3 species that are found in temperate regions of the world. Mare's-tails are perennial aquatic or amphibious plants with unbranched stems rising from a creeping rhizome. The stalkless entire leaves appear in whorls of 4 to 12. Flowers are of 2 types and are borne in leaf axils. Male flowers, found near the top of the stem, are composed of 4 sepals and a single stamen with a large anther. Flowers containing both male and female reproductive parts are found lower on the stem. They are composed of 4 sepals, 1 stamen, and 1 style. The style is often found between the 2 lobes of the anther. The fruit is nut-like and 1-seeded.

The mare's-tail family is of little economic importance.

Mare's-Tail Family

mare's-tail,
Hippuris vulgaris L.

Hippuridaceae

mare's-tail

Hippuris vulgaris L.

A perennial native to North America.

Also known as: marsh horsetail

French names: hippuride vulgaire

- Semi-aquatic plant
- Leaves in whorls of 6 to 12
- Flowers appear in leaf axils

Distribution: Found throughout Canada and the United States, except the southeastern states.

Weed Designation
Canada: MB

seed

DESCRIPTION

Seed: Seeds are nut-like and about 2 mm long.

Leaves: Leaves, 1 to 5 cm long and 1 to 2 mm wide, appear in whorls of 6 to 12. The stalkless leaves are dark green. Leaves above water are firm and have smooth margins. Submersed leaves are flaccid and up to 6 cm long; they collapse when taken from the water.

Flower: Small green flowers, less than 3 mm long, are borne in the axil of leaves. The flowers are sessile and composed of a single stamen and pistil. Sepals and petals are absent.

Plant: Mare's-tail is an aquatic or semi-aquatic plant with several unbranched stems rising from an extensive creeping rhizome. The hairless stems, up to 30 cm tall, have numerous dark-green leaves.

Fruit: The fruit, an elliptical capsule 2 to 3 mm long, contains a single seed.

REASONS FOR CONCERN

Mare's-tail is a weed of slow-moving water, such as drainage ditches and irrigation canals. Large colonies of this plant may impede water flow.

SIMILAR SPECIES

Mountain mare's-tail (*H. montana* Ledeb.) is found from Alaska and the Northwest Territories to Alberta, British Columbia, and Washington. Leaves appear in whorls of 5 to 8 and are less than 1 cm long and 1 mm wide. Flowers are of 3 types: male, female, and both male and female.

habitat

fruit

flower

The milkweed family has about 2,000 species worldwide. It is a diverse group of plants with growth habits ranging from herbs to trees to cactus-like succulents. All parts of the plant contain milky sap. The simple, entire leaves are arranged oppositely on the stem. Stipules are absent. Flowers, borne in umbels, are unusual and highly modified. The 5 sepals and 5 petals are turned back when the flower is fully opened; the 5 stamens are fused to the stigma and form a structure called a corona. The base of the corona is fused to the petals. The fruit, called follicles, often appear in pairs. Each follicle contains numerous flat seeds with a winged margin and a tuft of silky white hairs.

A few members of the milkweed family are grown for ornamental purposes.

Milkweed Family

Left: showy milkweed,
Asclepias speciosa Torr.
Right: showy milkweed,
Asclepias speciosa Torr.

Asclepiadaceae

showy milkweed

Asclepias speciosa Torr.

A perennial native to western North America.

Also known as: milkweed

French names: belle asclépiade

QUICK ID

- Milky juice
- Leaves opposite
- Flowers purplish pink in globe-shaped clusters

Distribution: Found from Manitoba to British Columbia and states west of Minnesota to Texas.

Weed Designation
Canada: MB, ON
USA: HI

DESCRIPTION

Seed: Seeds, 5 to 8 mm long and 2 to 5 mm wide, are flat with a prominent margin. Seeds are reddish brown and have a tuft of long, white, silky hairs at 1 end.

Seedling: Cotyledons, 11 to 19 mm long and 3 to 5.5 mm wide, are dull green above, shiny and distinctly veined beneath. The stem below the cotyledons is brownish purple at the soil surface. The first leaves are opposite and have hairy margins.

Leaves: Leaves are opposite, 7 to 15 cm long, short-stalked, ovate, with a heart-shaped base; they are covered with downy hairs.

Flower: Flesh-coloured to purplish pink flowers, about 1 cm across, appear on the ends of densely woolly stalks in globe-shaped clusters, 5 to 7 cm in diameter. These sweet-smelling flowers are composed of 5 sepals, 5 petals, 5 stamens, and 2 short styles. Sepals and petals are turned backwards. The stamens are highly modified and united to form a tube around the styles; the structure is often referred to as a corona. The scent of the flower and nectar is reported to have a stupefying effect on insects.

Plant: This milky perennial has coarse stems, up to 2 m tall, and often forms large colonies. The creeping underground rhizomes produce numerous buds that give rise to new shoots, thus enlarging the colony.

Fruit: The fruit is a spindle-shaped pod, 6 to 10 cm long. It is covered with dense white-woolly hairs. The stalks of the pod are curled backwards. Each pod contains more than 150 seeds.

REASONS FOR CONCERN

Showy milkweed is a common weed of roadsides, pastures, and zero-till fields. It is unable to survive in highly cultivated fields. Showy milkweed is POISONOUS to cattle and sheep, but poisonings are rare because large amounts of the leaves must be ingested.

fruit

SIMILAR SPECIES

Silky milkweed (*A. syriaca* L.) is similar to showy milkweed, and can be distinguished by the rounded shape of the leaf base. The flowers of silky milkweed are dull pinkish purple to white. It is found throughout Canada, except for British Columbia, Alberta, and Saskatchewan. Another species, green milkweed (*A. viridiflora* Raf.), has greenish white flowers and stems up to 60 cm tall. Green milkweed is found from British Columbia to Ontario.

fruit

Also known as Labiatae, the mint family is a large group of plants with more than 3,200 species worldwide. Primarily herbs and shrubs, the mints are distinguished from other families by their opposite leaves and square stems. The simple, opposite leaves are aromatic due to tiny glands on the surface, which contain strongly scented compounds. Stipules are absent. The irregularly shaped flowers appear in terminal and axillary clusters. They are composed of 5 united sepals, 5 united petals, 2 or 4 stamens, and a single style. The corolla is 2-lipped, with 2 upper and 3 lower petals. The fruit are called nutlets.

Several spices used to flavour food are members of the mint family, including lavender, mint, basil, sage, oregano, and thyme. A few other species—such as coleus and salvia—are grown for their ornamental value.

Mint Family

Left: water horehound, *Lycopus asper* L.
Right: marsh hedge nettle,
Stachys palustris L.

Lamiaceae

American dragonhead

Dracocephalum parviflorum Nutt.

An annual or biennial native to North America.

Also known as: dragonhead, small-flowered dragonhead

French names: dracocéphale d'Amerique

Scientific synonyms: *Moldavica parviflora* (Nutt.) Britt.

QUICK ID

- Stems square
- Leaves opposite
- Petals light blue or violet

Distribution: Found throughout Canada and the northern two-thirds of the United States.

Weed Designation
Canada: MB

DESCRIPTION

Seed: Seeds are ovate, brown to black, less than 3 mm long. Each plant is capable of producing 500 seeds.

Seedling: Cotyledons, 10 to 22 mm long and 5 to 9 mm wide, are ovate, with 2 basal, backward-pointing lobes. The stem below the cotyledons has a few short hairs at or near the soil surface. The first leaves are opposite and ovate with rounded teeth.

Leaves: Leaves are opposite, ovate to oblong, 2 to 6 cm long. The stalked leaves are coarsely toothed and hairy below. Leaf pairs are set 90° to those pairs above and below.

Flower: Blue to purple flowers are found in dense terminal clusters or in axils of the upper leaves. The terminal spike is 2 to 5 cm long and 2 to 3 cm across. Below each flower are leafy, spine-tipped bracts. The calyx, 10 to 14 mm long, is 5-lobed and 15-nerved. The corolla is 5-lobed and slightly shorter than the calyx. There are 4 stamens and 1 style.

Plant: American dragonhead has square stems with several branches. Smooth to hairy stems, up to 90 cm tall, rise from a thick taproot. In late summer, plants become stiff and bristly.

Fruit: The fruit is a single-seeded nutlet. Each flower produces 4 nutlets.

REASONS FOR CONCERN

American dragonhead is a serious competitor in cultivated fields and row crops.

SIMILAR SPECIES

Thyme-leaved dragonhead (*D. thymiflorum* L.), another introduced species, is found from Ontario to the Yukon and in scattered locations throughout the United States. It may be distinguished from American dragonhead by its bracts, which are not spine-tipped. Another distinguishing characteristic is that its flowers are whorled in interrupted clusters along the upper stem.

hemp nettle

Galeopsis tetrahit L.

An annual introduced from Europe and Asia, hemp nettle was common in Canada by 1884.

Also known as: dog nettle, bee nettle, wild hemp, flowering nettle, ironweed, brittle-stem hemp nettle, ironwort, simon's-weed

French names: ortie royale, chardonnet, galéopside à tige carrée

QUICK ID
- Stem square with opposite leaves
- Stems bristly
- Flowers pink with 5 united petals

Distribution: Found throughout Canada and the northeastern quarter of the United States. Small areas are also found in eastern Washington, northern Idaho, and western Montana.

Weed Designation
Canada: AB, MB, PQ
USA: AK

DESCRIPTION

Seed: Seeds are egg-shaped, mottled greyish brown, 3 to 4 mm long. The seeds of hemp nettle can remain dormant in soil for several years. Each plant is capable of producing up to 2,800 seeds. Germination occurs at 1 to 4 cm depth.

Seedling: Cotyledons, 5 to 10 mm long and 2 to 5 mm wide, are ovate with 2 pointed lobes at the base. A small notch can be found at the tip of the cotyledons. The stem below the cotyledons is often purplish at soil level. The first leaves are opposite, ovate, coarsely toothed, and prominently veined. Leaves are rough to touch because of fine, wiry hairs.

Leaves: Leaves, 3 to 12 cm long, are opposite, ovate to lance-shaped, and bristly haired. The stalked leaves have 5 to 10 coarse teeth on either side. Leaf stalks are 1 to 3 cm long. The stem is usually swollen below the leaf node, where numerous stiff, downward-pointing hairs are located.

Flower: The flowers of hemp nettle appear in terminal or axillary clusters. The flowers, about 1 cm across, can be white, pink, or variegated, with 2 yellow spots. The 5-lobed calyx, 7 to 11 mm long, has 10 prominent ribs. The calyx lobes, each about 5 mm long, are spine-tipped and elongate as the fruit mature. The tube-shaped corolla is 15 to 22 mm long. Four hairy stamens and a single pistil are found inside the corolla.

Plant: Bristly haired stems, up to 100 cm tall, are square in cross-section. Stems have several branches originating from the lower leaf axils. Hemp nettle has a slender taproot.

Fruit: Each flower produces 4 nutlets. Seeds are usually shed before crops are harvested.

REASONS FOR CONCERN

Hemp nettle is a serious competitor with crops for both moisture and soil nutrients. Yield losses of 24% in wheat and 25% in canola have been reported. Hemp nettle often forms dense stands in pastures, roadsides, and waste ground.

SIMILAR SPECIES

Yellow hemp nettle (*G. speciosa* Mill.) is a more robust plant than hemp nettle. It is distinguished by larger yellow flowers that feature a purple spot. Yellow hemp nettle is known from only 4 sites in North America: 1 in Alberta and 3 in Quebec.

fruit

henbit

Lamium
amplexicaule L.

An annual or biennial introduced from Europe and western Asia.

Also known as: dead nettle, blind nettle, bee nettle

French names: lamier amplexicaule, pain de poule

QUICK ID
- Stems square with opposite leaves
- Flowers pink to purple
- Leaves stalkless

Distribution: Found throughout Canada (except Prince Edward Island) and throughout the United States (except the north-central plains).

Weed Designation
Canada: AB, MB

DESCRIPTION
Seed: Seeds are ovate, 1.6 to 2 mm long and less than 1 mm wide, resembling a quarter-circle in cross-section. The speckled, greyish brown surface is smooth and dull. Each plant can produce up to 200 seeds. Germination occurs in shallow depths—usually in the top 2 cm of soil.

Seedling: Cotyledons, 3 to 12 mm long and 1 to 4 mm wide, are ovate with 2 basal lobes at the base. Seed leaves are usually notched at the tip. The stem below the cotyledons is usually purplish near the soil surface. The first leaves are opposite and ovate, with rounded teeth on the margins. The leaves are covered with soft hairs.

Leaves: Leaves are opposite, ovate to round, 5 to 30 mm long and 10 to 30 mm across. Lower leaves are long-stalked and have 2 to 4 rounded teeth on either side of the leaf. The upper leaves are stalkless and appear to surround the stem. Leaves are prominently veined and sparsely hairy.

Flower: Flowers appear in whorled clusters of 6 to 10 in the axils of the stalkless upper leaves. Flowers are stalkless and helmet-shaped. The calyx, 5 to 8 mm long, is 5-nerved and hairy. The corolla, 12 to 18 mm long, is pink to dark purple and hairy on the outside. Four stamens and a single pistil are found inside the corolla.

Plant: Henbit has square stems that are branched from the base. These weak stems may be up to 40 cm tall. Roots are shallow and fibrous. Reproduction is by seed only.

Fruit: The fruit is a single-seeded nutlet. Each flower produces 4 nutlets.

REASONS FOR CONCERN

Henbit is not a common weed of cultivated crops as it is not shade tolerant and competes poorly in areas where it is found. It is commonly found in row crops and gardens. Henbit is POISONOUS to livestock, especially sheep; the poison causes the animal to stagger. Henbit is an alternate host for aster yellows, tobacco etch, and tobacco mosaic viruses.

SIMILAR SPECIES

Ground-ivy (*Glechoma hederacea* L.), another introduced member of the mint family, resembles henbit. It is distinguished by stalked purple flowers and leaves. The calyx of ground-ivy has 15 nerves, unlike that of henbit, which has 5.

ground-ivy

marsh hedge nettle

Stachys palustris L.

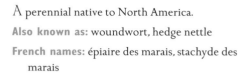

A perennial native to North America.

Also known as: woundwort, hedge nettle

French names: épiaire des marais, stachyde des marais

QUICK ID
- Stems square with opposite leaves
- Flowers mottled pink and purple
- Leaves hairy on both surfaces

Distribution: Found throughout Canada and the United States.

Weed Designation
Canada: MB, NS
USA: ME

DESCRIPTION

Seed: Seeds are ovate, dark brown, 1.8 to 2.2 mm long and 1.2 to 1.8 mm wide.

Seedling: Cotyledons, 3.5 to 10 mm long and 2 to 5 mm wide, are ovate. Cotyledons and the stem below have several minute hairs. The first leaves are opposite and ovate with rounded, toothed margins. By the third pair of leaves, creeping rhizomes have started to develop at the base of the plant.

Leaves: Opposite, oblong to lance-shaped leaves are 3 to 15 cm long and 1 to 4 cm wide. The leaves are stalkless and hairy on both surfaces. The margins have rounded teeth.

Flower: The terminal flower cluster, 2.5 to 25 cm long, is composed of whorls of flowers in axils of upper leaves. The funnel-shaped calyx, 6 to 9 mm long, is 5-lobed and sharp-tipped. The calyx has 5 to 10 prominent nerves. The corolla, 11 to 16 mm long, is mottled pinkish purple and hairy. The 4 stamens are of 2 lengths, the upper shorter than the lower. One pistil is present.

Plant: Marsh hedge nettle reproduces by seeds and spreading rhizomes. The white rhizomes are branched, succulent, and tuber-bearing. The square stems are rarely branched and up to 1 m tall. The plant is covered with short, stiff hairs.

Fruit: The fruit is a single-seeded nutlet. Each flower produces 4 nutlets that are surrounded by the dried calyx.

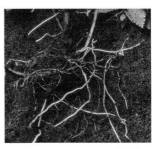

REASONS FOR CONCERN

Marsh hedge nettle is a serious weed in moist, low-lying areas of cultivated fields and row crops. Once established, it is difficult to eradicate.

root system

SIMILAR SPECIES

Several species of hedge nettle are found in North America. River hedge nettle (*S. tenuifolia* Willd.) closely resembles marsh hedge nettle. The stem of river hedge nettle is nearly hairless. The calyx is also hairless except for bristly hairs on the nerves. It is found from Manitoba to Quebec and in states east of the Mississippi River.

fruit

The morning-glory family is found throughout the world and contains over 1,500 species. Species range from twining herbs to shrubs or trees with milky sap. The alternate leaves are simple to compound. In the genus *Cuscuta*, the leaves are reduced to small scales. Flowers are composed of 5 sepals, 5 united petals, 5 stamens, and 1 style. The corolla is tube or funnel-shaped. The fruit is a capsule.

The morning-glory family is of limited economic importance, although some genera are grown for their horticultural and ornamental value. A few species are troublesome weeds in agricultural land.

plant

Morning-Glory Family

Left: ivy-leaved morning-glory,
Ipomoea hederacea (L.) Jacq.
Right: field bindweed,
Convolvulus arvensis L.

Convolvulaceae

field bindweed

Convolvulus arvensis L.

QUICK ID
- Stems twining
- Leaves arrowhead-shaped
- Flowers white

Distribution: Found throughout Canada (except Newfoundland and Prince Edward Island) and the northern three-quarters of the United States.

Weed Designation
Canada: FEDERAL, AB, MB, NS, ON, PQ, SK
USA: FEDERAL, AND ALL EXCEPT KY

A perennial introduced from Europe into New England in 1739, field bindweed had spread to California by 1900; the first Canadian report was from Ontario in 1879 and had spread to western Canada by the 1890s.

Also known as: European bindweed, small-flowered morning-glory, creeping Jenny, European glorybind, cornbine, lesser bindweed, barbine, corn bind, devil's-guts, greenvine, corn-lily, laplove, hedge-bells

French names: liseron des champs, liseron

DESCRIPTION

Seed: Seeds are egg-shaped and 3-sided, greyish brown, 3 to 5 mm long. The surface is dull and covered with rough bumps. Each plant is capable of producing in excess of 500 seeds. These seeds remain viable in the soil for up to 50 years. Seeds germinate in the top 2 cm of soil when temperatures are between 5 and 40°C.

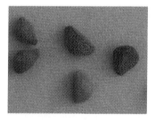

Seedling: Cotyledons, 9 to 22 mm long and 3.5 to 10 mm wide, are heart to kidney-shaped and long-stalked. The stem below the cotyledons is often red at or near the soil surface. The first leaves are stalked and arrowhead-shaped with a rounded tip. Seedlings can tolerate frost temperatures of -8°C.

Leaves: Leaves are alternate, arrowhead-shaped to triangular, 2 to 6 cm long and about 3 cm

wide. The long-stalked leaves have a rounded tip and smooth margins.

Flower: Funnel-shaped flowers, 2 to 3 cm across and 1.5 to 2 cm long, appear in groups of 1 to 4 in the axils of leaves. Flowers are composed of 5 fused sepals (about 3 mm long), 5 fused, pinkish white petals (1.5 to 3 cm long), 5 stamens, and 1 pistil. There are 2 small bracts below the flower. The flower stalks are 4-sided; flowers last only a single day. Seeds are viable 10 days after pollination.

Plant: Field bindweed is a hairless, twining, or trailing plant with deep, cord-like roots. These creeping white rhizomes have been reported to grow up to 30 m in length and 9 m deep. The twining stems twist counter-clockwise and may grow up to 7 m long. Under favourable conditions, plants may flower within 6 weeks of germination. A severe infestation of bindweed is capable of producing over 800 kg of seed per acre. Plants are quite frost tolerant and can survive -10 °C.

Fruit: The fruit is an egg-shaped capsule, about 3 mm long. The 2 chambers contain 1 to 4 seeds.

REASONS FOR CONCERN

Field bindweed has been known to reduce crop yields by 50%. It competes with crops for moisture and nutrients, and once established, it is difficult to eradicate. The twining nature of the plant also hampers harvesting of crops. Field bindweed is a serious weed of orchards and vineyards, where it entwines with the crop.

SIMILAR SPECIES

Hedge bindweed (*C. sepium* L.), also called wild morning-glory, is a larger perennial vine. It is distinguished from field bindweed by its larger flowers, 3 to 6 cm across, and 2 large green bracts below the flower (see pp 258-59). Wild buckwheat (*Polygonum convolvulus* L.), a member of the buckwheat family, is often confused with field bindweed. Wild buckwheat is distinguished by greenish pink flowers that are less than 5 mm across and leaves with pointed tips.

hedge bindweed

hedge bindweed

Convolvulus sepium L.

QUICK ID
⚬ Stems climbing
⚬ Leaves alternate
⚬ Flowers white, funnel-shaped

Distribution: Found throughout Canada, the eastern half of the United States, and the Pacific Northwest.

Weed Designation
Canada: AB, MB
USA: AL, AR, GA, HI, KS, LA, MI, MO, MS, NC, ND, NJ, OH, OK, PA, RI, SC, SD, TN, TX, UT, WA

A perennial native to North America; some introduced subspecies are also found in North America.

Also known as: devil's-vine, great bindweed, bracted bindweed, wild morning-glory, Rutland beauty, hedge-lily

French names: liseron des haies, gloire du matin, grand liseron

Scientific synonyms: *Calystegia sepium* (L.) R.Br.; *Convolvulus repens* L.

DESCRIPTION
Seed: Seeds are round, dark brown to black, about 5 mm across. Seeds can remain dormant for long periods of time and may not germinate even under favourable conditions.

Seedling: Cotyledons, 26 to 50 mm long and 16 to 22 mm wide, are rectangular and prominently veined on the underside. The stem below the cotyledons is often dull red. The first leaf is arrowhead-shaped and prominently veined below.

Leaves: Leaves are alternate, triangular to arrowhead-shaped, 4 to 15 cm long. The dark-green leaves have pointed tips and long stalks.

Flower: Large bell to funnel-shaped flowers appear in leaf axils on stalks, 5 to 15 cm long. The stalks are 4-angled. Flowers are composed of 5 united sepals, 5 united petals, 5 stamens, and a single pistil. The corolla is white to pink, 4 to 8 cm long and up to 8 cm across. The stamens are 2 to 3.5 cm long. Below each flower, and enclosing the calyx, are 2 large heart-shaped bracts, 1 to 5 cm long.

Plant: A large perennial vine with fleshy creeping rhizomes, hedge bindweed has stems up to 3 m long. Stems have numerous branches that climb on vegetation, cling to structures, or spread along the ground. Reproduction is by seed and rhizomes. Buds on the rhizome give rise to numerous shoots.

Fruit: The fruit is a globe-shaped capsule, 8 to 10 mm across. The capsule has 2 compartments, each with 1 or 2 seeds.

REASONS FOR CONCERN

Hedge bindweed is a serious weed in orchards and vineyards, where it entwines with the crop. It is also a weed of cultivated crops, fencerows, and roadsides. Hedge bindweed is an alternate host for cucumber mosaic and tobacco streak viruses.

fruit

SIMILAR SPECIES

Field bindweed (*C. arvensis* L.), an introduced species, is closely related to hedge bindweed. It is distinguished by smaller pinkish white flowers, about 2 cm across, and 2 small bracts below the flower (see pp 256-257).

field bindweed

dodder

Cuscuta spp.

An annual; introduced and native species occur in North America.

Also known as: goldthread-vine, love-tangle, coral-vine. There are several common names specific to individual species that are hosts for this parasite (i.e., onion dodder, large alfalfa dodder, etc.).

French names: cuscute

QUICK ID

- Stem climbing, parasitic
- Leaves reduced to small scales or absent
- Roots absent

Distribution: About 15 species of dodder are found throughout Canada, and several more are found in the United States.

Weed Designation

Canada: FEDERAL, BC, MB, ON, PQ
USA: FEDERAL, AND ALL EXCEPT AK, DC, UT

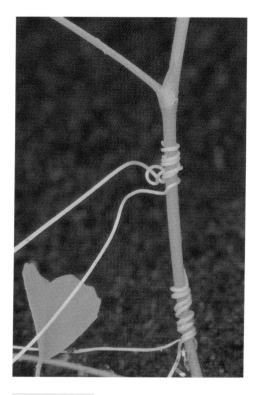

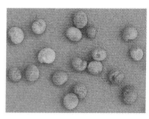

DESCRIPTION

Seed: Seeds are round, less than 1.5 mm in diameter, and found in a variety of colours ranging from white to brown. The surface is usually dull and covered with small scales. Germination occurs at the soil surface.

Seedling: Cotyledons are absent. Seeds germinate and produce slender, twining stems without leaves. The seedling must attach itself to a host plant within a short period of

time, or the young plant will wither and die.
When the seedling comes into contact with
an acceptable host, the stem develops
suckers that penetrate the tissue of the host
plant. Once the suckers are attached, food is
taken from the host plant, and the seedling
loses contact with the soil.

Leaves: Leaves are alternate, very small, and
scale-like.

Flower: Small yellow to white flowers, up to 5
mm across, appear in compact axillary clusters. The flowers are composed of a 4 to
5-lobed calyx, a 4 to 5-lobed, bell to globe-
shaped corolla, 5 stamens, and a single style.

Plant: An annual plant, dodder is a parasite on
herbaceous plants and occasionally trees and
shrubs. The yellow to reddish brown, thread-
like stems spread rapidly and form large mats.
Research has shown that a single seed can
produce over 720 m of stem in 4 months.
Dodder plants do not root in soil.

flower

Fruit: The fruit is a round capsule containing 4
to 8 seeds.

REASONS FOR CONCERN

Dodder is a parasite on agricultural crops and
drastically reduces yield. The twining stems
also hamper harvest of the crop. It also is an
alternate host for beet yellows, cucumber
mosaic, and tobacco etch viruses.

SIMILAR SPECIES

Another native parasitic plant, pine mistletoe
(*Arceuthobium americanum* Nutt.), is found on
branches of pines. The yellowish green
stems, 2 to 10 cm long, have numerous
branches and small green flowers. A problem
in nurseries and tree plantations, pine
mistletoe causes trees to develop witches'-
brooms on their branches. Pine mistletoe,
also called dwarf mistletoe, spreads by explo-
sively ejecting sticky seeds onto nearby trees.
The seeds are thrown up to 5 m from the
plant.

pine mistletoe

ivy-leaved morning-glory
Ipomoea hederacea
(L.) Jacq.

An annual introduced from tropical North America.

Also known as: morning-glory

French names: gloire du matin

QUICK ID
- Stems twining, up to 2 m long
- Leaves alternate, 3 to 5-lobed
- Flowers pale blue and funnel-shaped, turning to pinkish purple upon opening

Distribution: Found in southern Ontario and throughout the eastern and southern United States.

Weed Designation
USA: AR, AZ, KS, LA, MI, NE, NM, NC, OK, TX

DESCRIPTION
Seed: Seeds are disc-shaped, dark brown to black, 4.8 to 5.6 mm long and 3.4 to 4.2 mm wide. The surface is dull and somewhat wrinkled.

Seedling: Cotyledons, 16 to 57 mm long and 15 to 40 mm wide, are butterfly-shaped and shiny. The stem below the cotyledons is dull purple with a ridge running from the base of each seed leaf. Flowers may appear by the 4-leaf stage.

Leaves: Leaves, 5 to 12 cm long and wide, are alternate and deeply 3-lobed. Occasionally leaves are 5-lobed. These long-stalked, hairy leaves have heart-shaped bases.

Flower: Funnel-shaped flowers are borne in axillary clusters of 1 to 3. The lance-shaped sepals, 15 to 25 mm long, are densely haired to bristly. The corolla, 3 to 5 cm long, is pale to sky-blue and turns pinkish purple upon opening. Flowers have numerous stamens and 3 pistils.

Plant: An annual vine reproducing by seed, ivy-leaved morning-glory has hairy stems that climb on surrounding vegetation or spread on the ground. The stems are up to 2 m long.

Fruit: The fruit is an egg-shaped capsule that is partly surrounded by the calyx. The capsule has 3 compartments and is 4 to 6-seeded.

REASONS FOR CONCERN

Ivy-leaved morning-glory is a serious weed in orchards and vineyards, where it entwines with the crop. When found in cultivated fields and row crops, it hampers harvest of the crop. Ivy-leaved morning-glory is an alternate host for sweet potato internal cork virus.

SIMILAR SPECIES

Purple morning-glory (*I. purpurea* (L.) Roth) closely resembles ivy-leaved morning-glory. It is distinguished by shorter sepals (10 to 15 mm long) and larger flowers (4 to 6 cm long). The leaves are heart-shaped. Purple morning-glory is found in Ontario, Quebec, and Nova Scotia and throughout the United States.

fruit

The mustard family, also known as Cruciferae, refers to the 4 petals that, when viewed from above, form a cross or crucifix. A large family with more than 3,000 species of herbaceous plants, its greatest diversity occurs in the north temperate regions. Simple to compound alternate leaves often have numerous branched hairs on the surface. Stipules are absent. The flowers are composed of 4 sepals, 4 petals, 6 stamens (4 long and 2 short), and a single style. The fruit is a silicle or silique.

The mustard family is economically important. Species grown as food crops include radish, canola, broccoli, cabbage, rutabaga, and kohlrabi. Many species can be troublesome weeds in cultivated fields.

Mustard Family

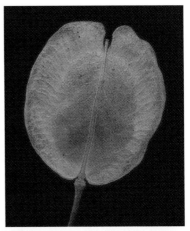

Clockwise from top left: wormseed mustard,
Erysimum cheiranthoides L.; stinkweed,
Thlapsi arvense L.; wild radish,
Raphanus raphanistrum L.

Brassicaceae

wild mustard

Brassica kaber
(DC.) L.C. Wheeler

An annual or winter annual introduced from Europe and Asia, wild mustard was common in New York state in 1748; the first Canadian report was from Nova Scotia in 1829, and it had spread to Manitoba by 1860.

Also known as: charlock, crunchweed, field kale, kraut-weed, water cress, yellow-flower, herrick, yellow mustard

French names: moutarde des champs, moutarde sauvage, séneué

Scientific synonyms: *Brassica arvensis* (L.) Kuntze; *Sinapis arvensis* L.

QUICK ID
- Stems bristly
- Flowers yellow
- Stems purplish at the nodes of branches

Distribution: Found throughout Canada and the United States.

Weed Designation
Canada: FEDERAL, AB, BC, MB, PQ, SK
USA: AK, CO, IL, IN, KS, MI, MN, NE, NV, PA, SD, TX, VA, WA, WI, WV

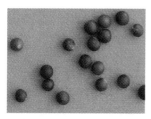

DESCRIPTION

Seed: Seeds are round, dark brown to black, 1 to 2 mm in diameter; at magnification, the seed surface is wrinkled. Each plant can produce up to 3,500 seeds, and seeds can remain dormant in the soil for up to 60 years. Germination occurs to a depth of 2 cm and is sporadic over the lifetime of the seeds.

Seedling: Cotyledons, 6 to 20 mm long and 6 to 12 mm wide, are kidney to heart-shaped and hairless. The stalks of the first leaves are bristly haired. These leaves are oblong with shallow lobes. Roots can be up to 87 cm long just 5 days after germination, and 12 m by day 21.

Leaves: Leaves are alternate with lower leaves differing from the upper. Lower leaves are stalked and have small lateral lobes and 1 large terminal lobe. The upper leaves are coarsely lobed and stalkless and do not clasp the stem. Leaves are prominently veined and somewhat hairy, especially on the veins of the underside.

Flower: Yellow flowers, 10 to 15 mm across, are borne on stalks, 2 to 6 mm long. Flowers are found in long terminal clusters. Flowers are composed of 4 green sepals, 4 yellow petals, 6 stamens, and 1 style.

Plant: Wild mustard has a slender taproot. The stems, up to 1.8 m tall, are bristly haired at the base of the plant and nearly hairless at the top. The hairs at the base of the stem are stiff and point downwards. The junction of the main stem and side branches is often purplish green.

Fruit: Smooth to somewhat hairy pods, 2 to 5 cm long, have short stalks about 5 mm long. These purplish pods are round in cross-section and constricted above the uppermost seed. Pods are prominently ribbed and contain 10 to 18 seeds. A single seed is found in the flattened beak of the pod.

REASONS FOR CONCERN

Wild mustard is a strong competitor with crops, especially in canola, where it may go unnoticed. Besides using moisture and nutrients, wild mustard seeds will lower the quality of canola oil.

Polish canola *seedling*

SIMILAR SPECIES

Two introduced mustards, Polish and Argentine canola, are cultivated for the oil content of their seeds. Polish canola (*B. rapa* L.) and Argentine canola (*B. napus* L.) are easily distinguished from wild mustard with their nearly hairless stems and clasping stem leaves.

small-seeded false flax

Camelina microcarpa
Andrz. ex DC.

An annual or winter annual introduced from Europe and Asia.

Also known as: false flax, Dutch flax, western flax, Siberian oilseed

French names: caméline à petits fruits, caméline à petites graines

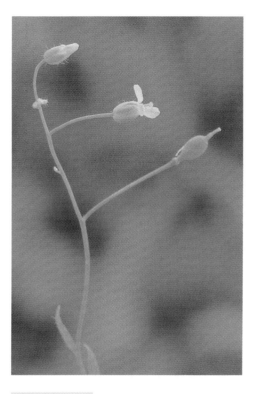

QUICK ID
- Flowers pale yellow
- Fruit round to pear-shaped
- Leaves alternate with simple to branched hairs

Distribution: Found throughout Canada and the northern two-thirds of the United States.

Weed Designation
Canada: MB

DESCRIPTION

Seed: Seeds are oblong, triangular in cross-section, 0.8 to 1.4 mm long. The reddish brown seeds are smooth and slightly glossy.

Seedling: Cotyledons, 3.5 to 6 mm long and 2 to 3 mm wide, are ovate and pale green. The stalk of the cotyledons have 2 or 3 short hairs. The first leaves are spatula-shaped and covered with simple and branched hairs.

Leaves: Basal leaves are spatula-shaped and bristly-hairy. These basal leaves have smooth margins. The lower leaves are covered with grey, star-shaped hairs, about 2 mm long. Stem leaves, 9 to 15 mm long and 4 to 6 mm wide, are alternate and clasp the stem with a broad, arrowhead-shaped base.

Flower: Small, pale-yellow flowers are borne in terminal clusters. Flowers are composed of 4 erect sepals, 4 spatula-shaped petals, 6 stamens, and 1 pistil. The petals, 4 to 7 mm long and 4 to 5 mm wide, are dark-veined. The fruiting stem is usually over 20 cm long.

Plant: An erect and somewhat branched plant, small-seeded false flax has stems up to 1 m tall. The plants are greyish green due to the presence of simple and star-shaped hairs that are rough to touch. Seeds are often shed while the plant is still flowering.

Fruit: The fruit, a round to pear-shaped capsule, 4 to 6 mm long, contains 10 or more seeds. The pod has a slender beak, less than 2 mm long. The stalks of the pods spread from the stem and are 6 to 25 mm long.

fruit

REASONS FOR CONCERN

Small-seeded false flax is a common weed of cultivated and abandoned fields, roadsides, and waste areas. It is often a contaminant in livestock feed. Small-seeded false flax is an alternate host for cabbage black ring spot, cauliflower mosaic, turnip crinkle, and turnip rosette viruses.

SIMILAR SPECIES

Large-seeded false flax (*C. sativa* (L.) Crantz), also called gold-of-pleasure, is another introduced species that closely resembles small-seeded false flax. A species found throughout Canada and the United States, its pods, 6 to 9 mm long, contain about 10 yellowish brown seeds, each about 2 mm long. Plants are usually hairless.

shepherd's-purse

Capsella bursa-pastoris
(L.) Medic.

An annual or winter annual introduced from southern Europe, shepherd's-purse was reported in North America prior to 1672.

Also known as: pepper plant, shepherd's-pouch, pick pocket, mother's-heart, St. James weed, caseweed, pick-purse, witches'-pouches, toothwort, shovel-plant

French names: bourse-à-pasteur, tabouret

QUICK ID
- Flowers white
- Pods triangular
- Leaves with wavy to deeply lobed margins

Distribution: Found throughout Canada and the United States.

Weed Designation
Canada: AB, MB

DESCRIPTION
Seed: Seeds are round to oblong, dull orange, about 1 mm in diameter. The surface is smooth with a slight sheen. Each plant may produce up to 40,000 seeds. Germination occurs in the top 2 cm of soil.

Seedling: Cotyledons, 2.5 to 5 mm long and 1 to 2 mm wide, are ovate to egg-shaped and long-stalked with a grainy appearance. The stem below the cotyledons is dull green and stained with purple. The first 4 leaves appear opposite and have numerous simple, star-shaped hairs.

Leaves: Shepherd's-purse has basal leaves as well as alternate stem leaves. Basal leaves, 3 to 15

cm long and up to 4 cm wide, vary greatly
between plants. Some plants have leaves with
wavy margins while others are deeply lobed.
The clasping stem leaves are stalkless and
reduced in size upwards. Stem leaves have
smooth to lobed margins.

Flower: Small white flowers appear in terminal
clusters. Flowers, up to 8 mm across, are
composed of 4 green sepals, 4 white petals, 6
stamens, and 1 pistil. The petals are 2 to 4 mm
long. The flowering stalk increases in length
during fruit development.

Plant: Shepherd's-purse has erect stems, up to
80 cm tall, and several branches. The plant
can be smooth or somewhat hairy. The
taproot is thin and branched.

Fruit: The fruit is a triangular pod, 5 to 8 mm long.
The 2 compartments contain about 20 seeds.
The fruiting stem elongates as fruit mature.

rosette

rosette

REASONS FOR CONCERN
Shepherd's-purse is a serious weed of cultivated
fields, row crops, gardens, and waste areas. It
can drastically reduce crop yields. Shepherd's-
purse is an alternate host for several viral
diseases: aster yellows, beet curly top, beet
mosaic, beet ring spot, beet yellow, cabbage
black ringspot, cabbage ring necrosis, cauliflower mosaic, cucumber mosaic, radish
mosaic, and tobacco mosaic. It also harbours
fungi that attack cabbage, turnips, and other
members of the mustard family.

fruit

SIMILAR SPECIES
Lyre-leaved rock cress (*Arabis lyrata* L.), a native
mustard with white flowers, is commonly
found in dry, open areas. It is similar in
appearance to shepherd's-purse. The distinguishing feature between the species is the
shape of the fruit. The narrow pod of lyre-
leaved rock cress is 1.5 to 4 cm long and 1 to
1.5 mm wide. It is found throughout Canada
(except the Atlantic provinces) and the
United States.

lens-podded hoary cress

Cardaria chalapensis
(L.) Handel-Mazzetti

QUICK ID
- Flowers white
- Leaves clasping the stem
- Fruit lens-shaped

Distribution: Found in all Canadian provinces west of and including Ontario, and throughout the northern two-thirds of the United States.

Weed Designation
Canada: FEDERAL, AB, BC, MB, SK
USA: FEDERAL, CA, NE, UT

A perennial introduced from western Asia (Uzbekistan to Israel) into California in 1918; the first Canadian report is from Grande Prairie, Alberta in 1926 as a contaminant in alfalfa seed from Turkestan.

Also known as: creeping hoary cress, white top, perennial peppergrass, white weed

French names: cranson rampant

Scientific synonyms: *C. draba* (L.) Desv. var. *repens* (Schrenk) O.E. Schulz

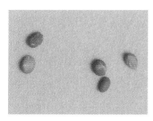

DESCRIPTION

Seed: Seeds are ovate, reddish brown, 2 mm long and 1.5 mm wide. Each plant is capable of producing 3,400 seeds, about 52% of which are viable after 3 years. Research shows that sunlight increases the germination rate.

Seedling: Cotyledons, 7 to 9 mm long and 2.5 mm wide, are club-shaped and dull greyish green. The stem below the cotyledons is usually brownish green. The first 3 pairs of

leaves are opposite and club-shaped. The
second pair and later leaves have short,
downward-pointing hairs on their margins.

Leaves: Stem leaves are alternate, up to 8 cm
long and 3 cm wide. The clasping stem leaves
have heart to arrowhead-shaped bases. Leaves
are not reduced in size upwards. The basal
leaves vary from smooth to irregularly
toothed margins; they are slightly hairy.

Flower: Small white flowers, 4 to 6 mm across,
are borne in flat-topped clusters from late
May to early June. Flowers, composed of 4
sepals, 4 petals, 6 stamens, and 1 style, are
found on stalks up to 1.5 cm long. The sepals, 2
to 2.5 mm long, are green with white margins.
The petals, 3 to 4 mm long, are white.

Plant: The most serious weed species of
Cardaria, lens-podded hoary cress spreads by
seeds, root fragments, and an extensive
underground creeping root system. It often
forms large colonies in ditches, cultivated
fields, and pastures. The stems, up to 50 cm
tall, are often branched above.

Fruit: The fruit, a lens to kidney-shaped pod, 2.5
to 6 mm long, contains 2 to 4 seeds. Each
stem may have up to 850 fruits.

REASONS FOR CONCERN

Lens-podded hoary cress is a serious weed in
cultivated crops, forages, and pastures. Once
established, it is difficult to eradicate.

SIMILAR SPECIES

Heart-podded hoary cress (*C. draba* (L.) Desv.), a
native species of eastern Europe, is closely
related to lens-podded hoary cress. As the
common name implies, the heart-shaped
fruit is the distinguishing characteristic
between these species. Another species,
globe-podded hoary cress (*C. pubescens* (C.A.
Mey.) Rollins), also called Siberian mustard,
is distinguished from the other species by its
fruit: globe-shaped and covered with short,
simple hairs. Both species are found
throughout most of North America.

heart-podded   globe-podded
hoary cress   hoary cress

flixweed

Descurainia sophia
(L.) Webb.

An annual, winter annual, or biennial introduced from Europe, Asia, and north Africa, flixweed was first observed in North America at Montreal in 1821; the first American report was from North Dakota in 1910.

Also known as:

French names: sagesse-des-chirurgiens, sisymbre Sophia

Scientific synonyms: *Sophia multifida* Gilib.; *Sisymbrium sophia* L.

QUICK ID
- Flowers yellow
- Leaves divided into narrow segments
- Plants greyish green

Distribution: Found throughout Canada and the northern third of the United States.

Weed Designation
  Canada: AB, MB

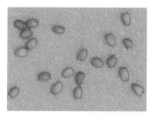

DESCRIPTION

Seed: Seeds are oblong, dull orange, less than 0.6 mm wide and 1 to 1.3 mm long. The seed surface is smooth. Some seeds have a thin, transparent wing on the rounded end. Each plant may produce up to 75,600 seeds, and most of the seeds will have germinated by the end of the third growing season. Germination is at or near the surface.

Seedling: Cotyledons, 4 to 12 mm long and 1 to 1.5 mm wide, are club-shaped, long-stalked and densely haired. The stem below the cotyledons has a few star-shaped hairs. The first 2 leaves are opposite, 3-lobed, and covered with star-shaped hairs. Later leaves are alternate and divided into narrow segments.

Leaves: Leaves are alternate, stalked, 2 to 10 cm long. The leaves are divided 2 to 3 times into narrow segments and covered with fine, grey, star-shaped hairs. A rosette of basal leaves is produced in the winter annual or biennial life cycles.

Flower: Flowers, 2 to 4 mm across, are pale yellow and appear in clusters at the ends of stems. These stems elongate and continue to flower while lower fruit mature. Flowers are composed of 4 sepals, 4 petals, 6 stamens, and 1 pistil.

Plant: Flixweed may have stems up to 1 m tall with numerous branches. The plant looks greyish green due to the star-shaped hairs on the stems and leaves. Flixweed is a prolific seed producer.

Fruit: The fruit is a narrow pod, 15 to 30 mm long and 1 mm wide. The pod usually contains 20 to 40 seeds. The stalks of the pods are 6 to 12 mm long and make an wide angle with the stem.

REASONS FOR CONCERN

Flixweed is a serious weed that robs crops of moisture and nutrients. It has been reported to reduce crop yields drastically in winter wheat and fall rye.

SIMILAR SPECIES

Grey tansy mustard (*D. richardsonii* (Sweet.) O.E. Schulz) is easily distinguished from flixweed. The pale-yellow flowers of grey tansy mustard produce pods (5 to 10 mm long) that are held close to the stem. The leaves of grey tansy mustard are divided once into narrow segments.

rosette

yellow whitlow-grass

Draba nemerosa L.

An annual native to North America.

Also known as: yellow draba

French names: drave de bois

Scientific synonyms: *D. lutea* Gilib.

QUICK ID
- Leaves primarily basal, densely haired
- Flowers yellow
- Flowers appear in early spring

Distribution: Found throughout Canada (except the Atlantic provinces) and the northwestern half of the United States.

Weed Designation
  Canada: MB

DESCRIPTION
Seed: Seeds are ovate, light brown, less than 0.5 mm across. Each plant is capable of producing up to 2,500 seeds.

Seedling: Cotyledons are elliptical and very small. The first leaves are elliptical; later leaves form a basal rosette.

Leaves: Elliptical leaves are primarily basal, with fewer than 5 small stem leaves. Leaves on the lower third of the stem are 2 to 45 mm long and 1 to 20 mm wide. The stem leaves often have 2 to 6 pairs of teeth.

Flower: An open terminal cluster of pale-yellow to white flowers appears in early spring. The flowering stem has 10 to 50 flowers, each composed of 4 sepals 2 to 2.5 mm long, 4 petals 2.5 to 4 mm long, 6 stamens, and a single pistil.

Plant: A small plant with unbranched stems, 3 to 35 cm tall, yellow whitlow-grass has fibrous roots. The stems and leaves are covered with simple or forked hairs. Yellow whitlow-grass is commonly found on dry, sandy sites.

Fruit: The fruit, an elliptical hairless pod, 3 to 10 mm long and 1 to 2 mm wide, opens at maturity. The stalk of the pod is about 15 mm long. Pods usually contain 30 to 50 seeds.

REASONS FOR CONCERN

Yellow whitlow-grass is a serious weed in cultivated fields and row crops. Its early spring growth competes with crop seedlings for moisture and nutrients; it does not trouble established crops and forages.

SIMILAR SPECIES

Pygmyflower (*Androsace septentrionalis* L.) is often confused with yellow whitlow-grass. Both species have a similar growth habit, but pygmyflower has leafless flowering stems and white flowers (see pp 348-49). The flowers of pygmyflower have 5 petals, unlike those of yellow whitlow-grass, which have 4.

rosette

dog mustard

Erucastrum gallicum
(Willd.) Schulz

An annual or winter annual introduced from Europe into the United States in 1903; the first Canadian report was from Emerson, Manitoba in 1922.

Also known as: rocketweed

French names: moutarde des chiens, fausse roquette

QUICK ID
- Flowers pale yellow
- Leaves deeply lobed with large terminal lobe
- Stem with stiff, downward-pointing hairs on lower part

Distribution: Found throughout Canada and the northern half of the United States.

Weed Designation
Canada: FEDERAL, AB, MB

DESCRIPTION

Seed: Seeds are ovate, reddish to light brown, 1.2 mm long and 0.8 mm wide.

Seedling: Cotyledons are round to club-shaped, 4 to 5 mm across, and long-stalked. A small notch can be found at the tip of the cotyledon. The first 2 or 3 leaves are entire with wavy to shallowly lobed margins. Later leaves are divided into several lobes.

Leaves: Leaves are alternate, oblong to lance-shaped, 3 to 25 cm long and 1 to 6 cm wide.

Leaves are deeply lobed, often to the midrib. The basal and lower leaves have a distinct lobe at the base. Stem leaves have several lateral lobes and a large terminal segment. All leaves are covered with stiff, simple hairs.

Flower: Pale-yellow flowers, about 6 mm across, appear in leafy clusters at the ends of branches. Flowers are composed of 4 sepals, 4 petals, 6 stamens, and a single pistil. The petals, 4 to 7 mm long, have greenish veins. As the fruit mature, the flowering stalk lengthens.

Plant: Dog mustard has branched stems, up to 1 m tall, that rise from a slender taproot. The lower part of the stem has stiff, downward-pointing hairs.

Fruit: The fruit is a 4-sided pod, 2 to 5 cm long. It is usually curved upwards on stalks 6 to 10 mm long. The beak of the pod is about 3 mm long.

REASONS FOR CONCERN

Dog mustard has the potential to be a serious weed in canola crops. It is a common weed of orchards, railways, roadsides, and disturbed ground.

SIMILAR SPECIES

Garden rocket (*Eruca sativa* L.), an introduced plant that has escaped cultivation, is easily distinguished from dog mustard. Garden rocket has whitish yellow petals, 12 to 20 mm long. The petals are conspicuously veined. Pods are 12 to 25 mm long and 3 to 5 mm wide. Leaves, 5 to 15 cm long, are fiddle-shaped and deeply lobed. Garden rocket has been reported from most Canadian provinces. Another introduced species, tumbling mustard (*Sisymbrium altissimum* L.), resembles dog mustard. Tumbling mustard, an annual with pale-yellow flowers, is distinguished by its narrowly lobed leaves and pods that are 5 to 10 cm long (see pp 290-91).

garden rocket

wormseed mustard

Erysimum cheiranthoides L.

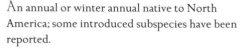

An annual or winter annual native to North America; some introduced subspecies have been reported.

Also known as: treacle mustard, treacle erysimum

French names: vélar fausse giroflée, vélar giroflée

Scientific synonyms: *Cheirinia cheiranthoides* (L.) Link

QUICK ID
- Flowers yellow
- Leaves with wavy margins, not lobed
- Plant covered with branched hairs

Distribution: Found throughout Canada and the northern two-thirds of the United States.

Weed Designation
Canada: AB, MB
USA: KS

DESCRIPTION

Seed: Oblong to elliptical seeds are light orange to brown, 1 to 1.2 mm long and less than 0.6 mm wide. The surface is slightly rough and somewhat shiny. Each plant can produce up to 3,500 seeds. Germination occurs in the top 2 cm of soil.

Seedling: Cotyledons, 1.5 to 5 mm long and 1 to 2 mm wide, are spatula-shaped and pale green. Tips of the cotyledons are slightly indented. The first 2 leaves appear opposite and are angularly lobed, with a few simple to star-shaped hairs.

Leaves: Leaves are alternate, oblong to lance-shaped, up to 8 cm long and 2 cm wide. The dark-green leaves have smooth to wavy margins and are covered with numerous forked hairs. The upper leaves are stalkless and distinctly toothed.

Flower: Numerous yellow flowers, 6 to 10 mm across, appear in dense terminal clusters, up to 3 cm across. Flowers are composed of 4 sepals 2 to 3.5 mm long, 4 petals 3.5 to 5.5 mm long, 6 stamens, and 1 pistil. As the fruit mature, the flowering stem lengthens.

Plant: An erect annual weed, wormseed mustard rises from a short taproot. The purplish green stems grow up to 1 m tall and are occasionally branched. The stem is covered with short hairs that have 2 to 3 branches.

Fruit: The pod-like fruit, 1.5 to 3 cm long, is 4-angled. The short-beaked pods are held erect and parallel to the stem. The stalks of the fruit are 6 to 12 mm long.

REASONS FOR CONCERN

Wormseed mustard is not a concern in most crops, but it has the potential to be weedy in canola, where it is not easily controlled. It is a common weed in gardens, lawns, pastures, and roadsides. The seeds of wormseed mustard are bitter-tasting, and pigs refuse to eat any feed that is contaminated with it. It is also an alternate host for cucumber mosaic, turnip crinkle, turnip rosette, and turnip yellow mosaic viruses.

SIMILAR SPECIES

Prairie rocket (*E. asperum* (Nutt.) DC.), a native plant of western North America that inhabits dry, sandy prairie grasslands, is closely related to wormseed mustard. Prairie rocket is distinguished by bright-yellow petals, 15 to 25 mm long, and erect pods 6 to 10 cm long and 2 mm thick.

prairie rocket

dame's rocket

Hesperis matronalis L.

A perennial introduced from Europe as a garden flower.

Also known as: dame's violet, mother-of-the-evening

French names: julienne des dames, julienne des jardins, julienne

QUICK ID
- Flowers purple and fragrant
- Leaves alternate and hairy
- Fruit 2 to 14 cm long, constricted between seeds

Distribution: Found throughout Canada and the United States.

Weed Designation
Canada: MB
USA: TN

DESCRIPTION
Seed: Seeds are slightly rounded, dark reddish brown, 3 to 4 mm long. Each plant is capable of producing up to 20,000 seeds.

Seedling: Cotyledons, 8 to 15 mm long and 5 to 8 mm wide, are ovate and dull green. The cotyledons are covered with short, white, branched hairs. The first leaves are ovate and appear opposite. Later leaves are alternate.

Leaves: Leaves are alternate, lance-shaped, 5 to 15 cm long. The stalkless stem leaves are shallowly toothed and hairy on both sides.

Flower: Showy, fragrant, pinkish purple flowers, 1.4 to 2.5 cm across, are found in elongated racemes. Flowers are composed of 4 sepals, 4 petals (15 to 25 mm long), 6 stamens, and 1 style. Flowers are reported to be more fragrant during the evening hours.

Plant: Dame's rocket reproduces by seed only. Its branched stems rise up to 90 cm tall from a shallow root system. Leaves and stems are covered with simple to forked hairs.

Fruit: The fruit is a cylindrical pod, 2.5 to 14 cm long. The erect to ascending pods are somewhat constricted between the seeds. Each pod produces between 20 and 35 seeds. The seeds appear in a single row.

REASONS FOR CONCERN

Dame's rocket is a common weed of ditches, fencelines, and orchards. It is an alternate host for beet mosaic, cauliflower mosaic, radish mosaic, squash mosaic, and turnip mosaic viruses.

common peppergrass

Lepidium densiflorum Schrad.

An annual or winter annual native to North America, common peppergrass has spread as a contaminant in seed and feed.

Also known as: peppergrass, poor man's pepper, prairie peppergrass, green-flowered peppergrass, wild tongue-grass

French names: lépidie densiflore, passerage, passerage densiflore

Scientific synonyms: *L. apetalum* A. Grey

QUICK ID
- Pods heart-shaped
- Flowers densely arranged along the stem
- Leaves basal, deeply lobed

Distribution: Found throughout Canada and the United States.

Weed Designation
    Canada: FEDERAL, MB

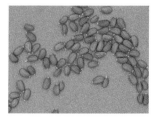

DESCRIPTION
Seed: Seeds are ovate, orange, 1.4 to 1.8 mm long and less than 1.2 mm wide. The surface is slightly rough and shiny. Each plant may produce up to 5,000 seeds.
Seedling: Cotyledons are ovate, long-stalked, and hairless. The first leaves are deeply lobed,

long-stalked and hairless. The first pair of leaves appears opposite.

Leaves: Peppergrass has basal and alternate leaves. The basal leaves are stalked and may be toothed to deeply lobed. They are 3 to 10 cm long and 1 to 2 cm wide. Stem leaves are alternate and stalkless with smooth margins. Leaves are reduced in size upward.

Flower: Flowers are small, inconspicuous, less than 2 mm wide. They are composed of 4 green sepals, 4 pinkish white petals, each about 1 mm long, 6 stamens, and 1 pistil. Petals are occasionally absent. Flower stalks are 2 to 3 mm long.

Plant: Common peppergrass has numerous branches, 20 to 50 cm tall. It is a bushy plant covered with dense, short hairs, giving it a greyish green appearance. Reproduction is by seed only.

Fruit: Heart-shaped to round pods, 2 to 3.5 mm long, each contain 2 seeds. The pod has a papery margin and a notch at the top. An average of 9 to 15 pods are produced for every 1 cm of flowering stem.

REASONS FOR CONCERN

Common peppergrass is a serious weed of cultivated fields and can drastically reduce crop yield. It is common in roadsides, waste areas, and farmyards.

SIMILAR SPECIES

Garden cress (*L. sativum* L.), an introduced plant that has escaped cultivation, is closely related to common peppergrass. The leaves of garden cress are dissected into narrow segments. The basal leaves wither soon after the flowering stalk has emerged. Petals are reddish white and twice as long as the sepals. Pods are 5 to 7 mm long and have a deep notch at the top. Garden cress has been reported from all Canadian provinces.

rosette

ball mustard

Neslia paniculata
(L.) Desv.

An annual or winter annual introduced from southern Europe or north Africa; the first Canadian report was from Portage La Prairie, Manitoba in 1891.

Also known as: yellow-weed, neslia

French names: neslie paniculée, neslie

QUICK ID
- Fruit round, containing a single seed
- Flowers yellow
- Leaves lance-shaped

Distribution: Found throughout Canada, the northeastern United States, and Montana.

Weed Designation
Canada: AB, MB, SK

DESCRIPTION
Seed: Seeds are ovate, yellowish brown, 2.2 mm long.

Seedling: Cotyledons are round, 6 to 8 mm across, with a small indentation at the tip. The cotyledons are hairless. The first leaves are oblong with pointed or rounded tips, stalked, and covered with star-shaped hairs.

Leaves: Leaves are alternate, lance-shaped, 1 to 6 cm long. Basal leaves are stalked, while stem leaves are stalkless. The upper leaves are arrowhead-shaped and clasp the stem. The leaves have numerous star-shaped hairs.

Flower: Bright-yellow flowers, 2 to 3 mm wide, appear near the ends of the stems and branches. The flower stalks are 6 to 10 mm long. Flowers are composed of 4 green sepals, 4 yellow petals, 6 stamens, and 1 pistil.

Plant: An erect annual with several branches, ball mustard can grow up to 1 m tall. The plant has a yellowish green appearance because of numerous star-shaped hairs on the stem and leaves.

Fruit: The fruit is a round pod, 3 mm in diameter, with 1 or 2 seeds. The surface of the pod is prominently veined. The fruit has a thick wall, and the seeds are not released when mature. Pods remain attached to the stem when ripe.

REASONS FOR CONCERN

Ball mustard causes concerns for canola growers. The pods are similar in size to canola seeds, making them difficult to separate and reducing the quality of canola oil. Ball mustard is also an alternate host for cabbage ring necrosis, cauliflower mosaic, turnip crinkle, turnip mosaic, and turnip yellow mosaic viruses.

SIMILAR SPECIES

Sand bladder-pod (*Lesquerella arenosa* (Richards.) Rydb.), a prostrate-growing native perennial found in sandy open areas, may be confused with ball mustard. Sand bladder-pod has bright-yellow flowers, about 6 mm across, and a round pod; each pod contains 2 to 7 seeds. It is found on the Canadian prairies and the central plains of the United States.

sand bladder-pod

wild radish
Raphanus raphanistrum L.

An annual or winter annual introduced from Europe and Asia.

Also known as: jointed charlock, jointed radish, wild kale, wild turnip, cadlock, wild rape, runch

French names: radis sauvage, ravenelle

DESCRIPTION

Seed: Seeds are egg-shaped, reddish brown, 4 to 6 mm long and 2 mm wide. Each plant produces about 160 seeds. Germination usually occurs in the top 2 cm of soil.

Seedling: Cotyledons are heart to kidney-shaped and distinctly veined. The stem below the cotyledons has stiff hairs. The first leaves are ovate with prominent veins and a large terminal lobe. These toothed leaves have hairy margins and undersides.

Leaves: Leaves are alternate, oblong to ovate with wavy irregularly toothed margins. Basal leaves, 5 to 20 cm long, have 5 to 15 oblong segments. The lobes increase in size towards the tip of the leaf, with the terminal segment being the largest. Leaves are reduced in size upwards. Stem leaves, up to 7.5 cm long, have 2 to 5 toothed lobes. Both sides of the leaves have scattered stiff hairs.

Flower: Clusters of bright to pale-yellow flowers, 18 to 20 mm across, appear at the ends of branches. Flowers are composed of 4 sepals, 4 petals, 6 stamens, and 1 pistil. The petals, 10 to 20 mm long, are often tinged with purple or conspicuously purple-veined. Flower stalks are 10 to 25 mm long.

Plant: A stout annual weed, wild radish has a thick taproot. The stems, 30 to 90 cm tall, are bristly near the base. Plants may have a few long branches from the base.

Fruit: The fruit, a pod 3 to 7.5 cm long, is 4 to 10-seeded. The pods are strongly ribbed and constricted between the seeds, breaking into segments at the joints. These barrel-shaped segments are single-seeded. Seeds are rarely seen because the pod segments do not open at maturity.

fruit segments

rosette

REASONS FOR CONCERN

Wild radish can drastically reduce crop yields, especially in canola, where it may go unnoticed. It competes with crops for moisture, nutrients, and sunlight. Wild radish is also a concern in wheat because pod segments are similar in size to the grain, making them difficult to separate. It is an alternate host for cabbage black ring spot, cauliflower mosaic, turnip crinkle, turnip rosette, and turnip yellow mosaic viruses. The seeds of wild radish are reported to be POISONOUS to livestock if eaten in large quantities.

SIMILAR SPECIES

Wild radish is occasionally confused with wild mustard (*Brassica kaber* (DC.) L.C. Wheeler), another introduced species. Wild mustard is distinguished by its smaller flowers (10 to 15 mm across) and smooth pod (see pp 266-67). The pod of wild mustard does not break into segments like that of wild radish.

wild mustard

tumbling mustard

Sisymbrium altissimum L.

An annual, winter annual, or biennial introduced from the western Mediterranean region and north Africa.

Also known as: Jim Hill mustard, tall sisymbrium, tall hedge mustard

French names: sisymbre élevé, moutarde roulante

QUICK ID

⌀ Flowers pale yellow
⌀ Leaves divided into thread-like segments
⌀ Pods 5 to 10 cm long

Distribution: Found throughout Canada and the United States.

Weed Designation
Canada: MB, SK

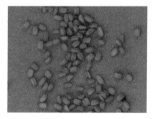

DESCRIPTION

Seed: Seeds are oblong, dull orange, 1.1 to 1.3 mm long and less than 0.8 mm wide. The surface of the seed is smooth. Each plant may yield as many as 2,700 seeds. Germination occurs in the top 2 cm of soil.

Seedling: Cotyledons, 2 to 6 mm long and 1 to 2 mm wide, are ovate to club-shaped, pale green. The first leaves are ovate with angular lobes and bristly hairs on the leaf margin.

Leaves: The basal and lower leaves are up to 30 cm long and have 5 to 8 pairs of broad triangular lobes. The lower leaves have usually withered by the time the plant flowers. Stem leaves are alternate, triangular in outline, and divided into thread-like segments. The upper leaves are smaller and have 2 to 5 thread-like segments. The terminal lobe of leaves is smaller than the lateral lobes. Upper and lower leaves are pale green and bristly haired.

Flower: Pale-yellow flowers, 6 to 14 mm wide, are clustered at the ends of branches. Flowers are composed of 4 sepals 4 to 5 mm long, 4 petals 6 to 8 mm long, 6 stamens, and 1 pistil.

Plant: Tumbling mustard, a pale-green plant, has numerous branches that may reach 1.2 m in height. The erect stems have white hairs near the base. Plants become woody and brittle with age; they break off at the ground at maturity. The broken stems form tumble-weeds, scattering seeds as they travel.

Fruit: The fruit, a pod 5 to 10 cm long, may contain as many as 100 seeds. The pods are wide-spreading and resemble branches. At maturity, the pod is about the same size as its stalk.

REASONS FOR CONCERN

Tumbling mustard is a common weed of road-sides, fencelines, and pastures. Infestations in cultivated fields have recently been reported, which coincides with changes in cultivation practices. Tumbling mustard is an alternate host for cabbage ring necrosis, cauliflower mosaic, and turnip mosaic viruses.

SIMILAR SPECIES

Tall hedge mustard (*S. loeselii* L.) is very similar to tumbling mustard. It is distinguished by shorter petals (5 to 6 mm long) and shorter pods (1 to 4 cm long). At maturity, the pod is thicker than its stalk. The divisions of the upper leaves are lance-shaped, not thread-like as in tumbling mustard. Tall hedge mustard is found throughout Canada, except the Atlantic provinces.

tall hedge mustard

stinkweed

Thlapsi arvense L.

An annual or winter annual introduced from the eastern Mediterranean region of Europe and Asia into Detroit in 1701; the first Canadian report was from Manitoba in 1860.

Also known as: pennycress, frenchweed, fanweed, field pennycress, bastardweed, bastard cress, dish mustard, mithridate mustard

French names: tabouret des champs, monayère

QUICK ID
- Fruit heart-shaped and flat
- Plant with distinctive odour (garlic, mustard, or turnip)
- Flowers white

Distribution: Found throughout Canada and the United States.

Weed Designation
Canada: FEDERAL, AB, MB, PQ, SK
USA: IN, KS, MI, MN, NE, NV, OH, SD, WA

DESCRIPTION

Seed: Seeds are ovate, purplish brown, 1.7 to 2 mm long and less than 0.7 mm thick. The seed surface has 6 fingerprint-like ridges on each face. Each plant is capable of producing more than 15,000 seeds, which are viable for about 20 years.

Seedling: Cotyledons are ovate to spoon-shaped, 4 to 10 mm long and 2 to 6 mm wide, and hairless. The stalk of the cotyledons can be up to 7 mm long. The first leaves appear opposite and have wavy margins, with 1 to 3 indentations per side.

Leaves: Leaves are alternate with basal leaves withering soon after the flowering stems emerge. Basal leaves are stalked and ovate with the widest part of the leaf near the tip. These leaves are up to 10 cm long with a few teeth on each side. Stem leaves are stalkless and clasp the stem. Auricles, small, ear-like appendages at the base of the leaf, almost encircle the stem. Stem leaves are oblong with toothed or smooth margins.

Flower: Small white flowers, less than 3 mm across, appear in terminal clusters. The flowering stem elongates as the plant matures. Flowers are composed of 4 green sepals 1 to 2 mm long, 4 white petals 3 to 4 mm long, 6 stamens, and 1 pistil. Stinkweed flowers April to October and during warm periods in the winter months.

Plant: A pale-green, hairless plant, stinkweed turns yellow soon after flowering. Stems are often branched at the base and can grow up to 80 cm tall. Stinkweed, as the common name implies, has a strong turnip odour. Research has determined that the winter annual life cycle produces more prolific plants than the annual life cycle.

Fruit: The fruit is a flat, heart-shaped pod, 1 to 2 cm long; each fruit produces 4 to 16 seeds. Pods have a broad, papery membrane on the edges.

REASONS FOR CONCERN

Stinkweed is a serious weed of cultivated fields, row crops, gardens, and waste areas. It has been reported to drastically reduce yields in all crops. When eaten by livestock, stinkweed causes off-flavours in milk and meat, but the plants are not readily eaten because of the bitter mustard oils. Feed containing large amounts of seed may be POISONOUS to livestock. Research has shown that a lethal dose for cattle is 65 mg/kg of body weight.

fruit

rosette

SIMILAR SPECIES

Shepherd's-purse (*Capsella bursa-pastoris* (L.) Medic) is occasionally confused with stinkweed. Shepherd's-purse is distinguished by its triangular fruit (see pp 270-71).

black henbane,
Hyoscyamus niger L.

The nightshade family, often referred to as the potato family, contains more than 2,800 species worldwide. Species in this family may be herbs, shrubs, or trees. The simple to compound alternate leaves lack stipules. Flowers are composed of 4 to 7 sepals, 4 to 7 petals, 5 stamens, and a single style. The petals may be partly or completely fused and form a funnel-shaped corolla. The fruit is a berry or capsule.

The nightshade family is a very important group of plants. Many species are grown for food, including potatoes, tomatoes, eggplants, and peppers. Several other species are grown as ornamental plants. These include petunias, Chinese lanterns, and angel's trumpets. Tobacco is probably the most important crop species of this family. The poisonous members of this family include henbane and belladonna.

Nightshade Family

Clockwise from top left: wild tomato,
Solanum triflorum Nutt.; black nightshade,
Solanum nigrum L.; black henbane,
Hyoscyamus niger L.

Solanaceae

jimsonweed

Datura stramonium L.

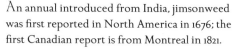

An annual introduced from India, jimsonweed was first reported in North America in 1676; the first Canadian report is from Montreal in 1821.

Also known as: Jamestown-weed, thorn apple, mad apple, stinkwort, angel's-trumpet, devil's-trumpet, dewtry, whitcman's weed

French names: stramoine commune, pomme épineuse, herbe du diable

QUICK ID
- Flowers white, trumpet-shaped
- Fruit a spiny capsule
- Leaves alternate

Distribution: Found throughout Canada (except Alberta and Newfoundland) and the United States (except for the north-central plains).

Weed Designation
Canada: MB, NS
USA: MI, NC, SC

DESCRIPTION

Seed: Seeds are black, disc-shaped with 1 flat side, 3.4 to 3.8 mm long, 2.8 to 3.2 mm wide and less than 1.5 mm thick. The surface is dull and slightly wrinkled. The seeds are EXTREMELY POISONOUS. Each plant is capable of producing up to 35,000 seeds. Germination occurs in the top 8 cm of soil.

Seedling: Cotyledons, 20 to 40 mm long and 4 mm wide, are lance-shaped with a prominent midrib. The stem below the cotyledons is often purplish. The first leaves are opposite, egg-shaped, and prominently veined beneath. Leaves have scattered minute hairs. Cotyledons wither and remain attached to the developing stem.

Leaves: Leaves are alternate, ovate to triangular, and 7 to 20 cm long. These long-stalked leaves have irregularly toothed margins. When crushed, the leaves release a strong scent.

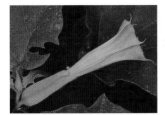

Flower: White or purplish, trumpet-shaped flowers, 5 to 12.5 cm long and 5 cm across, are borne singly in the axils of leaves. The flowers are composed of 5 sepals fused into a tube, 5 united petals, 5 stamens, and a single pistil. The funnel-shaped corolla has 5 points. A single plant may produce up to 50 fruit.

Plant: The leaves and stems of jimsonweed release an unpleasant odour when crushed. Stems, up to 2 m tall, rise from thick, shallow roots. The smooth stems are thick, 3 to 5 cm in diameter, and branched near the top. Stems are often purplish green.

fruit

Fruit: The fruit is a spiny, egg-shaped capsule, 3 to 6 cm wide. The capsule is 4-celled and contains many seeds. At maturity, the capsule breaks into 4 sections, releasing the seeds; each capsule contains 600 to 700 seeds.

REASONS FOR CONCERN

Jimsonweed is a serious weed of cultivated fields, row crops, and farmyards. It has been reported to reduce yields by 45% in beans and 77% in tomatoes. All parts of the plant are POISONOUS, especially the seeds. It is reported that the plant has a narcotic affect that may result in death to livestock or humans that ingest it. Less than 0.1% of body weight is considered a lethal dose. The nectar of jimsonweed flowers contains several alkaloid compounds that are reported to contaminate honey. Over 55 viral diseases have been identified with jimsonweed, including beet curly top, cucumber mosaic, and several potato, tobacco, and tomato viruses.

datura *or* thorn-apple

SIMILAR SPECIES

Datura or thorn-apple (*D. innoxia* Small.), an ornamental plant, is closely related to jimsonweed. It is distinguished by flowers 12 to 20 cm long and lance-shaped leaves.

black henbane

Hyoscyamus niger L.

An annual or biennial introduced from Europe.

Also known as: fetid nightshade, henbane

French names: jusquiame noire

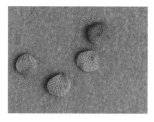

DESCRIPTION

Seed: Seeds are egg to pear-shaped, light greyish brown, 1.5 mm long, 1.2 mm wide and less than 0.8 mm thick. At low magnification, the surface features a network of raised veins. Each plant is capable of producing up to 100,000 seeds, which are viable for up to 5 years.

Seedling: Cotyledons, 3.5 to 5 mm long and 1 to 1.5 mm wide, are ovate with a few hairs near the base. The first leaves are elliptical and have numerous hairs on the leaf stalks. The leaves have a clammy texture and are unpleasant smelling when bruised.

Leaves: Leaves are alternate and reduced in size upwards. Basal leaves produced in the first growing season may be up to 45 cm long and 15 cm wide. These leaves have shallow lobes and wavy margins. Stem leaves are stalkless and irregularly lobed. These clasping stem leaves are 7 to 20 cm long. All leaves are covered with long, sticky hairs.

rosette

Flower: Yellowish green flowers with purple veins are borne singly in leaf axils. These short-stalked flowers appear to be borne on 1 side of the stem. Flowers, 25 to 35 mm wide, are composed of 5 united sepals, 5 united petals, 5 stamens, and a single pistil. The funnel to tube-shaped corolla is 2.5 to 4.5 cm long. The anthers, the pollen-producing portion of the stamens, are purple in this species.

Plant: A strong-scented weed with branched stems up to 1 m tall, black henbane is covered with long, sticky hairs. The robust taproot is spindle-shaped.

Fruit: The fruit is a globe-shaped capsule, 1 to 1.5 cm long, that opens at the top. The urn-shaped calyx, 2 to 2.5 cm long, is bristle-tipped and surrounds the seed capsule. A single capsule may contain up to 200 seeds.

REASONS FOR CONCERN

Black henbane is a common weed of waste areas, roadsides, and pastures. It is rarely found in cultivated fields. Black henbane is TOXIC to livestock and man. Poisonings are rare as the sticky hairs make it unpalatable. It is an alternate host for cucumber mosaic, lucerne mosaic, and several potato, tobacco, and tomato viruses.

fruit

black nightshade

Solanum nigrum L.

An annual introduced from South America; the first Canadian report is from New Brunswick in 1877.

Also known as: deadly nightshade, poison-berry, garden nightshade, hound's-berry, garden huckleberry

French names: morelle noire, crêve-chien

Scientific synonyms: *S. americanum* Mill.

QUICK ID
- Leaves alternate
- Flowers white with yellow centres
- Fruit black and berry-like

Distribution: Found throughout Canada and the eastern half of the United States.

Weed Designation
Canada: MB   USA: KS, MI

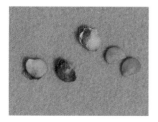

DESCRIPTION
Seed: Seeds are disc-shaped, light brown, 1.3 mm across and 0.6 mm thick. Up to 178,000 seeds per plant may be produced. Seeds are viable in soil for 8 years.

Seedling: Cotyledons, 3 to 9.5 mm long and 1 to 4 mm wide, have minute hairs on the upper surface and the midvein beneath. The stem below the cotyledons has several short, sticky hairs. The first leaves are egg-shaped and hairy. The upper surface of the leaves becomes smooth with age. The underside remains hairy.

Leaves: Leaves are alternate, ovate to triangular, up to 8 cm long and 5 cm wide. Dark-green leaves have wavy or irregularly toothed margins. The leaves are long-stalked.

Flower: Clusters of 5 to 10 white flowers with a yellow centre appear on a short stalk that is connected directly to the stem and not in the leaf axil. The flowers, 3 to 8 mm across, are composed of a 5-lobed calyx, 5-lobed corolla, 5 stamens, and a single pistil. Each plant produces up to 100 berries.

Plant: An erect annual with fibrous roots, black nightshade has widely branched stems, 10 to 100 cm tall. The plant is somewhat hairy.

Fruit: The fruit is a globe-shaped berry, 9 to 15 mm across. Young berries are green and turn bluish black at maturity. The fruit has many seeds.

REASONS FOR CONCERN

A weed of cultivated fields and waste areas, black nightshade is not easily controlled by herbicides. The fruit are often harvested with beans and peas and lower the quality of the crop. The unripe fruit of black nightshade are POISONOUS to man and livestock. It is also an alternate host for cucumber mosaic, tobacco mosaic, tomato spotted wilt, beet curly top, chili mosaic, petunia mosaic, and potato A viruses.

SIMILAR SPECIES

Hairy nightshade (*S. sarrachoides* Sendt.), another introduced species, is often confused with black nightshade. It is distinguished from black nightshade by bristly and sticky hairs on the stem, and fruit that are yellowish green at maturity.

fruit

wild tomato

Solanum triflorum Nutt.

An annual native to North America.

Also known as: cutleaf nightshade, three-flow-ered nightshade

French names: morelle à trois fleurs

QUICK ID
- Plant ill-smelling
- Flowers white with yellow centres
- Fruit green and berry-like

Distribution: Found throughout Canada (except the Atlantic provinces) and the western half of the United States.

Weed Designation
Canada: MB

DESCRIPTION
Seed: Seeds are disc-shaped, yellowish brown, 2 to 2.2 mm long and less than 1.5 mm wide and 0.5 mm thick. The surface is dull and rough-ened.

Seedling: Cotyledons, 4 to 9 mm long and 0.5 to 2 mm wide, are lance-shaped and slightly hairy. The stem below the cotyledons has several short, sticky hairs. The first leaves are alternate with wavy margins and slightly hairy.

Leaves: Leaves are alternate, oblong, 2 to 10 cm long. The leaves are deeply lobed with a few scattered hairs. Leaves release an unpleasant odour when crushed.

Flower: White flowers, 8 to 15 mm across, appear in clusters of 3 in leaf axils. The flowers are composed of 5 united sepals, 5 united petals, 5 stamens, and 1 pistil. Flowers are similar in appearance to the cultivated tomato.

Plant: A low-spreading plant with several branches from the base, wild tomato forms small mats about 60 cm across. Stems are often zig-zagged, purplish green, and hairy. Stems in contact with the soil often root, making this plant difficult to eradicate by cultivation. The whole plant has an unpleasant odour.

Fruit: The fruit is a globe-shaped berry, 8 to 14 mm across. The small "tomato" is green at maturity. The fruit has 2 compartments and contains numerous seeds.

REASONS FOR CONCERN

Wild tomato is a common weed of cultivated fields and waste areas. Wild tomato has been reported to be the cause of livestock POISONING. It has been determined that 0.1% of body weight is a lethal dose. It is an alternate host for cucumber mosaic, tobacco ring spot, tobacco streak, and turnip mosaic viruses.

fruit

SIMILAR SPECIES

Black nightshade (*S. nigrum* L.), another member of the nightshade family, is closely related to wild tomato. Black nightshade has ovate to lance-shaped leaves and fruit that turns black at maturity (see pp 300-01).

black nightshade

dissected flower

loment

legume

The pea family is often referred to by its old name, Leguminosae. It is a large family, with worldwide distribution of more than 20,000 species. Species may be herbs, shrubs, vines, or trees with alternate compound leaves. Stipules are absent. Irregularly shaped flowers are composed of 5 sepals, 5 petals, 10 stamens (9 fused and 1 free), and a single style. The upper petal of the flower is often called the banner or standard; the 2 side petals are referred to as the wings, while the lower 2 petals are fused to form a keel. There are 2 types of fruit: legumes and loments.

The pea family is the second most important plant family, second only to the grasses. The family includes such important crop species as peanuts, beans, peas, and lentils. Other species, including alfalfa and clover, are grown for their important forage value.

Pea Family

caragana,
Caragana arborescens
Lam.

Fabaceae

black medick

Medicago lupulina L.

An annual, winter annual, biennial, or short-lived perennial introduced from eastern Europe, western Asia, and north Africa, black medick was first reported in Canada in 1792.

Also known as: trefoil, black clover, none-such, hop medic, spotted burclover, blackseed

French names: lupuline, luzerne lupuline, minette

QUICK ID
- Leaves compound with 3 leaflets
- Leaves alternate
- Flowers yellow, borne in globe-shaped clusters

Distribution: Found throughout Canada and the United States.

Weed Designation
Canada: MB

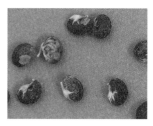

DESCRIPTION
Seed: Seeds are ovate to kidney-shaped, yellowish brown with a green tinge, 1.2 to 1.6 mm long and less than 1.2 mm wide. The surface is smooth. Each plant is capable of producing over 6,000 seeds which are viable in soil for up to 11 years. No dormant period is required for seeds to germinate.

Seedling: Cotyledons, 4 to 9 mm long and 2 to 4 mm wide, are dull green above and pale beneath. The first leaf is simple and spatula-shaped. All later leaves are compound and have 3 leaflets.

Leaves: Leaves are alternate, compound, and composed of 3 ovate, hairy leaflets. Leaflets are 5 to 30 mm long. The terminal leaflet is stalked, while the laterals are nearly stalkless. Stipules, small papery appendages at the leaf base, are lance or awl-shaped and spine-tipped.

Flower: Globe-shaped clusters of 20 to 50 yellow flowers, about 12 mm across, appear in leaf axils. Flowers may appear as early as 6 weeks after germination. Flowers, 3 to 4 mm long, are composed of 5 united sepals, 5 united petals, 10 stamens, and a single pistil.

Plant: Black medick has hairy prostrate stems up to 80 cm long. The roots are thick and shallow, and are often difficult to pull from the ground.

Fruit: The fruit, a black, kidney-shaped pod, 1.5 to 3 mm long, contains a single seed.

REASONS FOR CONCERN

Black medick is a weed of lawns, gardens, roadsides, and pastures. It is occasionally found in cultivated crops. Black medick is an alternate host for bean yellow mosaic, pea mottle, pea wilt, potato yellow dwarf, and red clover mosaic viruses.

SIMILAR SPECIES

Alfalfa (*M. sativa* L.), another introduced species, is distinguished from black medick by its blue or purple flowers and spirally coiled pod containing several seeds (see pp 308-09). Stems, up to 1 m tall, rise from a deep taproot. Alfalfa was introduced from southeastern Europe as a forage crop in the early 1800s.

alfalfa

alfalfa

Medicago sativa L.

A perennial introduced from Europe as a forage plant, alfalfa is now widespread throughout areas where it has been cultivated.

French names: luzerne

QUICK ID
- Leaves compound with 3 leaflets
- Leaves alternate
- Flowers blue to purple, borne in globe-shaped clusters

Distribution: Found throughout Canada and the United States.

Weed Designation
  None

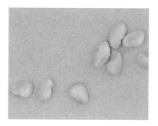

DESCRIPTION
Seed: Seeds are ovate to kidney-shaped, yellowish brown, 1.5 to 3 mm long.

Seedling: Cotyledons, 3 to 10 mm long and 2 to 5 mm wide, are dull green above and pale beneath. The first leaf is simple and spatula-shaped. All later leaves are compound and have 3 leaflets.

Leaves: Leaves are alternate, compound, and composed of 3 ovate, hairy leaflets. Leaflets are 10 to 35 mm long. The terminal leaflet is stalked, while the laterals are nearly stalkless. Stipules, small papery appendages at the leaf base, are lance-shaped.

Flower: Ovate clusters of blue to purple flowers, 1 to 4.5 cm long, appear in leaf axils or terminal clusters. Flowers, 5 to 11 mm long, are composed of 5 united sepals, 5 united petals, 10 stamens, and a single pistil.

Plant: Alfalfa has erect to ascending stems up to 1 m long; the stems rise from a thick, somewhat woody, crown.

Fruit: The fruit, a brown, spirally coiled pod, 5 to 8 mm long, contains several seeds.

REASONS FOR CONCERN

Alfalfa is a common weed of roadsides, fencelines, and waste areas. It can be weedy in cultivated crops that were previously forage and hay fields.

SIMILAR SPECIES

Yellow lucerne (*M. falcata* L.), another introduced species, is distinguished from alfalfa by its yellow flowers and straight pod. Stems of yellow lucerne are up to 1 m tall, rising from a deep taproot. Yellow lucerne was introduced from Europe as a forage crop in the 1800s.

fruit

yellow lucerne

white
sweet clover

Melilotus alba Desr.

An annual or biennial introduced from Europe and Asia as a forage crop in the mid-1600s.

Also known as: white melilot, honey clover, honey-lotus, tree clover, white millet

French names: mélilot blanc

QUICK ID
- Flowers white
- Leaves compound with 3 leaflets
- Plants sweet-smelling

Distribution: Found throughout Canada and the United States.

Weed Designation
Canada: PQ
USA: TN

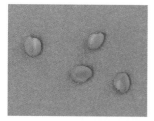

DESCRIPTION

Seed: Seeds are yellow, ovate to kidney-shaped, 2 to 2.5 mm long and 1.5 mm wide. Each plant is capable of producing up to 350,000 seeds. Seeds remain viable in the soil for up to 81 years.

Seedling: Cotyledons, 5 to 8.5 mm long and 2 to 2.5 mm wide, are oblong, whitish green above and pale green below. The first leaf is simple with a round or kidney-shaped blade. All later leaves are compound with 3 leaflets.

Leaves: Leaves are alternate, 1.5 to 5 cm long, and compound with 3 club-shaped leaflets, 12 to 25 mm long. The margins of the leaflets are finely toothed. Small papery structures called stipules, 7 to 10 mm long, are found at the base of the leaf.

Flower: Fragrant white flowers, 4 to 6 mm long, appear in terminal and axillary clusters called racemes. The raceme, 5 to 15 cm long, has 40 to 80 flowers that resemble those of cultivated peas. Flowers are composed of 5 united sepals, 5 united petals, 10 stamens, and a single pistil. Flower stalks are 1.5 to 2 mm long.

Plant: A sweet-scented plant, white sweet clover has stems up to 2.5 m tall. These branched, leafy stems rise from roots that extend to 1.2 m depth.

Fruit: The fruit is a smooth, papery pod, 3 to 4 mm long, black to dark grey. The fruit is normally single-seeded, but occasionally 2 seeds are produced.

REASONS FOR CONCERN

White sweet clover is a common weed of roadsides and waste areas. The plant contains coumarin, a compound reported to be TOXIC to livestock. Seeds are a CONTAMINANT in cereal grains and adversely affect flour quality. White sweet clover is associated with over 28 viral diseases, including aster yellows, bean yellow mosaic, beet curly top, cucumber mosaic, pea mosaic, pea mottle, and tobacco streak.

SIMILAR SPECIES

Yellow sweet clover (*M. officinalis* (L.) Lam.) is distinguished from white sweet clover by its yellow flowers and wrinkled pod. Each plant is capable of producing over 100,000 seeds. Other common names for *M. officinalis* are king's-crown, plaster clover, Hart's clover, king's clover, and yellow millet.

yellow sweet clover

late yellow loco-weed

Oxytropis monticola
A. Grey

A perennial native to North America; several subspecies occur across the continent.

Also known as: crazyweed

French names: oxytropis jaune tardif

Scientific synonyms: *O. campestris* (L.) DC.

QUICK ID

- Leaves basal
- Flowers yellowish white
- Leaves compound, with 17 to 33 leaflets

Distribution: Found throughout Canada (except Prince Edward Island) and the western United States.

Weed Designation
Canada: MB
USA: HI

DESCRIPTION

Seed: Seeds are brown to black, kidney-shaped, 2 to 3 mm long and 2 mm across. Each plant is capable of producing over 1,500 seeds.

Seedling: Cotyledons are 4 to 6 mm long and 2 to 3 mm wide. The stem below the cotyledons is pale green and succulent. The first leaf is simple, lance-shaped, and densely haired. Compound leaves, composed of 3 leaflets, appear from the second to sixth leaf stage. All later leaves have 17 to 33 leaflets.

Leaves: Leaves, 6 to 23 cm long, are basal and composed of 17 to 33 oblong leaflets, each 6 to 25 mm long. The leaves are covered with short, silky hairs. Small papery appendages, called stipules, are found at the base of each leaf.

Flower: Flowering stems, 10 to 40 cm tall, have 10 to 30 creamy-white or occasionally pinkish blue flowers that resemble those of cultivated peas. The flower cluster is usually 5 to 10 cm long. The 5 sepals are united, 5 to 7 mm long, and covered with white and black hairs. The 5 petals are united and 12 to 17 mm long. There are 10 stamens and a single pistil. Bracts below each flower are black-haired. Flowers appear in June and July.

Plant: A native plant of grassland and open forests, late yellow loco-weed has flowering stems up to 40 cm tall. The flowering stem and leaves rise from a short, thick taproot.

Fruit: The fruit, an oblong, papery pod, 16 to 20 mm long, is covered with black and white hairs. The pod is several-seeded.

REASONS FOR CONCERN

Late yellow loco-weed contains a POISONOUS agent that affects the nervous system of animals that ingest it. The common names loco-weed and crazyweed refer to the behaviour of animals that have been poisoned by this plant.

SIMILAR SPECIES

Early yellow loco-weed (*O. sericea* Nutt.) is often confused with late yellow loco-weed. Early yellow loco-weed blooms from late April to early May. Its leaves are 4 to 30 cm long with 11 to 17 leaflets. The fruit is a leathery pod about 20 mm long. Another native species, showy loco-weed (*O. splendens* Dougl. ex Hook.), is often found growing alongside late yellow loco-weed. It has blue to reddish purple flowers and leaves with 21 to 60 leaflets.

showy loco-weed

showy loco-weed

white clover

Trifolium repens L.

A perennial introduced from Europe and Asia as a forage crop, white clover was common in Canada prior to 1749.

Also known as: alsike clover, Dutch clover, wild white clover

French names: trèfle blanc

QUICK ID
- Leaves alternate, compound, with 3 leaflets
- Flowers white
- Stems often rooting at nodes

Distribution: Found throughout Canada and the United States. White clover is often found north of the Arctic Circle.

Weed Designation
None

DESCRIPTION
Seed: Seeds are round, dull yellow to orangish brown, and 0.8 to 1.1 mm across. The surface of the seed is smooth. Soil temperatures of at least 10 °C are required for germination.

Seedling: Cotyledons are 2.4 to 4.1 mm long and 1 to 2 mm wide. The first leaf is spatula-shaped. Later leaves are composed of 3 ovate leaflets. The stem does not begin to elongate until the seventh leaf stage.

Leaves: Leaves are alternate and compound with 3 ovate leaflets, each 1 to 3.5 cm long. Small pointed appendages, called stipules, are found at the base of the leaf. The stipules often form a tube around the stem.

Flower: White to pinkish white flowers appear in terminal clusters 15 to 20 mm across. Each globe-shaped cluster has 20 to 40 flowers, 7 to 11 mm long. Similar to cultivated peas, the flowers are composed of 5 sepals 3.5 to 7 mm long, 5 petals 7 to 11 mm long, 10 to 15 stamens, and 1 style. Seeds mature about 28 days after pollination, but are viable at day 12.

Plant: A weed of waste areas, lawns, and ditches, white clover reproduces by seed and creeping stems. The stems, up to 50 cm long, rise from a shallow root system and often root at leaf nodes. The distribution of white clover in North America is restricted to drought-free areas, as the shallow root system is vulnerable to drought.

Fruit: The fruit, a pod 4 to 5 mm long, contains 3 to 6 seeds.

REASONS FOR CONCERN
White clover is a serious weed in lawns, waste areas, and abandoned fields. When white clover exceeds 20 to 40% of cattle feed, death from bloat may occur. It is an alternate host for alfalfa mosaic and pea mottle viruses.

red clover

SIMILAR SPECIES
Red clover (*T. pratense* L.), another introduced forage crop, is often found growing beside white clover. As the common name implies, it has reddish pink flowers in a globe-shaped cluster. The flowers are 12 to 20 mm long. Each flower produces a pod containing 1 yellow or purple seed. The leaves of red clover are composed of 3 leaflets, each 2 to 5 cm long; leaflets often have an inverted V on the upper surface.

plant

The pink family is occasionally called the carnation family. With worldwide distributions, it has over 2,000 species. Primarily annual and perennial herbs, this family's most distinguishing characteristic is swollen stem nodes. The simple leaves are opposite and entire. Flowers are composed of 4 to 5 sepals, 0 to 5 petals, 3 to 10 stamens, and 2 to 5 styles. The fruit, a capsule, opens at the top to release numerous kidney-shaped seeds.

The pink family contains a number of showy flowers and plants that are often cultivated for their ornamental value. They include carnations, baby's-breath, maltese cross, and bouncing bet. Several other species in this family may be troublesome weeds.

Pink Family

Left: common chickweed,
Stellaria media (L.) Cyrill.
Right: white cockle, *Silene pratensis*
(Rafn) Godron & Gren.

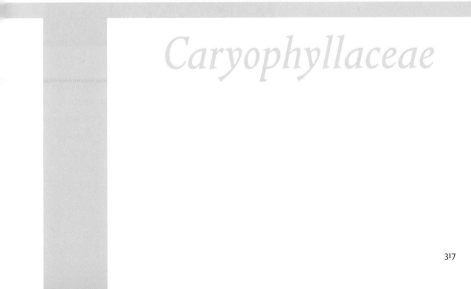

Caryophyllaceae

mouse-ear chickweed

Cerastium arvense L.

A perennial native to North America.

Also known as: field chickweed

French names: céraiste des champs

- Leaves opposite
- Flowers white
- Stem swollen at leaf nodes

Distribution: Found throughout Canada and the northern two-thirds of the United States.

Weed Designation
   Canada: FEDERAL, AB, MB

DESCRIPTION

Seed: Seeds are triangular, orange to brown, less than 1 mm long and wide. The surface is covered with small bumps or projections.

Seedling: Cotyledons, 2 to 8 mm long and less than 2 mm wide, often have a few hairs on the upper surface. The first pair of leaves is spatula-shaped and may be hairy above and on the midveins below.

Leaves: Leaves are opposite, narrowly elliptical, 2 to 7 cm long and 1 to 15 mm wide. The leaves are somewhat hairy.

Flower: White flowers, about 2 cm across, appear at the ends of the stems in early summer. Flowers are composed of 5 lance-shaped sepals 5 to 8 mm long, 5 petals 10 to 16 mm long, 10 stamens, and 5 styles. Petals are deeply notched at the tip. The bracts below the flowers are small and papery.

Plant: Erect to ascending stems, up to 60 cm tall, often root at lower nodes. The numerous stems and branches give the plant a densely matted appearance. This species is highly variable in hairiness: some plants are densely hairy, while others are hairless. Where present, hair is downward-pointing on the stem.

Fruit: The fruit is a single-celled, cylindrical capsule containing many seeds.

REASONS FOR CONCERN

Mouse-ear chickweed is not a concern in cultivated fields as it does not survive tillage. However, it is a problem in pastures and rangeland, where it invades overgrazed areas. Mouse-ear chickweed is an alternate host for strawberry yellow dwarf virus.

flower, C. vulgatum

SIMILAR SPECIES

Mouse-ear chickweed (*C. vulgatum* L.), a short-lived, introduced perennial, is often confused with the native mouse-ear chickweed (*C. arvense*). It is distinguished from the native species by petals that are the same length or shorter than the sepals. Upper leaves are oblong to lance-shaped and 1 to 2 cm long. Introduced mouse-ear chickweed is an alternate host for tobacco mosaic and tobacco streak viruses.

fruit, C. vulgatum

baby's-breath

Gypsophila paniculata L.

A perennial introduced from Europe and Asia as an ornamental plant, baby's-breath was first reported in Manitoba in 1887.

Also known as: perennial baby's-breath, perennial gypsophila, tall gypsophill, maiden's-breath

French names: gypsohile paniculée

QUICK ID

- Many small, white flowers
- Leaves opposite
- Stems and branches bluish green

Distribution: Found throughout Canada (except for the Atlantic provinces) and United States.

Weed Designation
Canada: MB
USA: WA, CA

DESCRIPTION

Seed: Seeds are kidney-shaped, black, 1.5 to 2 mm long. The surface is covered with rows of rounded bumps. Plants are capable of producing up to 14,000 seeds. Seeds require little or no dormancy to germinate.

Seedling: Cotyledons are lance-shaped, 10 to 15 mm long and 3 to 5 mm wide. The first leaves are opposite and lance-shaped. The cotyledons and first leaves are similar in shape and appearance.

Leaves: Leaves are opposite, lance-shaped, 3 to 10 cm long and 1 cm wide. The hairless leaves have a single prominent vein. Leaves are reduced in size upward, with the upper leaves usually less than 1 cm long. Very few leaves are present when the plant is in flower.

Flower: Numerous white flowers, 3 to 6 mm wide, appear at the ends of branches. The sweet-scented flowers, on stalks 3 to 12 mm long, are composed of 5 sepals, 5 petals, 10 stamens, and 2 styles. The sepals are about 2 mm long; the petals, 2.5 to 4 mm long.

Plant: Stems with numerous branches, up to 1 m tall, are hairless and covered with a powdery white film. Although reproduction is by seed only, the number of stems from the rootstalk increases with the age of the plant. The woody rootstalk, up to 4 m deep, has sufficient reserves to survive up to 2 years of adverse growing conditions. At maturity, the plant often breaks off at base and tumbles in the wind, spreading seeds. Baby's-breath is often cultivated in gardens and flower beds.

Fruit: The fruit, an egg-shaped capsule containing 2 to 5 seeds, has 4 compartments.

REASONS FOR CONCERN

Baby's-breath is a serious weed of roadsides, waste areas, and pastures. It does not withstand any cultivation, however, and is rarely found in crops. Baby's-breath is reported to be an alternate host for aster yellows and beet curly top viruses.

SIMILAR SPECIES

Annual baby's-breath (*G. elegans* Bieb.), another introduced garden plant, is closely related to perennial baby's-breath. It is distinguished from its perennial relative by longer petals (8 to 10 mm long) and shorter stems; the stems, up to 50 cm long, have numerous branches. Leaves, 2 to 7 cm long and 3 to 10 mm wide, are obscurely 1 to 3-veined.

fruit

knawel

Scleranthus annuus L.

An annual or winter annual introduced from Europe.

Also known as: annual knawel, German knotwort

French names: scléranthe annuel

QUICK ID
- Leaves opposite
- Flowers green
- Plants tufted, often forming mats

Distribution: Found throughout Canada (except Manitoba and Newfoundland), the west coast of the United States, and states east of the Mississippi River.

Weed Designation
Canada: AB

DESCRIPTION

Seed: Seeds are light brown, ovate, 2 mm long, and enveloped by the calyx. Each plant is capable of producing up to 100 seeds. Optimal seed germination occurs when temperatures are between 18 and 20 °C.

Seedling: Cotyledons, 8 to 12 mm long and less than 5 mm wide, are somewhat fleshy and about twice as wide as the first leaves. The first leaves are 5 to 20 mm long.

Leaves: Leaves are opposite, 5 to 20 mm long and 1 to 1.5 mm wide. These awl-shaped leaves are stalkless and borne in pairs at swollen leaf nodes along the stem. A few hairs may be found on the leaf margin. The leaves have transparent, papery edges near the base.

Flower: Small green flowers, about 5 mm across, are found in leaf axils and at the ends of stems. Flowers are composed of 5 sepals, 8 to 10 stamens, and 2 styles. Petals are absent. The sepals are partly fused and 3 to 4 mm long.

Plant: Knawel has weak, spreading stems that often form mats on the ground. The brownish green stems can be 2.5 to 25 cm long. Knawel prefers acidic soils and can be used as an indicator species for those soil types.

Fruit: The fruit is an ovate capsule containing a single seed. The fruit is enclosed by the hardened calyx.

REASONS FOR CONCERN

The roots of knawel are tough and fibrous and can survive light cultivation; thorough cultivation in the fall is required to control the winter annual plants. Knawel can survive light shade and may be found in some crops.

SIMILAR SPECIES

Knawel could be confused with low whitlow-wort (*Paronychia sessiliflora* Nutt.), a perennial native to western North America. Low whitlow-wort is common on dry prairie hillsides and ridges. The leaves of low whitlow-wort are awl-shaped, 4 to 6 mm long, and overlap the leaves above. Flowers are composed of 5 sepals, 5 stamens, and a 2-lobed style. Densely branched stems, rarely exceeding 15 cm tall, give the plant a cushion-like appearance. Deep woody roots enable the plant to survive long periods of drought.

low whitlow-wort

bladder campion

Silene cucubalus Wibel

A perennial introduced from Europe and Asia.

Also known as: white bottle, bubble-poppy, sea pink, maiden's-tears, devil's-rattlebox, cowbell, white hen, bird's-eggs, snappery, rattleweed

French names: silène bisannuel, pétards, silène gonflé

Scientific synonyms: *S. vulgaris* (Moench) Garcke; *S. latifolia* (Mill.) Britten & Rendle; *S. inflata* Sm.

QUICK ID
- Calyx inflated
- Leaves opposite
- Flowers white

Distribution: Found throughout Canada and the United States.

Weed Designation
Canada: FEDERAL, AB, MB, PQ, SK
USA: WA

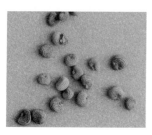

DESCRIPTION
Seed: Seeds are kidney-shaped, brown to grey, 1 to 1.5 mm long. The surface is covered with rows of rounded bumps.

Seedling: Cotyledons, 3 to 12 mm long and 1 to 2.5 mm wide, are elliptical and yellowish green. The stem below the cotyledons is pale green and translucent. The first pair of leaves is lance-shaped and yellowish green; the second pair has finely toothed margins.

Leaves: Leaves are opposite, ovate to lance-shaped, 3 to 8 cm long and 1 to 3 cm wide. The stalkless leaves appear pale green because of a white, powdery film.

Flower: Branched clusters of 5 to 30 white flowers, 10 to 20 mm across, are found at the ends of branches. Flowers are composed of 5 united sepals, 5 petals, 10 stamens, and 3 styles. The inflated calyx, 15 to 20 mm long, is bladder-like with 20 pinkish white veins. The deeply notched petals are 14 to 16 mm long.

Plant: A hairless plant with deep, penetrating roots, bladder campion has swollen stem nodes. The stems, up to 1 m tall, are branched from the base. Bladder campion reproduces by seeds and root fragments.

Fruit: The fruit is a round capsule about 1 cm long, enclosed by the inflated calyx. The 3-celled capsule contains numerous seeds.

REASONS FOR CONCERN

Bladder campion is not a serious weed in cultivated crops. However, it has the potential to be weedy in zero to minimum-till fields, pastures, roadsides, and gardens. Once established on these sites, bladder campion crowds beneficial plants.

SIMILAR SPECIES

Smooth catchfly (*S. cserei* Baumg.), a biennial or short-lived perennial weed from Asia, is often confused with bladder campion. It is distinguished from bladder campion by its non-inflated, obscurely veined calyx, 8 to 12 mm long. Smooth catchfly seeds are less than 1 mm long.

night-flowering catchfly

Silene noctiflora L.

An annual or winter annual introduced from Europe in clover or grass seed, night-flowering catchfly was first reported in North America in 1822; the first Canadian report was from Hamilton, Ontario in 1862, and the weed had spread to the Canadian prairies by 1883.

Also known as: sticky cockle, night-flowering silene, night-flowering cockle, clammy cockle

French names: silène noctiflore, silène de nuit, attrape-mouche

QUICK ID
- Plants sticky-hairy throughout
- Leaves opposite
- Calyx with 10 prominent veins

Distribution: Found throughout Canada and the northern half of the United States.

Weed Designation
Canada: FEDERAL, AB, BC, MB, SK

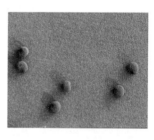

DESCRIPTION

Seed: Seeds are kidney-shaped, grey, about 1 mm long. Seeds are covered with several rows of warty bumps. Each plant is capable of producing up to 2,600 seeds, over 82% of which are viable after 5 years. Soil temperatures of 20°C are required for germination.

Seedling: Cotyledons, 5.5 to 15 mm long and 3 to 4.5 mm wide, are club-shaped, with short, stiff hairs on the stalk. The first pair of leaves is spatula-shaped, with hairy stalks and margins.

Leaves: Leaves are opposite and covered with sticky hairs. Basal leaves are stalked, oblong, 4 to 12 cm long. Stem leaves are stalkless, 2 to 8 cm long and up to 4 cm wide. Leaves are reduced in size upwards and may be alternate near the top of the stem.

Flower: Fragrant flowers, in terminal clusters of 3 to 8, open at night. The calyx is sticky-haired and 15 mm long when the flowers open. As the fruit matures, the calyx elongates to 25 to 40 mm long. The calyx has 10 prominent dark-green veins. The 5 deeply notched petals, 20 to 35 mm long, are white to pink. There are 10 stamens and 3 styles.

Plant: Night-flowering catchfly is hairy throughout. Sticky hairs on the upper stems and flowers trap small insects. One to 3 woody stems, up to 1 m tall, rise from the root. Stem nodes are swollen where the leaves are attached, and the stems have numerous branches in the flowering clusters.

Fruit: The fruit is a capsule with 3 compartments, each containing up to 185 seeds. When mature, the capsule opens by 6 backwards-curling teeth. There are 10 distinct green veins on the seed capsule.

juvenile

REASONS FOR CONCERN

Night-flowering catchfly is a serious weed in cultivated crops and pastures. It competes for moisture, nutrients, and sunlight. The seeds, similar in size to clover, are difficult to separate. Night-flowering catchfly is an alternate host for tobacco streak virus.

SIMILAR SPECIES

White cockle (*S. pratensis* (Rafn) Godron & Gren.) is often confused with night-flowering catchfly. Both species bloom in the evening, but white cockle has male and female plants, unlike night-flowering catchfly. Male plants have flowers with 10 stamens and a calyx with 10 prominent veins, while female plants have flowers with 4 or 5 styles and a calyx with 20 prominent veins (see pp 328-29).

fruit

white cockle

Silene pratensis
(Rafn) Godron & Gren.

An annual, biennial, or short-lived perennial introduced from Europe into United States in the early 1800s, white cockle was first reported in Ontario in 1875.

Also known as: campion, white campion, evening campion, evening lychnis, snake cuckoo, thunder flower, bull rattle, white robin

French names: lychnide blanche, compagnon blanc, oeillet de Dieu, floquet

Scientific synonyms: *S. alba* (Mill.) E.H.L. Krause; *Lychnis alba* Mill.; *Melandrium album* Garcke

QUICK ID
- Leaves opposite
- Calyx with 10 or 20 prominent veins
- Flowers white, opening at night

Distribution: Found throughout Canada and the northern half of the United States.

Weed Designation
Canada: FEDERAL, AB, BC, MB, NS, SK
USA: CT, WA, WI

DESCRIPTION
Seed: Seeds are kidney-shaped, grey to brown, about 1.5 mm long. The seeds are covered with rows of warty bumps. Each female plant is capable of producing over 24,000 seeds. White cockle requires light for germination, but also cool temperatures (as low as 2°C), which limits its distribution in the United States. Immature seeds are viable 2 to 3 weeks after pollination.

Seedling: Cotyledons, 5 to 10 mm long and 1 to 4 mm wide, are slightly hairy and pointed at the tip. The stem below the cotyledons is yellowish green. The first leaves are ovate and hairy, with longer hairs on the leaf margin.

Leaves: Leaves are opposite, oblong, 2 to 10 cm long and 2 cm wide. Lower leaves are stalked, while the upper are stalkless.

Flower: Fragrant flowers, 2 to 3 cm across, appear in the evening and close in the morning. The calyx is tube-shaped and 15 to 20 mm long. Male plants produce flowers composed of a calyx with 10 prominent veins, 5 deeply notched white petals, and 10 stamens. Female plants have flowers composed of a calyx with 20 prominent veins, 5 deeply notched white petals, and 4 or 5 styles. The calyx is often sticky-haired.

Plant: White cockle presents male and female plants. Both types of plants have coarse, somewhat sticky, hairs. Plants rise up to 1 m tall from a stout fleshy taproot that may be 1.2 m deep. White cockle is a prolific seed producer that matures in about 40 days.

Fruit: The fruit is an ovate capsule, 10 to 15 mm long. The fruit opens by 10 teeth and releases about 500 seeds.

REASONS FOR CONCERN

White cockle is a serious weed in cultivated crops and pastures, where it competes for moisture, nutrients, and sunlight. The seeds, similar in size to clover, are difficult to separate. It is also an alternate host for *Lychnis* ringspot virus, which infects sugar beets and spinach crops. Other viral diseases, such as cucumber mosaic, tobacco necrosis, tobacco ring spot, and tobacco streak, are associated with this weed.

fruit

SIMILAR SPECIES

Night-flowering catchfly (*S. noctiflora* L.) is often confused with white cockle. Night-flowering catchfly has perfect flowers, with both stamens and styles present in the same flower (see pp 326-27).

corn spurry

Spergula arvensis L.

An annual introduced from Europe as a forage crop.

Also known as: stickwort, starwort, devil's-guts, sandweed, pickpurse, yarr, pinecheat, poverty-weed, cow-quake

French names: spargoute des champs, herbe à Bolduc

QUICK ID
- Leaves appear in whorls of 12 to 16
- Stems and leaves somewhat fleshy
- Flowers with 5 white petals

Distribution: Found throughout Canada (except Manitoba and Saskatchewan), in the United States on the west coast, and in most states east of the Mississippi River.

Weed Designation
Canada: AB, MB, PQ

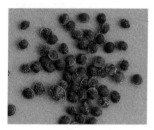

DESCRIPTION
Seed: Seeds are round to lens-shaped, black, 1.5 mm in diameter. The seed is often pitted and has a white ring around the centre. Each plant can produce up to 10,000 seeds, which may be viable in soil for up to 10 years. Seeds germinate in 0.5 to 3 cm soil depth.

Seedling: Cotyledons, 10 to 15 mm long and less than 1 mm wide, are needle-like with a blunt tip. The first leaves are similar in appearance to the cotyledons.

Leaves: Leaves are opposite but appear whorled, as 6 to 8 pairs originate at a single node. These thread-like leaves, 2 to 5 cm long, are somewhat fleshy; they are slightly round in cross-section.

Flower: White flowers appear in loosely branched clusters at the end of stems. The flower, less than 6 mm across, opens only in bright light. Flowers are composed of 5 sepals, 5 petals, 5 or 10 stamens, and 5 styles. Flowers have an unpleasant odour and are rarely pollinated by insects.

Plant: Corn spurry has several branches originating near the base, giving the plant a bushy appearance. Spreading stems, up to 60 cm long, have swollen nodes and are somewhat sticky and fleshy. Plants may produce seeds within 10 weeks of germination. Corn spurry is readily eaten by livestock and poultry.

Fruit: The fruit, a round capsule with 5 compartments, contains many seeds; as the seeds mature, the capsule turns towards the ground, releasing the seeds. Large plants may produce as many as 500 capsules. Capsules produced early in the growing season will have up to 25 seeds, while those produced in late summer may have only 5.

REASONS FOR CONCERN

Corn spurry is a serious weed in cultivated fields and row crops. It is an alternate host for beet yellows, lucerne mosaic, and tobacco streak viruses.

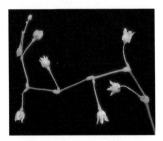

SIMILAR SPECIES

Knawel (*Scleranthus annuus* L.) is often confused with corn spurry because of its growth habit. It is distinguished by awl-shaped leaves that appear in pairs at stem nodes. The flowers of knawel do not have petals, and the fruit is 1-seeded and surrounded by an enlarged calyx (see pp 322-23). The seedling of Russian thistle (*Salsola kali* L.; see pp 162-63) is often mistaken for the seedling of corn spurry. The distinguishing feature between the seedlings is that Russian thistle leaves are spine-tipped.

knawel

common chickweed

Stellaria media
(L.) Cyrill.

An annual or winter annual introduced from Europe into New England in 1672, common chickweed was widely distributed in Quebec and Nova Scotia by the 1820s.

Also known as: chickwhirtles, cluckenweed, mischievous Jack, skirt buttons, tongue-grass, star-weed, winter weed, satin flower, cyrillo, starwort, bindweed, white bird's-eye

French names: stellaire moyenne, mouron des oiseaux

QUICK ID

- Leaves opposite, succulent
- Plant with prostrate growth
- Flowers with 5 white petals

Distribution: Found throughout Canada and the United States.

Weed Designation
Canada: FEDERAL, AB, MB, PQ

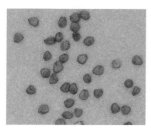

DESCRIPTION

Seed: Seeds are oblong, pale yellow to reddish brown, 1 to 1.2 mm long. The surface of the seed is covered with rows of small, rounded projections. Each plant is capable of producing over 15,000 seeds, and after 10 years, 22% of seeds are still viable. Germination takes place in the top 3 cm of soil and can occur at temperatures of 2 °C, although 12 to 20 °C is optimal.

Seedling: Cotyledons, 1 to 12 mm long and less than 2 mm wide, are ovate with pointed tips. The seed leaves occasionally have a few clear hairs on the stalk. The first pair of leaves, ovate with a pointed tip, has a fringe of white hairs on the leaf stalk.

Leaves: Leaves are opposite, ovate, 1 to 3 cm long and 3 to 15 mm wide. The leaf stalks of lower leaves, 5 to 20 mm long, usually have a single line of hairs. The upper leaves are often stalk-less and about 1 cm wide.

Flower: White flowers, 6 mm across, are found in small clusters near the ends of branches. The 5 sepals are green, 4 to 6 mm long, and hairy. The 5 white petals, when present, are 3 to 5 mm long. The deeply notched petals often look like 10. Stamens are reddish purple and vary between 3 and 10, depending on the amount of light present. There are 3 styles. Common chickweed flowers when temperatures are above 2°C.

Plant: Found on all continents, including Antarctica, common chickweed has weak, trailing stems up to 80 cm long. Plants are shade tolerant and quite leafy. A line of fine white hairs can be found on the stem. Common chickweed is capable of producing seed 5 to 7 weeks after germination. With 4 generations possible in a growing season, a single seed can produce over 15 billion offspring! Common chickweed can survive temperatures of -10°C with little or no frost damage.

Fruit: The fruit, a single-chambered capsule about 7 mm long, opens by 6 teeth and releases 8 to 10 seeds.

REASONS FOR CONCERN

Chickweed is a major pest in fields where there is abundant organic matter and large amounts of rainfall. It is able to compete with crops because of its shade tolerance, and it leaches valuable moisture and nutrients.

SIMILAR SPECIES

Long-stalked chickweed (*S. longipes* Goldie), a native species often found growing in moist woods and meadows, is easily distinguished by lance-shaped leaves that are stalkless and 1 to 3 cm long.

long-stalked chickweed

COW cockle

Vaccaria pyramidata
Medic.

An annual introduced from Europe and Asia.

Also known as: cow herb, China cockle, cow soapwort, spring cockle

French names: saponaire des vaches, vaccaire

Scientific synonyms: *V. segetalis* (Neck.) Garcke; *V. vulgaris* Host; *Saponaria vaccaria* L.

QUICK ID
◢ Leaves opposite
◢ Flowers pink
◢ Plants bluish green

Distribution: Found throughout Canada (except Newfoundland and Prince Edward Island) and the United States.

Weed Designation
Canada: FEDERAL, AB, MB

DESCRIPTION
Seed: Seeds are round, grey to black, 1.7 to 2.5 mm across. The seed surface is covered with rounded projections, giving it a pebbly appearance. The seeds are often included in "wildflower" garden packages.

Seedling: Cotyledons, 9 to 32 mm long and 3.5 to 8 mm wide, are oblong, hairless, and some-

what fleshy. The cotyledons have a prominent lower midrib. The stem below the
cotyledons is often stained with purple. The
first leaves are similar in appearance to the
cotyledons.

Leaves: Leaves are opposite, lance-shaped, 2 to 10
cm long. Leaves clasp the stem and are bluish
green, hairless, and somewhat fleshy.

Flower: Bright-pink flowers, about 12 mm across,
appear singly at the end of stems. Five sepals,
10 to 15 mm long, are fused to form a flask-
shaped, 5-ribbed calyx; the calyx becomes
enlarged as the fruit matures. The 5 pink
petals, each toothed at the tip, are about 20
mm long; the 10 stamens are longer than the
petals and stick out of the flower. There are 2
styles.

Plant: An annual with numerous branches, cow
cockle rises from a slender taproot. The hairless, bluish green stems, up to 60 cm tall,
have swollen leaf nodes.

Fruit: The fruit is a round capsule, 6 to 8 mm
long. It opens at the top by 4 teeth. The
capsule is often enclosed by the calyx.

REASONS FOR CONCERN

Cow cockle is an occasional weed of cultivated
fields, roadsides, and waste areas. It competes
with the crop for moisture and nutrients.
The seeds of cow cockle contain saponin, a
substance reported to be TOXIC to livestock.
It has been determined that 112 g of seed per
45 kg of body weight can be fatal to livestock.

SIMILAR SPECIES

Soapwort or bouncing bet (*Saponaria officinalis* L.)
is often confused with cow cockle. The
species may be distinguished by 2 features:
the calyx of soapwort is tube-shaped, and its
petals have a claw-like appendage. Soapwort
is found throughout Canada and the United
States.

bouncing bet

flower

dissected fruit

The plantain family has over 250 species of herbs and shrubs with worldwide distribution. The herbaceous species are found in temperate regions and have simple basal leaves. The leaves are prominently ribbed and have winged petioles. The flowers, borne on leafless flowering stalks, are composed of 4 sepals, 4 petals, 2 to 4 stamens, and a single style. The fruit is a capsule whose top falls off at maturity. The seeds of plantain are sticky when wet.

The plantains are of limited economic importance, and several species of this family are common weeds in populated areas.

Plantain Family

hoary plantain,
Plantago media L.

Plantaginaceae

common plantain

Plantago major L.

An annual, biennial, or perennial introduced from Europe, common plantain was first observed in North America in 1748; the first Canadian report was from Montreal in 1821, and by 1899, common plantain had spread to British Columbia.

Also known as: whiteman's-foot, ground plantain, greater plantain, major plantain, dooryard plantain, English plantain, birdseed plantain, rippleseed plantain, waybread

French names: plantain majeur, grand plantain

QUICK ID
- Leaves basal, prominently 3 to 5-ribbed
- Flowers greenish white, borne in dense clusters
- Rootstalk short and thick

Distribution: Found throughout Canada and the United States.

Weed Designation
Canada: MB, PQ
USA: AK, CT, WA

DESCRIPTION
Seed: Seeds are triangular to 4-sided, brownish black, about 1 mm long and less than 0.7 mm wide. The surface is rough and dull. Seeds are sticky when wet, which may assist in their dispersal. Each plant is capable of producing up to 14,000 seeds. Seeds are viable in soil for up to 60 years and require light for germination.

Seedling: Cotyledons are spatula-shaped, 1.5 to 7 mm long and less than 1 mm wide. The cotyledons have 3 faint veins and wither soon after the appearance of the first leaves. The first leaves are elliptical, strongly 3 to 5-ribbed, and hairless.

Leaves: Leaves appear in a basal rosette of ovate leaves with smooth margins. These stalked leaves are 5 to 30 cm long and up to 12 cm wide. They have 3 to 5 prominent ribs on the leaf underside. The edges of the leaf stalks curve upward. Upon close examination, leaves in the basal rosette are alternately arranged.

Flower: The flower cluster, 7 to 30 cm long, appears on a leafless stalk, 10 to 60 cm tall. The numerous small greenish white flowers, 2 to 3 mm across, are short-stalked. The calyx is 4-lobed and 1.5 to 2 mm long. The corolla is 4-lobed and papery. The 4 stamens are longer than the calyx and corolla, and stick out of the flower. There is a single style. Flowers are wind-pollinated.

Plant: A perennial plant reproducing by seeds, common plantain has a short, thick rootstalk with fibrous roots, up to 80 cm deep and wide. Flowering stalks are up to 60 cm tall. Common plantain is hairless, except for leaf undersides that may be slightly hairy. Common plantain is found within 200 km of the arctic treeline.

Fruit: The fruit, an egg-shaped capsule, 2 to 4 mm long, splits around the middle and contains 5 to 30 seeds.

juvenile

REASONS FOR CONCERN

Common plantain is a common weed in cultivated fields, lawns, roadsides, and waste areas. It is an alternate host for tobacco mosaic, aster yellows, beet curly top, beet yellows, tobacco streak, and tomato spotted wilt viruses.

SIMILAR SPECIES

Ribgrass (*P. lanceolata* L.), another introduced plantain, is closely related to common plantain. It is distinguished by narrow leaves 8 to 30 cm long and 1 to 4 cm wide. The brownish flowers, 3 to 5 mm across, are composed of 4 sepals, 4 petals, 4 yellow stamens, and 1 style. Ribgrass is found throughout Canada (except Alberta) and the United States.

ribgrass (juvenile)

hoary plantain

Plantago media L.

A perennial introduced from Europe.

Also known as: lamb's-tongue

French names: plantain moyen

QUICK ID

- Leaves basal with prominent veins
- Flowers pinkish, borne in dense clusters
- Rootstalk short and thick

Distribution: Found throughout Canada (except the Atlantic provinces) and the United States.

Weed Designation
Canada: MB
USA: AK, CT, WA

DESCRIPTION

Seed: Seeds are oblong, black, about 1 mm long. The surface of the seed is rough and dull. Each plant is capable of producing over 15,000 seeds. Germination occurs in the top 0.5 cm of soil.

Seedling: Cotyledons, 1.4 to 8 mm long and less than 2 mm wide, are club-shaped with very short stalks. The first leaves have 3 to 5 ribs on the underside.

Leaves: Leaves are basal, ovate to elliptical, 10 to 20 cm long. Leaves are covered with short, soft hairs. The leaf margins are smooth or finely toothed. Leaf blades are narrowed at the base to form a stalk.

Flower: Pinkish white flowers, up to 4 mm across, are borne in dense cylindrical spikes, 2 to 10 cm long. Flowers are composed of 4 united sepals, 4 united petals, 4 long-stalked stamens, and 1 style. Papery bracts, found below each flower, are the same length as the sepals. The white corolla and pinkish purple stalks of the stamens make the flowering stalk quite showy.

Plant: A perennial with a fibrous rootstalk, hoary plantain has leafless flowering stems, 20 to 40 cm tall. The stem bears numerous short, soft hairs.

Fruit: The fruit, a capsule about 3 mm long, contains 4 seeds.

REASONS FOR CONCERN

Hoary plantain is a weed of roadsides, pastures, and waste areas. Its prolific seed production allows it to spread rapidly.

SIMILAR SPECIES

Common plantain (*P. major* L.) closely resembles hoary plantain. It is distinguished by hairless leaves (5 to 30 cm long and up to 12 cm wide) and greenish brown flowers (about 3 mm across). Leaves have 3 to 5 prominent ribs on the underside (see pp 338-39).

common plantain

flower

habit

The pondweed family consists of a single genus with 100 species; several other small aquatic plant families are often included with the pondweeds. Aquatic herbs with jointed stems, species of this family are found throughout the world. The alternate leaves are simple and entire with several membraneous sheaths that are stipule-like. Whorls of small green flowers appear in spikes that may rise above the surface of the water. Flowers are composed of 4 tepals (indistinguishable sepals and petals), 4 stamens, and 4 styles. The fruit is an achene or drupe. Pondweeds reproduce by seeds, tubers, rhizomes, and winter buds.

The pondweed family is of little economic importance.

Pondweed Family

clasping-leaved
pondweed,
Potamogeton richardsonii
(Benn.) Rydb.

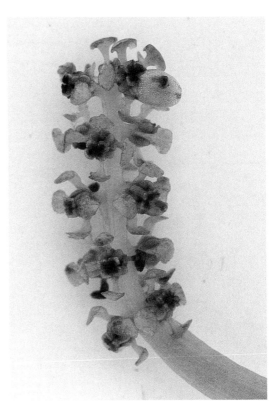

Potamogetonaceae

clasping-leaved pondweed

Potamogeton richardsonii
(Benn.) Rydb.

A perennial native to North America.

Also known as: Richardson pondweed

French names: potamot de Richardson

QUICK ID
- Plants aquatic
- Leaves alternate, with numerous prominent veins
- Flowers appear in whorls of 6 to 12

Distribution: Found throughout Canada and the northern half of the United States.

Weed Designation
Canada: MB

DESCRIPTION

Seed: Seeds are ovate, greyish to olive green, 2.5 to 4 mm long and 2.3 mm wide. A prominent beak on 1 end is about 1 mm long.

Seedling: Seedlings are rarely produced in nature.

Leaves: Leaves are alternate, ovate to lance-shaped, 1.5 to 12 cm long and 5 to 20 mm wide.

Stalkless leaves that clasp the stem are submersed and reduced in size upwards; the margins are wavy. Leaves have 7 to 33 nerves, of which 3 to 7 are prominent. Lance-shaped structures, called stipules, are located at the base of the leaf. These stipules, 1 to 2 cm long, shred into stringy white fibres as the plant matures.

Flower: Flower clusters, 1.5 to 25 cm long, are borne on stalks, 2 to 10 cm long, and may emerge from the water. The clusters are composed of 6 to 12 whorls of green flowers. Flowers are composed of 4 tepals, which are sepals and petals that are similar size and appearance, 4 stamens, and 4 styles.

Plant: A submersed aquatic plant, clasping-leaved pondweed has leafy, branched stems, 1 to 2.5 mm thick. Plants have branched, jointed rhizomes. The primary method of reproduction is by spreading rhizomes.

Fruit: The fruit, a single-seeded nutlet, is about 3 mm long.

REASONS FOR CONCERN

Pondweeds are a concern in waterways, irrigation canals, and drainage ditches, because large colonies of plants may impede water flow.

SIMILAR SPECIES

Several species of pondweed are native to North America. Pondweeds are aquatic plants that have jointed rhizomes, alternate leaves, and small greenish flowers. Flowers appear in interrupted whorls on the stem. A closely related species, slender-leaved pondweed (*P. gramineus* L.), has both submersed and floating leaves. The submersed leaves, 1 to 12 cm long, have 3 to 9 nerves. The leathery floating leaves are 2 to 6 cm long and 13 to 19-nerved.

slender-leaved pondweed

fruit

The primrose family has over 1,000 species worldwide, with most occurring in cool northern climates. All species are herbaceous annuals or perennials with alternate, opposite, or whorled leaves. Stipules are absent. The flowers are composed of 4 or 5 united sepals, 4 to 9 petals, 4 to 9 stamens, and a single style. The fruit is a capsule that opens by 2 to 6 valves.

The family is of little economic importance. Several species are grown for their ornamental value, including primroses, shooting stars, cyclamen, and pimpernel.

plant

Primrose Family

Left: pygmy flower,
Androsace septentrionalis L.
Right: shooting-star,
Dodecatheon pulchellum (Raf.) Merr.

Primulaceae

pygmyflower

Androsace septentrionalis L.

An annual or winter annual native to North America.

Also known as: fairy candelabra

French names: androsace septentrionale

QUICK ID

- Leaves basal
- Flowers white
- Plants less than 30 cm tall

Distribution: Found throughout Canada and the United States.

Weed Designation
   Canada: MB

DESCRIPTION

Seed: Seeds are ovate, light brown, less than 1 mm long.

Seedling: Cotyledons, 4 to 6 mm long, are oblong and distinctly stalked. Lance-shaped leaves, covered with short hairs, form tight rosettes.

Leaves: Leaves are basal, oblong to lance-shaped, 1 to 4 cm long and up to 3 mm wide. Leaf margins are smooth to finely toothed.

Flower: One to several flower stems, 2 to 30 cm
tall, rise from the middle of the basal leaves.
Each flowering stem has 3 to 40 small white
flowers, 3 to 5 mm across. Flowers are
composed of 5 united sepals, 5 united petals,
5 stamens, and a single pistil. The corolla is
funnel-shaped. Below each flower are lance-
shaped bracts, 1 to 3 mm long.

Plant: Pygmyflower has flowering stems up to
30 cm tall. These branched stems are yellow
to reddish green and have scattered reddish
hairs.

Fruit: The fruit is a 5-valved capsule with a few
seeds.

REASONS FOR CONCERN

In early spring, pygmyflower is a serious weed in
cultivated fields and row crops. Its early
growth competes with newly seeded crops
for nutrients and moisture.

SIMILAR SPECIES

Western fairy candelabra (*A. occidentalis* Pursh), a
closely related native species of western
North America, prefers sandy soil. It has
ovate bracts, 3 to 4 mm long, below each
flower. Basal leaves are 6 to 12 mm long, and
stems are 2 to 5 cm tall. Pygmyflower may
also be mistaken for yellow whitlow-grass
(*Draba nemerosa* L.; pp 276-77) when not in
flower. Both species form a basal rosette of
leaves and almost leafless flowering stems.
Leaves of yellow whitlow-grass are covered
with short, branched hairs, while the leaves
of pygmyflower are hairless. Yellow whitlow-
grass has yellow flowers with 4 petals, unlike
pygmyflower, whose flowers are white and 5-
petalled.

rosette

yellow whitlow-grass

fruit

The purslane family is a small family of herbs and shrubs with more than 500 species worldwide. The distinguishing characteristic of this family is simple, succulent leaves that are alternate, opposite, or basal. The flowers have 2 sepals, 3 to 6 petals, 2 to 5 stamens, and 2 to 8 styles. The fruit is a capsule whose top falls off to release numerous seeds.

Members of the purslane family are often grown as ornamentals, including portulaca, rose-moss, pygmyroot, and miner's-lettuce.

Purslane Family

Top: spring beauty,
Claytonia megarhiza (A. Gray) Parry
Right: western spring beauty,
Claytonia lanceolata Pursh

Portulacaceae

purslane

Portulaca oleracea L.

An annual introduced from southern Europe or northern Africa as a garden plant, purslane was first reported in Massachusetts in 1672 and Canada in 1863.

Also known as: wild portulaca, pusley, low pigweed

French names: pourpier portager, pourpier gras

QUICK ID
- Leaves fleshy
- Flowers yellow
- Plant with prostrate growth habit

Distribution: Found throughout Canada (except Newfoundland) and the United States.

Weed Designation
Canada: MB
USA: AZ

DESCRIPTION

Seed: Seeds are ovate to triangular, reddish brown to black, and shiny. Seeds are less than 1 mm across. Each plant is capable of producing up to 240,000 seeds, which are viable for up to 40 years. Light and temperatures over 24 °C are required for seeds to germinate.

Seedling: Cotyledons, 2 to 10 mm long and 1 to 2 mm wide, are succulent and tinged with bright red. The stem below the cotyledons is bright red and succulent. The first pair of leaves is ovate, 14 mm long and 7 mm wide, and appears opposite.

Leaves: Leaves are alternate but appear opposite. They are ovate to wedge-shaped, 4 to 28 mm long and 6 to 20 mm wide. The succulent leaves are green above and pale purple below. These hairless leaves are crowded near the ends of branches.

Flower: Small, star-shaped yellow flowers, 3 to 10 mm across, are borne in axillary clusters of 1 to 3. Flowers are inconspicuous and open only on sunny mornings. Stalkless flowers are composed of 2 sepals (3 to 4 mm long), 4 to 6 petals, 6 to 12 stamens, and a single pistil. The petals are shorter than the sepals and fall off soon after the flower opens. Flowering begins 1 month after germination—at or about the 10 to 12-leaf stage. Seeds are produced 7 to 12 days after the flower opens.

Plant: A hairless annual with numerous stems and branches, purslane forms large, circular mats up to 1.2 m across. The succulent stems are red and often root at the nodes. Uprooted plants are able to ripen seeds from the reserves in the stems and leaves, and may survive long enough to produce new roots.

Fruit: The fruit is a small, globe-shaped capsule, 4 to 8 mm long, which opens around the middle, releasing a few seeds.

REASONS FOR CONCERN

Purslane is not shade tolerant and is rarely a weed of cultivated crops. It is more of a concern in row crops, home gardens, and flower beds. A prolific seed producer, purslane is not controlled by cultivation, as the stems and leaves store enough reserves to produce seeds even after being uprooted. Stem fragments may also root and produce more plants. Purslane is an alternate host for beet nematode, as well as the following viral diseases: tobacco mosaic, tobacco streak, tobacco etch, beet curly top virus, and aster yellows.

SIMILAR SPECIES

Prostrate pigweed (*Amaranthus graecizans* L.) is often confused with purslane. It is distinguished by its greenish white flowers and non-fleshy, spoon-shaped leaves. The prostrate reddish stems, up to 120 cm long, do not root at leaf nodes (see pp 4-5).

prostrate pigweed

A large family with more than 3,000 species worldwide, the rose family is diverse and occasionally separated into 4 to 6 smaller subfamilies. Species may be herbs, shrubs, or small trees with alternate, simple, or compound leaves. Stipules are present. Flowers are composed of 5 sepals, 5 petals, and numerous stamens and pistils; 5 bractlets are often associated with the sepals. The fruit range from achenes to drupes and pommes.

The rose family is very important economically. Members of the family include roses, raspberries, strawberries, apples, peaches, plums, cinquefoil, hawthorn, and mountain-ash. Several species are weedy.

Rose Family

Top: prickly rose, *Rosa acicularis* Lindl.
Right: prairie rose, *Rosa arkansana* Porter

Rosaceae

rough cinquefoil

Potentilla norvegica L.

An annual, biennial, or short-lived perennial native to North America; some introduced subspecies may be present.

Also known as: tall five finger, Norwegian cinquefoil, upright cinquefoil

French names: potentille de Norvège
Scientific synonyms: *Potentilla monspeliensis* L.

QUICK ID
- Flowers yellow
- Leaves compound with 3 leaflets
- Stems and leaves covered with stiff hairs

Distribution: Found throughout Canada and the northern two-thirds of the United States.

Weed Designation
Canada: AB, MB

DESCRIPTION

Seed: Seeds are ovate, yellowish brown, 1 mm long and less than 0.8 mm wide. Seeds require light for germination.

Seedling: Cotyledons are 1.3 to 4 mm long and 1 to 2 mm wide. The first leaf is simple, ovate with 3 terminal lobes, and covered with soft hairs. Compound leaves with 3 leaflets appear by the fifth leaf stage.

Leaves: Leaves are alternate and compound with 3 ovate, coarsely toothed leaflets. The leaves, 2 to 10 cm long, are covered with long hairs. Basal leaves are long-stalked and hairy on both sides. Leaves are reduced in size upwards and often reddish.

Flower: Yellow flowers, 7 to 12 mm across, are borne in dense, leafy clusters. Flowers are composed of 5 sepals, 5 petals, 15 to 20 stamens, and numerous styles. Sepals and petals are about the same length. Below the sepals are 5 small bractlets that give the flower the appearance of having 10 sepals.

Plant: A robust plant, rough cinquefoil has branched stems up to 90 cm tall. The stem is usually covered with long, stiff hairs. The range of rough cinquefoil is climatically controlled: it is only found in areas where rainfall exceeds 500 mm. Reproduction is by seed only.

Fruit: Several single-seeded fruits, called achenes, are produced by each flower. The brown achenes are enclosed by the enlarged sepals at maturity.

REASONS FOR CONCERN

Rough cinquefoil is a problem weed in pastures, roadsides, gardens, and row crops. It is occasionally found in cultivated fields.

SIMILAR SPECIES

The basal leaves of rough cinquefoil are often mistaken for strawberry (*Fragaria* spp.). Strawberry leaves have teeth on the lower half of the leaflets, unlike those of rough cinquefoil, which are toothed to the tip of the leaflet. Strawberry leaves have very few hairs. Sulphur cinquefoil (*P. recta* L.), an introduced species from Europe, was first reported in North America in 1897. It is distinguished from rough cinquefoil by its leaves and larger flowers. Leaves are composed of 5 to 7 leaflets, each with 7 to 17 triangular teeth on the margin. Sulphur yellow flowers, 15 to 25 mm wide, appear at the ends of branches. Silverweed (*P. anserina* L.), a species native to North America, has 7 to 21 leaflets, silver below and green above. Plants produce several runners that root and form leaf clusters at the nodes.

rosette

silverweed

prairie rose

Rosa arkansana Porter

A perennial native to western North America.

Also known as: Arkansas rose

French names: rosier des prairies

QUICK ID
- Low shrub with spiny stems
- Flowers pink, fragrant
- Leaves compound, with 7 to 11 leaflets

Distribution: Found in Canadian provinces west of and including Manitoba, and throughout the northern half of the United States.

Weed Designation
Canada: MB

DESCRIPTION
Seed: Seeds are elliptical, brown, 5 to 5.5 mm long. Seeds are angular and covered with short, fine hairs.

Leaves: Leaves are alternate and compound, with 7 to 11 ovate leaflets. Leaflets are sharply toothed and 1 to 5 cm long.

Flower: Fragrant pink to white flowers, 3 to 7 cm across, are borne at the ends of stems. Each stem has 2 or 3 flowers. Flowers are composed of 5 sepals, 5 petals, and numerous stamens and styles. Flowers are flat when open.

Plant: Prairie rose reproduces by seeds and underground rhizomes. The coarse, woody, deep-penetrating roots give rise to unbranched stems, up to 50 cm tall, covered with prickles about 3 mm long. Prairie rose stems die back to ground level each autumn.

Fruit: The fruit, a red "hip," 2 to 3 cm long and up to 15 mm in diameter, contains several hard, brown, irregularly shaped seeds. Each seed is a single fruit and often referred to as an achene.

REASONS FOR CONCERN

Prairie rose is a common plant of roadsides, pastures, and rangeland. With changes in cultivation practices, it has begun to appear in minimum and zero-till fields. The rhizomes are not killed during light cultivation.

SIMILAR SPECIES

Prickly rose (*R. acicularis* Lindl.), a native rose found throughout most of Canada and the northern United States, is closely related to prairie rose. It is distinguished by shrubby branched stems, up to 1.5 m tall, and compound leaves composed of 3 to 7 leaflets. Pink flowers, 5 to 7 cm across, produce a red hip, about 1.5 cm long.

fruit

prickly rose

3-ranked leaves

triangular stem

The sedge family is a large family, composed of more than 9,300 species worldwide. Found primarily in wetland areas, sedges are grass-like plants with stems that are usually triangular in cross-section. The leaves are commonly 3-ranked with closed leaf sheaths. Male and female flowers, often found in separate flower clusters, have sepals and petals reduced to scales or small bristles. Male flowers have 3 stamens, while female flowers have a single style with 2 or 3 branches. Some members of this family have perfect flowers. The fruit is a lens-shaped or 3-sided achene. Several species are important economically and include such plants as papyrus and Chinese water-chestnut. Many sedge species provide food and habitat for a variety of wildlife.

perfect flower

Sedge Family

awned sedge,
Carex rostrata L.

Cyperaceae

yellow nutsedge

Cyperus esculentus L.

A perennial native to North America.

Also known as: chufa, northern nutgrass, coco, coco sedge, rush nut, edible galingale, earth almond

French names: souchet comestible, amande de terre, souchet rampant

QUICK ID

- Stems triangular in cross-section
- Leaves grass-like
- Plants produce tubers on roots

Distribution: Found in all Canadian provinces east of and including Manitoba (except Prince Edward Island and Newfoundland) and throughout the United States.

Weed Designation
Canada: MB, NS, PQ
USA: AZ, CA, CT, GA, HI, LA, ME, MI, MS, NC, NH, NM, RI, TN, TX

seedling

DESCRIPTION

Seed: Seeds are ovate, 3-sided, whitish brown, 1.2 to 1.8 mm long. The surface of the seed is shiny. Each plant is capable of producing over 90,000 seeds. In greenhouse experiments, more than 51% of the seeds germinated.

Seedling: The seedling of yellow nutsedge resembles grass and is often overlooked. Seedlings are rarely produced in nature. The leaves of young plants are shiny. New plants are formed from the germination of underground tubers.

Leaves: Leaves are alternate, grass-like, 20 to 90 cm long and 4 to 9 mm wide; they are waxy and glossy with a prominent midrib. The tips of the leaves are sharply pointed. The sheath is closed and triangular. Auricles and ligules are not present.

Flower: Umbrella-shaped clusters of small, yellowish brown flowers are borne at the end of stems. Spikelets are 1 to 3 cm long and composed of several flowers. Flowers are composed of 3 stamens and a 3-lobed style. A whorl of 3 to 9 leaf-like bracts, 5 to 25 cm long, is found below the flower clusters. The longest bract is generally longer than the flower cluster. Seed production in yellow nutsedge is uncommon.

Plant: Yellow nutsedge has triangular stems, 15 to 90 cm tall. Plants have creeping, fibrous roots that produce underground tubers. These black tubers, 8 to 19 mm long, have a hard, woody shell and are produced at the ends of scaly rhizomes that originate at a stout basal bulb. Tubers are the only part of the plant that overwinters. Buds located at the end of a tuber can produce more than 10 fibrous roots, each about 20 cm long. These roots give rise to a basal bulb and ultimately new plants that produce more tubers. Tubers weigh about 2 grams and are viable for 3.5 years. Tubers are rarely found below 23 cm depth and are most common in the top 15 cm of soil. Research has shown that in a single growing season, 1 tuber can produce 1,900 plants and 7,000 new tubers, in an area 2.1 m in diameter. The range of yellow nutsedge is climatically controlled: soil temperatures below -6.5 °C kill most of the tubers.

Fruit: The single-seeded fruit is often referred to as an achene.

REASONS FOR CONCERN

Yellow nutsedge is a serious weed of cultivated fields and row crops. It is a major pest of corn, beans, and potatoes. Tubers of yellow nutsedge are capable of growing inside potato tubers, reducing the quality of the crop.

roots with young tubers

cyathium

The spurge family, a large group (approximately 7,500 species) of herbs, shrubs, and trees with milky sap, is found primarily in tropical regions of the world, although a few species are found in temperate regions. The simple, stipulate leaves are alternate, opposite, or whorled. The flower cluster of the largest genus, *Euphorbia*, is highly modified and resembles a flower. The cluster, called a *cyathium*, consists of 4 to 5 fused bracts and nectar-secreting glands. Each cyathium bears a single female flower, consisting of a 3-lobed nodding ovary and style, and several male flowers, consisting of a single stamen. Each cyathium has 5 groups of male flowers with 1 to many stamens per group. The fruit is a capsule.

The spurge family is a diverse group of economically important plants. Castor oil and tapioca are produced by tropical members of this family. Other species—such as crotons, poinsettias, crown-of-thorns, and castor bean—are grown as ornamental plants. Several species are designated as noxious weeds.

Spurge Family

leafy spurge,
Euphorbia esula L.

Euphorbiaceae

cypress spurge

Euphorbia cyparissias L.

A perennial introduced from Europe as an ornamental plant.

Also known as: salvers spurge, quack salvers grass, graveyard-weed, tree-moss, Irish moss, Bonaparte's crown, kiss-me-Dick, welcome-to-our-house

French names: rhubarbe des pauvres, euphorbe cyprès

Scientific synonyms: *E. virgata* Waldst. & Kit.

QUICK ID
- Milky juice
- Flowers greenish yellow
- Leaves alternate and narrow

Distribution: Found throughout Canada (except Alberta) and the northern half of the United States.

Weed Designation
Canada: AB, MB, ON, PQ

DESCRIPTION

Seed: Seeds are egg-shaped, yellow to bluish grey, 2 to 3 mm long.

Seedling: Cotyledons, 6.5 to 9 mm long and 2 to 2.5 mm wide, are larger than the first few pairs of leaves. The stem below the cotyledons is dull red. The first leaves are opposite and lance-shaped. The milky juice is present at early stages of growth.

Leaves: Leaves are alternate, slightly club-shaped, up to 2.5 cm long and less than 3 mm wide. The dark-green leaves of the branches are small and bristle-like. Leaves drop from the stems early in the season.

Flower: Flowers are produced in umbrella-shaped terminal clusters. Bracts below flower clusters appear in a whorl of 10 or more. The bracts are yellowish green and turn to bronze or purple with age. Flowers are of 2 types: male and female. Male flowers are composed of a single stamen with a small bract at the base; female flowers are composed of a single pistil.

Plant: Cypress spurge reproduces by seeds and creeping rhizomes. The rhizomes have numerous pink buds that give rise to new shoots. Plants are often clustered in areas where they form large patches. Both sterile and fertile plants are found in nature. The stems, up to 80 cm tall, are very leafy. The stem and leaves, if broken, exude a sticky, bitter-tasting, milky juice.

Fruit: The fruit is a 3-lobed capsule, about 3 mm long. The capsule contains 1 to 3 egg-shaped seeds.

REASONS FOR CONCERN

Cypress spurge is a serious weed of roadsides, waste areas, and pastures in dry, open areas. It is not a problem in cultivated fields or row crops. Cypress spurge causes SKIN IRRITATION in humans who come in contact with the plant. The plant is reported to be somewhat TOXIC to cattle and horses.

SIMILAR SPECIES

Leafy spurge (*E. esula* L.) is closely related to cypress spurge, but is distinguished by fewer, pale green leaves. The leaves are 1 to 3.5 cm long and 5 to 10 mm wide. Leafy spurge reproduces by seed and an extensive creeping rhizome (see pp 368-69).

leafy spurge

leafy spurge

Euphorbia esula L.

A perennial introduced from the Caucasus region of western Asia as a seed impurity in 1827 at Newbury, Massachusetts (another introduction in Minnesota occurred in 1890 in grain imported from Russia), leafy spurge was first reported in Ontario in 1889 and had spread to British Columbia by 1939.

Also known as: wolf's-milk, euphorbia, spurge, faitours-grass

French names: euphorbe ésule

QUICK ID

- Leaves alternate, whorled below the flower clusters
- Flower clusters greenish yellow
- Milky juice

Distribution: Found throughout Canada (except Newfoundland) and the northern half of the United States.

Weed Designation

Canada: FEDERAL, AB, BC, MB, NS, ON, SK

USA: FEDERAL, AK, AZ, CA, CO, HI, IA, ID, IL, KS, MI, MN, MO, MT, ND, NE, NV, NY, OH, OR, SD, UT, WA, WI, WY

DESCRIPTION

Seed: Seeds are ovate to oblong, greyish with yellow and brown flecks, 2 to 2.4 mm long and about 1.8 mm wide. The surface is smooth and somewhat glossy. Each stem is capable of producing 250 seeds. Seeds float on water, which assists in establishing new colonies on the shores of ditches, canals, and rivers. Seeds are viable for at least 6 years and germinate when air temperatures reach 26 °C.

Seedling: Cotyledons, 13 to 19 mm long and 2 to 4 mm wide, are narrowly oblong with a granular texture. The stem below the cotyledons is pale green and reddish brown at soil level. The first leaves are opposite, lance-shaped, and stalkless. Seedlings contain milky juice, a characteristic that assists in early identification.

Leaves: Leaves are alternate or opposite and sometimes whorled below the flowering cluster. The lance-shaped leaves are 2 to 7 cm long and 3 to 5 mm wide; they are stalkless with smooth margins.

Flower: Greenish yellow, umbrella-shaped clusters of flowers appear at the end of the stem and branches. Sepals and petals are absent. Male flowers, arranged in groups of 5, consist of a single stamen; female flowers, arranged in groups of 3, consist of a single pistil. Bracts are opposite, 1.2 cm long and 1 cm wide. Four crescent-shaped glands are present in each floral cluster. Seeds are produced 30 days after the first flowers appear.

Plant: Leafy spurge is a deep-rooted perennial with roots up to 5 m long. Small pink buds on horizontal roots give rise to new plants. Stems are somewhat woody, branched above, reaching a height of 1 m; they are filled with a milk-like juice. The plant is smooth, resulting in a bluish green tinge. Research has shown that root fragments from 2.8 m depth can produce new plants. Some reports indicate that decomposing plant tissue produces an ALLELOPATHIC response to sensitive crops like legumes and tomatoes.

root system

Fruit: The fruit is a 3-seeded nodding capsule, 4 mm long. At maturity, the capsule explodes, scattering seeds up to 5 m away.

REASONS FOR CONCERN

Leafy spurge is a serious weed of pastures, rangeland, and roadsides. If found in cultivated fields or row crops, it is difficult to eradicate because of its rhizome and seed dispersal mechanism. In North America, it is estimated that over 2.5 million acres are infested. Plants are POISONOUS to most livestock, except sheep who feed on it without harmful effects. The milky juice may cause SEVERE SKIN RASHES in humans.

thyme-leaved spurge

Euphorbia glyptosperma
Engelm.

An annual native to North America.

Also known as: ridge-seeded spurge

French names: euphorbe à feuilles de serpolet, euphorbe à feuilles de thym

QUICK ID
- Milky juice
- Plant with prostrate growth habit
- Leaves opposite

Distribution: Found throughout Canada (except Nova Scotia, Prince Edward Island, and Newfoundland) and the United States.

Weed Designation
Canada: MB

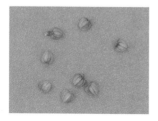

DESCRIPTION

Seed: Seeds are prism-shaped, greyish white to tan, 1.2 mm long. The surface of the seed is pitted or wrinkled. Seeds are very sticky when wet, which assists in their dispersal.

Seedling: Cotyledons, 4 to 6 mm long, are ovate and pinkish beneath. The first pair of leaves are opposite and resemble later leaves. The main stem appears from the axils of the first leaves.

Leaves: Leaves are opposite, narrowly oblong, 3 to 15 mm long. Leaves are dark green with a red midrib. Leaf margins are smooth, except for a few small teeth near the tip.

Flower: Clusters of small, greenish white flowers are found in the axils of leaves. Flowers are of 2 types: male and female. Male flowers, in clusters of 1 to 5, are composed of a single stamen and a small basal bract. Female flowers are composed of a single pistil.

Plant: A prostrate, freely branched annual, thyme-leaved spurge has reddish green stems up to 30 cm long. Plants often form large, circular mats, about 60 cm across. Stems and leaves, if broken, exude a white, milky juice. This species reproduces by seed only.

Fruit: The fruit is a 3-angled capsule, 1.5 to 2 mm long. Each capsule contains 3 grey seeds.

REASONS FOR CONCERN

Thyme-leaved spurge is a common weed of gravelled areas, railways, and roadsides. It is occasionally found in gardens and new or poorly maintained lawns.

SIMILAR SPECIES

A closely related species, also called thyme-leaved spurge (*E. serpyllifolia* Pers.), is distinguished from this species by wider, toothed leaves and clusters of 5 to 18 male flowers. Like *E. glyptosperma*, it is found throughout Canada and the United States. Purslane (*Portulaca oleracea* L.) may be confused with thyme-leaved spurge. It is distinguished from thyme-leaved spurge by its fleshy, alternate leaves, bright-yellow flowers, and lack of milky juice (see pp 352-53).

purslane

female flower

male flower

stinging hair

fruit

The stinging nettle family has about 1,000 species of plants worldwide. Many species in the tropics grow as small trees or shrubs, while those in temperate regions are herbaceous. Only a few genera have stinging hairs. The simple leaves are alternate or opposite and stipulate. Male flowers are composed of 3 to 5 sepals and 3 to 5 stamens. Female flowers are composed of 3 to 5 sepals and 1 style. Petals are absent. The fruit is an achene or drupe.

The stinging nettle family is of little economic importance, although a few species without stinging hairs are grown as ornamental plants.

Stinging Nettle Family

stinging nettle, *Urtica dioica* L.

Urticaceae

stinging nettle

Urtica dioica L.

A perennial native to North America; some introduced subspecies may be present.

Also known as: bigsting nettle, tall nettle, slender nettle

French names: ortie dioïque d'Amérique, ortie dioïque d'Europe

Scientific synonyms: *U. lyallii* S. Wats.; *U. gracilis* Ait.

DESCRIPTION

Seed: Seeds are ovate, dull orange to pale brown, 1 to 1.5 mm long and less than 1 mm wide. A narrow wing encircles the seed. Each plant can produce up to 20,000 seeds, which may remain viable for 10 years.

Seedling: Cotyledons, 2 to 4 mm long, are oblong and have a distinct midrib. The first pair of leaves has shallowly toothed margins and a few stinging hairs. Each tooth is tipped with a long hair. Seedlings survive only if kept out of direct sunlight. Stinging hairs are present at the 2-leaf stage.

Leaves: Leaves are opposite, heart to lance-shaped, 5 to 12 cm long and 2 to 3 cm wide. Leaves, with 3 to 7 prominent nerves, have stalks 10 to 15 mm long. At the base of each leaf are 2 green to pale-brown, papery structures called stipules; the stipules are 5 to 12 mm long.

Flower: Numerous small green flowers are borne in branched clusters in the axils of leaves. Flowers are of 2 types (male and female) and appear in separate clusters. Male flowers are greenish yellow and composed of 4 sepals and 4 stamens; female flowers are greenish and composed of 4 hairy sepals (2 inner sepals are larger and enclose the ovary) and a single pistil. The sepals of both flower types are 1 to 2 mm long. Petals are absent. Flowers are wind-pollinated.

Plant: Stinging nettle has an extensive creeping rhizome capable of spreading up to 2.5 m in diameter per year. Stinging nettle reproduces by spreading roots and seeds. Small pink buds on the rhizome give rise to new shoots. The stems, up to 3 m tall, are 4-sided and sparsely to densely haired. Stinging nettle is a long-lived perennial—some colonies are estimated to be more than 50 years old.

Fruit: The single-seeded fruit, called an achene, is surrounded by a papery covering.

juvenile

REASONS FOR CONCERN

Stinging nettle is a weed of disturbed areas, farmyards, roadsides, and pastures. It is rarely a problem in cultivated fields or row crops. Stinging hairs located on the stem and leaves cause a type of DERMATITIS. The sharp-pointed hairs have a bulbous base filled with irritating fluid. These hairs break when they penetrate the skin, releasing the fluid.

SIMILAR SPECIES

Small nettle (*U. urens* L.), an introduced annual, is distinguished by stipules 1 to 3 mm long and by flower clusters that include both male and female flowers.

flower

The sumac family is predominantly tropical, with a few temperate species. These shrubs, woody vines, or trees have alternate leaves that are simple to compound and estipulate. The flowers, borne in either terminal or axillary clusters, are composed of 3 to 7 fused sepals, 3 to 7 petals, 5 to many stamens, and 1 to 5 styles. A ring of nectaries is present. The fruit is a drupe or berry.

The sumac family is probably best known for a single species: poison ivy (*Rhus radicans* L.). The stems and leaves of poison ivy and poisonwood, another TOXIC species, contain a resinous substance that CAN IRRITATE THE SKIN of humans. Other species of the sumac family—such as cashew, pistachio, and mango—produce edible fruit and seeds. A few other species are cultivated as ornamentals.

Sumac Family

poison ivy,
Rhus radicans L.

Anacardiaceae

poison ivy

Rhus radicans L.

A perennial native to North America.

Also known as: poison oak, poison creeper, three-leaved ivy, picry, mercury, markweed

French names: herbe à la puce, sumac vénéneux, sumac grimpant, bois de chien

Scientific synonyms: *Toxicodendron rydbergii* (Small ex Rydb.) Greene; *Toxicodendron radicans* (L.) Kuntze

QUICK ID
- Shrub or climbing vine
- Leaves alternate and compound with 3 shiny leaflets
- Flowers yellowish green

Distribution: Found throughout Canada (except Newfoundland) and the United States.

Weed Designation
Canada: MB, NS, ON, PQ

DESCRIPTION

Seed: Seeds are round, white with grey stripes, 3 to 4 mm across. They are viable for at least 6 years. Each germinating seed produces a single vertical stem.

Leaves: Leaves are alternate, compound with 3 shiny leaflets, 6.5 to 40 cm long. Leaves are reddish purple in the spring, but turn a glossy green by midsummer. The margins of the leaflets may be smooth or toothed. The terminal leaflet is stalked, while the laterals are stalkless.

Flower: Yellowish green flowers, 2 to 5 mm across, are found in axillary clusters, 2.5 to 10 cm long. Flowers are composed of 5 sepals, 5 petals, 5 stamens, and a single pistil. Flowers may be of 3 types: male, female, or male and female. Not all plants bear fruit.

Plant: A shrub reaching 45 cm tall or a climbing vine reaching 1.2 m tall, poison ivy spreads by creeping underground roots that often produce large colonies. The roots spread at a rate of about 10 cm per year. Poison ivy reproduces by seed, rhizomes, and rooting of stem nodes.

Fruit: The fruit is a globe-shaped, creamy-white berry, 3 to 7 mm in diameter. The berry, technically called a drupe, is waxy and 1-seeded. The fruit generally remain on the stem throughout the winter.

REASONS FOR CONCERN

Some references indicate that simply touching the plant causes poisoning, while others indicate that the plant tissue must be ruptured. EXTREME CARE should be taken when travelling or working in areas where this plant is found. Burning the plant releases the poison in the ash and smoke, so AVOID INHALATION. The poisonous compound is found in the sap of leaves, stems, and roots. The poison, urushiol, initially causes severe itching; 24 to 48 hours later, the skin becomes red and blistered. Contaminated clothing should be hot-laundered to neutralize the poisons. Poisoning can also occur when using contaminated tools.

fruit

SIMILAR SPECIES

Poison oak (*R. toxicodendron* L.) is closely related to poison ivy. The leaflets of poison oak are 4 to 8 cm long. The leaflets have 2 to 7 deep teeth or shallow lobes, and resemble oak leaves. Poison oak has erect stems to up 1 m tall. It is found in the Pacific and southeastern states of the United States. Skunkbush (*R. trilobata* Nutt.) is found throughout western North America. An ill-scented shrub growing up to 2 m tall, skunkbush is common on south-facing slopes of coulees and river valleys. The leaves, 1 to 4 cm long, are composed of 3 leaflets. Clusters of small, yellowish green flowers appear before the leaves. The fruit is a round, red berry, 5 to 6 mm across.

skunkbush

skunkbush *(fruit)*

flower

The teasel family contains 250 species of herbaceous plants, found primarily in Africa and Eurasia. Leaves are opposite or whorled and may be simple to pinnately compound. The flowers are borne in heads and resemble those of the aster family. Flowers are composed of 5 sepals, 4 to 5 petals, 2 to 4 stamens, and 1 style. Teasels are distinguished from the aster family by the presence of sepals. The fruit is an achene.

The teasels are of little economic importance.

Teasel
Family

blue buttons, *Knautia arvensis* (L.) Duby

Dipsacaceae

blue buttons

Knautia arvensis
(L.) Duby

A perennial introduced from Europe.

Also known as: field scabious, knautia, pincushion, gypsy-rose, blue-caps

French names: scabieuse de champs

Scientific synonyms: *Scabiosa arvensis* L.

QUICK ID
- Leaves opposite
- Flowers heads blue to pale purple
- Lower part of the plant bristly-hairy

Distribution: Found throughout Canada (except Nova Scotia and Prince Edward Island) and the northeastern United States.

Weed Designation
Canada: MB

DESCRIPTION

Seed: Seeds are rectangular, light brown, 5 to 6 mm long and 2 mm wide. Seeds are 4-sided and covered with long hairs. Each plant may produce up to 2,000 seeds. Germination occurs at 1 to 2 cm depth.

Seedling: Cotyledons are club-shaped, about 15 mm long and 5 mm wide. The tip of the cotyledons is slightly indented. The first leaves are ovate with wavy margins. Scattered white hairs can be found on the early leaves. Later leaves are shallowly to deeply lobed.

Leaves: Leaves are opposite and deeply divided into 5 to 15 narrow segments. The terminal lobe is the largest segment of the leaf. The leaves, 6 to 25 cm long and 2 to 6 cm wide, are dull greyish green due to the presence of short, stiff hairs. Lower leaves are stalked and have toothed margins. Leaves are reduced in size upwards. Upper leaves are stalkless with toothed to deeply lobed margins.

Flower: Terminal flower heads, 1.5 to 4 cm across, are composed of numerous blue to purple, tube-shaped florets. Flowers are composed of a calyx with 8 to 12 teeth, a 4 to 5-lobed corolla 9 to 12 mm long, 4 stamens, and a single pistil. A row of floral bracts, 10 to 15 mm long, can be found below the flower head.

Plant: A rough-textured perennial herb, blue buttons has purple-spotted stems that grow up to 1.3 m tall. Near the base of the plant, the stem is covered with short, stiff hairs. The upper part of the stem is often hairless.

Fruit: A single-seeded fruit, called an achene, is produced by each floret. The seed is enclosed by a hairy, 4-ribbed bract.

REASONS FOR CONCERN

Blue buttons is not a weed of cultivated land but has the potential to be a serious weed of pastures and forage crops. Once established, it is difficult to eradicate.

juvenile

SIMILAR SPECIES

Blue buttons is often confused with several blue-flowered members of the aster family. It is distinguished from asters by the presence of the calyx, 4 stamens, and absent pappus. Members of the aster family have no calyx, 5 stamens, and a pappus of hairs or scales.

plant

The water milfoil family has about 100 species worldwide, with most occurring in the southern hemisphere. Species found in the northern hemisphere are aquatic herbs with alternate, opposite, or whorled leaves. The leaves are deeply divided into numerous thread-like segments. Male flowers, composed of 3 to 4 sepals, 4 petals, and 2 to 8 stamens, are found at or near the top of the flower cluster. Female flowers have similar sepals and petals, and 2 to 4 feathery styles. They are found near the bottom of the flower cluster. Sepals and petals often fall off when the flower opens. The fruit is nut-like and splits into 4 seeds.

Water milfoil
Family

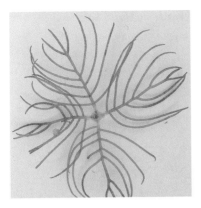

Left: northern water milfoil,
Myriophyllum exalbescens Fern.
Right: northern water milfoil,
Myriophyllum exalbescens Fern.

Haloragaceae

northern water milfoil
Myriophyllum exalbescens Fern.

A perennial native to North America.

Also known as: water-milfoil

French names: myriophylle blanchissant

Scientific synonyms: *M. spicatum* L. ssp. *squamosum* Laest. ex Hartm. f., *M. spicatum* L. ssp. *exalbescens* (Fern.) Hult.

QUICK ID
- Plants aquatic
- Leaves in whorls of 4
- Stems purplish red

Distribution: Found throughout Canada and the northern half of the United States.

Weed Designation
Canada: MB

DESCRIPTION
Seed: Seeds are 3-sided (2 flat and 1 round), 2.3 to 3 mm long.

Seedling: Seedlings are rarely observed in nature.

Leaves: Leaves appear in whorls of 4 at each node. The feather-like leaves, 1 to 3 cm long, are composed of 12 to 22 thread-like segments.

Flower: Flower clusters, 4 to 10 cm long, often remain under water during flowering.

Flowers of 2 types (male and female) appear whorled in an interrupted spike. Male flowers are purplish and appear at the end of the flowering stem. They are composed of 4 sepals, 4 petals, and 8 stamens, 1.2 to 1.8 mm long. The lower, whitish flowers are female. Female flowers are composed of 4 sepals, 4 petals, and 1 pistil with 2 to 4 feathery stigmas. The petals of both flowers are about 2.5 mm long and fall off soon after the flowers open. Small bracts, 1 to 1.8 mm long, are found below each flower.

Plant: A submersed aquatic plant, northern water milfoil has purplish red branching stems, up to 1.5 m long. Plants turn white when removed from water and left out to dry. Reproduction is by seeds, fragmentation, and winter buds. Fragmentation is the development of new plants from pieces of a former plant. Another method of vegetative reproduction is winter buds. Winter buds are clusters of tightly held leaves near the end of the stem; they develop when water temperatures drop and daylength shortens. The buds break off and fall to the bottom, where they overwinter. When temperatures and daylight increase in the spring, the buds rise and elongate to form new plants.

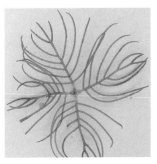

Fruit: The fruit is a globe-shaped, nut-like fruit, 2.3 to 3 mm long. The fruit breaks into 4 seeds at maturity. The floral bracts are shorter than the fruit.

REASONS FOR CONCERN
Northern water milfoil is a concern in waterways, irrigation ditches, and drainage canals, where it may impede water flow.

winter bud

SIMILAR SPECIES
Eurasian water milfoil (*M. spicatum* L.), a closely related species, is often mistaken for northern water milfoil. It is distinguished from northern water milfoil by its leaves, which have 28 to 48 thread-like divisions, and the numerous roots that appear along the length of the stem.

Eurasian water milfoil

A family of 100 submersed or floating aquatic plants, the waterweed family is found throughout the world. Plants may be male, female, or both. The simple leaves may be alternate, opposite, whorled, or basal, and sheathing or sheathless. Flowers may be male or female. Male flowers are composed of 3 green sepals, 3 petals, and 1 to many stamens; female flowers have 3 green sepals, 3 petals, and 2 to 15 styles. The fruit is a capsule or berry.

The waterweed family is of little economic importance.

plant *female flower*

Waterweed Family

Canada waterweed,
Elodea longivaginata
St. John

Hydrocharitaceae

Canada waterweed
Elodea longivaginata
St. John

A perennial native to western North America.

Also known as: water thyme, ditch moss

French names: élodée du Canada

Scientific synonyms: *E. canadensis* Michx.; *Anacharis canadensis* (Michx.) Rich.

QUICK ID

- Plants aquatic
- Leaves opposite or in whorls of 3
- Male and female plants produced

Distribution: Found throughout Canada (except Newfoundland and Prince Edward Island) and in the northern half of the United States.

Weed Designation
Canada: MB

seeds

fruit

DESCRIPTION

Seed: Seeds are cylindrical, brown, about 4.5 mm long. The surface of the seed is smooth.

Seedling: Seedlings are rarely produced in nature.

Leaves: Lower leaves are opposite, while the upper leaves appear in whorls of 3. Leaves, 6 to 20 mm long and 1 to 5 mm wide, are dark green and translucent. The stalkless leaves have finely toothed margins.

Flower: Flowers are of 2 types (male and female) and appear on separate plants. Female flowers appear in the upper leaf axils and reach the surface of the water surface on a thread-like stalk, 10 to 20 cm long. Female flowers appear before the male flowers.

These flowers are composed of 3 sepals (each 3.5 to 5 mm long and 2 to 2.5 mm wide), 3 white petals (each about 5 mm long and less than 1 mm wide), and a single pistil. Male flowers are borne on shorter stalks in leaf axils and break from the plant to float to the surface. Male flowers are composed of 3 sepals (each 3 to 5 mm long and 2 to 2.5 mm wide), 3 white petals (each about 5 mm long and less than 1 mm wide), and 9 stamens. The sepals are dark veined and fall off as the flower opens. The 6 outer stamens are stalkless and spread when the flower opens. The inner 3 stamens become petal-like once the pollen has been shed. There are also 3 sterile stamens called staminodes; these are needle-like and 0.7 mm long. A leaf-like bract, called a *spathe*, 2 to 15 mm long, is found below each male flower.

Plant: Canada waterweed is a submersed aquatic plant that roots in mud. This species has male and female plants. Male plants are rare. The stems of female plants branch in pairs. Creeping thread-like roots anchor the plant; roots often appear from the stem nodes. The primary form of reproduction is by winter buds, which develop when water temperatures drop and daylength shortens. Winter buds are clusters of tightly held leaves near the end of the stem. These buds break off and fall to the bottom, where they overwinter. When temperatures and daylight increase in the spring, these buds anchor to the bottom and produce new stems.

Fruit: The fruit is an ovate capsule, 6 to 9 mm long and 2 to 3 mm wide. The stalkless fruit is found in leaf axils. Each capsule contains 1 or 2 seeds; 3 seeds are rare.

REASONS FOR CONCERN

Canada waterweed is a major weed problem in irrigation canals and drainage ditches: large colonies often impede water flow.

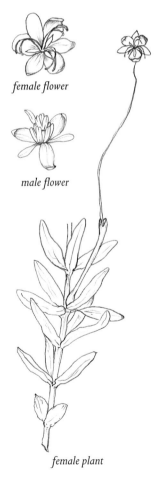

female flower

male flower

female plant

fruit

The woodsorrel family contains more than 900 species of herbaceous plants of tropical and subtropical zones. A few species are found in temperate zones. Leaves are alternate or basal and compound with 3 or more leaflets. Flowers are composed of 5 sepals, 0 to 5 petals, 10 to 15 stamens, and 3 to 5 styles. The fruit is a many-seeded capsule or berry.

A few woodsorrel species are cultivated for their ornamental value.

plant

Woodsorrel Family

creeping woodsorrel,
Oxalis corniculata L.

Oxalidaceae

creeping woodsorrel

Oxalis corniculata L.

A perennial introduced from Asia, Malaysia, or Australia about 1732.

Also known as: yellow woodsorrel, sour clover, creeping lady's sorrel

French names: oxalide cornue, oxalis corniculé

Scientific synonyms: *Xanthoxalis corniculata* (L.) Small.

QUICK ID
- Leaves alternate, compound with 3 heart-shaped leaflets
- Flowers yellow
- Stems often rooting at nodes

Distribution: Found throughout Canada and the United States.

Weed Designation
  USA: FL

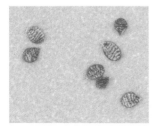

DESCRIPTION
Seed: Seeds are elliptical, brown, 1 to 1.4 mm long and about 1 mm wide. The dull surface of the seed has 9 cross ridges and 2 or 3 faint lengthwise ridges.

Seedling: Cotyledons are about 2.3 mm long and 1 mm wide. The stem below the cotyledons is very short, making the seed leaves appear to emerge from the soil. The first leaves are alternate and compound, composed of 3 heart-shaped leaflets. Leaves after the 4-leaf stage have hairy margins and petioles.

Leaves: Leaves are alternate and compound with 3 heart-shaped leaflets, each 1 to 2 cm across. Leaves are often purplish green. These long-stalked leaves taste sour, giving rise the common name "sour clover." Stipules—small, leafy appendages found at the base of the leaf—are present.

Flower: Yellow flowers, appearing in terminal and axillary clusters of 1 to 4, are 4 to 10 mm across. Flowers are composed of 5 sepals (each 3.5 to 7 mm long), 5 petals (each 7 to 11 mm long), 10 to 15 stamens, and 1 style.

Plant: Creeping woodsorrel reproduces by seed only. The greyish green stems, 10 to 50 cm tall, are erect to prostrate. The creeping stems often root at the nodes.

Fruit: The fruit is a hairy, cylindrical capsule, 1.2 to 2.5 cm long, containing numerous sticky seeds. At maturity, the capsule explodes and disperses the seeds up to 2 m away.

REASONS FOR CONCERN

Creeping woodsorrel is a common weed in lawns, gardens, and greenhouses. It has been reported to cause OXALATE POISONING in sheep. It is also an alternate host for beet curly top virus.

SIMILAR SPECIES

When not in flower, creeping woodsorrel may often be confused with either black medick (*Medicago lupulina* L.; see pp 306-07) or white clover (*Trifolium repens* L.; see pp 314-15). These species can be distinguished by the shape of the leaflet: the leaflets of black medick and white clover are not heart-shaped. Several other species of woodsorrel (*Oxalis* spp.) are found throughout North America.

black medick

achene

A dry, single-seeded fruit that does not open when ripe.

allelopathic

A plant that produces a chemical that suppresses the growth of other plants.

annual

A plant whose life-cycle is completed in a single growing season.

anthers

The pollen-producing sacs of the stamens.

apex

Tip of a leaf or petal.

apical

At the tip.

auricle

Ear-like appendages; in grasses, auricles are found at the junction of the blade and the sheath.

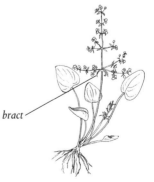

auricle *ligule*

awn

A stiff bristle.

axil

The angle formed between the leaf and the stem.

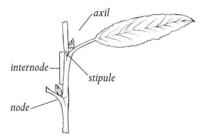

axil

internode

stipule

node

axillary

Refers to structures found in the axil of leaves.

basal

From the base; often refers to leaves.

biennial

A plant that takes two years to complete its life cycle.

bract

Leaf-like structure found below a flower or flower cluster.

bract

bracteole
　A small bract.

calyx
　The collective term for the sepals of a flower.

capitulum
　A head.

capsule
　A dry fruit that opens when mature.

caryopsis
　The fruit or grain of a grass.

cleft
　Deeply lobed.

collar
　In grasses, part of the leaf where the blade and sheath connect (see p 168).

compound leaf
　A leaf composed of two or more leaflets (see p XVIII).

corolla
　The collective term for the petals of a flower.

corona
　An appendage derived from petals and stamen filaments (see p 240).

cotyledons
　The seed leaves.

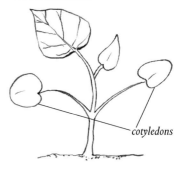

cotyledons

deciduous
　Having leaves that fall in autumn; also refers to seeds that are shed at maturity.

dicotyledon
　Plants whose seeds produce two cotyledons.

disc floret
　Small flowers, usually tube-shaped, in the aster family.

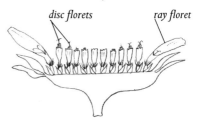

disc florets　　　*ray floret*

dormancy
　In reference to seeds, the period between seed maturity and germination.

drupe

A fleshy, usually single-seeded, fruit (e.g., cherry).

drupelet

Single section of an aggregate fruit (e.g., raspberry).

elliptical

Shaped like an ellipse.

emergent

A plant whose stem rises out of the water.

family

A group of plants that share many similar characteristics.

fibrous

Thread-like roots of plants.

fruit

The part of the plant that contains seeds.

genus (pl. genera)

A group of species that share similar characteristics.

glabrous

Lacking hair.

gland

A structure that usually produces nectar or another sticky substance.

glume

In grasses, a small bract at the base of a spikelet.

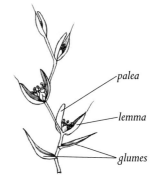

palea

lemma

glumes

herb

A plant that lacks woody stems.

host

An organism on which another organism lives as a parasite.

inflorescence

Flower cluster.

internode

The region of stem between two leaves. See *axil*.

involucre

A bract or group of bracts below a flower cluster.

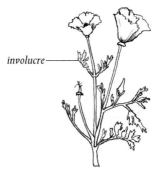

involucre

lemma

In grasses, one of two small bracts that enclose the flower. See *glume*.

ligule

In grasses, a small projection from the top of the sheath. See *auricle*.

margin

The edge of a leaf.

midrib

The main vein or rib of a structure (e.g., leaf, petal, etc.).

monocot

Term given to plants whose seeds produce a single cotyledon.

nerve

A vein of a leaf, petal, sepal, or other structure.

node

The point at which the leaf attaches to the stem. See *axil*.

noxious

A plant capable of causing damage to agricultural crops or animal health.

nutlet

A small nut.

ocrea

A sheath found at leaf nodes, derived from the fusion of two stipules.

ovary

Part of the pistil that contains the ovules.

ovate

Egg-shaped and broader at the base, usually in reference to leaves.

palea

In grasses, one of two small bracts that enclose the flower. See *glume*.

panicle

A branching flower cluster that is often pyramid-shaped.

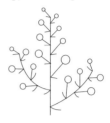

pappus

Hairs or bristles that are attached to the seeds of the aster family.

parasite

A plant that obtains food and nutrients from another living plant.

pepo

In the gourd family, a berry-like fruit with a thick rind and fibrous interior (e.g., pumpkin, cucmber).

perennial

A plant, or part of a plant, living more than two growing seasons.

perfect

Term given to flowers that have both stamens and pistils present.

petal

Part of a flower that is usually coloured to attract insects.

petiole

The stalk of a leaf.

pinna (pl. pinnae)
The primary division of a compound leaf.

pinna

pinnate
Compound leaf with leaflets arranged on both side of the stalk (see p XVIII).

pistil
The female part of the flower.

pistillate
Flowers containing female reproductive structures.

pod
A dry fruit that releases its seeds when mature.

prickle
A spiny structure on the surface of a plant.

prothallus
In ferns and fern allies, a small structure producing male and female sex organs.

raceme
Flower cluster with flowers attached along a central stalk with flower stalks of equal length.

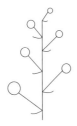

ray floret
Strap-like, often marginal flower type in the aster family. See *disc floret*.

recurved
Bent or curled backward.

rhizome
An elongated, underground stem.

rosette
A cluster of basal leaves.

schizocarp
A fruit that breaks into sections that contain one or more seeds.

semi-aquatic
A plant capable of living in water and on wet shorelines.

sepals
The outermost part of the flower; usually green and leaf-like.

serrated
Leaf margin with jagged edges.

sessile
Stalkless.

sheath

The base of the leaf that surrounds the stem.

shrub

Woody plant that has many stems arising from the root.

silicle

In the mustard family, a silique that is 2 to 3 times as long as it is wide (see *Thlapsi arvense*, pp 292-93).

silique

In the mustard family, a capsule whose compartments are separated by a membraneous wall.

simple leaf

A leaf with a single blade.

spathe

A large bract that encloses a flower cluster.

spatulate

Spoon-shaped; usually refers to leaves.

species

A group of similar plants capable of interbreeding to produce offspring like themselves.

spike

An unbranched flower cluster where flowers are attached directly to the main stem.

spikelet

A small spike; often refers to members of the grass and sedge families.

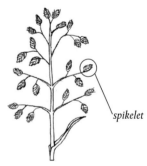

spikelet

spore

A reproductive structure in ferns and fern allies.

spur

A slender projection from the corolla or calyx.

stamen

The male part of the flower.

staminate

Flowers containing only male reproductive structures.

staminode

A sterile stamen.

sterile

A flower without functional reproductive structures.

stigma

The receptive surface to which pollen grains attach.

stipulate

Stems with stipules at the base of the leaf.

stipules

A pair of membraneous structures found at the base of a leaf. See *axil*.

strobilus (pl. strobili)

A cone.

style

The elongated part of the pistil between the stigma and the ovary.

subspecies

In taxonomy, the rank below species; this term is often used to distinguish between characteristics within the same species.

sucker

A stem that grows from the underground root of a plant.

taproot

The main root, like those of carrots.

tendril

A clasping or twining part of a leaf.

tepals

A collective term used to describe sepals and petals that are similar in size, appearance, and colour.

terminal

The end of the stem or leaf.

thallus (pl. thalli)

Plants without differentiation between stems and leaves.

tillers
In grasses, stems or branches originating at the base of the first stem.

tree
A woody plant having one stem
arising from the root.

true flower
Flower possessing stamens and/or
pistils.

umbel
Flower arrangement where the
flower stalks originate from one
point.

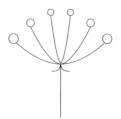

winter annual
A plant that germinates and
produces a leafy rosette in the fall,
then produces seeds and dies the
following growing season.

Bibliography

Agri-Growth Reasearch, Inc. 1993. *Southern Weed Seedling Identification.* Agri-Growth Research, Hollandale, Minnesota.

Alberta Agriculture. 1983. *Weeds of Alberta.* Alberta Agriculture and Alberta Environmental Centre, Edmonton, Alberta.

Alberta Agriculture. 1986. *Weed Seedling Identification.* Agdex 640-3. Alberta Agriculture, Edmonton, Alberta.

Alberta Environment. 1989. *An Identification Guide to Alberta Aquatic Plants.* Alberta Environment, Pesticide Management Branch, Edmonton, Alberta.

Alex, J. F. 1992. *Ontario Weeds: Descriptions, Illustrations and Keys to their Identification.* Ontario Ministry of Agriculture and Food, Publication 505 Agdex 640, Toronto, Ontario.

Alex, Jack F., Richard Cayouette, and Gerald A. Mulligan. 1982. *Common and botanical names of weeds in Canada.* Canadian Government Publishing Centre, Ottawa.

Auld, B.A. and R. W. Medd. 1987. *Weeds: An Illustrated Botanical Guide to Weeds of Australia.* Inkata Press, Melbourne.

Best, K.F. and J. Baden Campbell. 1971. *Prairie Grasses, Identified and Described by Vegetative Characters.* Canadian Department of Agriculture Publication 1413, Ottawa.

Cavers, P.B. 1995. *The Biology of Canadian Weeds.* Contributions 62-83. The Agriculture Institute of Canada, Ottawa.

Cheeke, P.R. and L.R. Shull. 1985. *Natural toxicants in feeds and poisonous plants.* AVI Publishing Company, Westport, Connecticut.

Cooper, M.R. and A.W. Johnson. 1984. *Poisonous plants in Britain and their effects on animals and man.* Her Majesty's Stationery Office, London, England.

Crockett, Lawrence J. 1977. *Wildly Successful Plants: A Handbook of North American Weeds.* MacMillan Publishing Co., New York.

Davis, Linda W. 1993. *Weed Seeds of the Great Plains: A Handbook for Identification.* University Press of Kansas, Lawrence, Kansas.

Duckworth, R.H. 1975. Poisoning of cattle by *Amaranthus. New Zealand Veterinary Journal* 23: 154-155.

Eilers, Raymond H. 1975. *South Dakota Weeds.* State Weed Control Commission.

Fernald, M.L. 1950. *Gray's Manual of Botany.* Eighth (centennial) edition—illustrated. American Book Company, New York.

Fleming, C.E. et al. 1920. The narrow-leaved milkweed and the broad-leaved or showy milkweed. *Plants poisonous to livestock in Nevada.* University of Nevada Agricultural Experimental Station Bulletin 99.

Frankton, Clarence and Gerald A. Mulligan. 1970. *Weeds of Canada*. Canada Department of Agriculture Publication 948, Ottawa.

Fuller, T. C. and E. McClintock. 1986. *Poisonous plants of California*. University of California Press, Berkeley, California.

Gilkey, Helen M. 1957. *Weeds of the Pacific Northwest*. Oregon State College.

Gleason, Henry A. 1963. *The New Britton and Brown Illustrated Flora of the Northeastern United States and Adjacent Canada*. Hafner Publishing Company, New York and London.

Gray, E. et al. 1968. *Hydrocyanic acid potential of* Sorghum *plants grown in Tennessee*. Tennessee Agriculture Experimental Station Bulletin 445.

Gwatkin, R. and I.W. Moynihan. 1943. Wild mustard seed poisoning in cattle. *Canadian Journal of Comparative Medicine* 7: 76-77.

Hanf, Martin. 1974. *Weeds and Their Seedlings*. BASF United Kingdom Limited, Agricultural Division, Ipswich, England.

Holm, LeRoy G. et al. 1977. *The World's Worst Weeds: Distribution and Biology*. The University Press of Hawaii, Honolulu, Hawaii.

Isley, Duane. 1960. *Weed Identification and Control in the North Central States*. Iowa State University Press, Ames, Iowa.

James, Lynn F. et al. 1991. *Noxious range weeds*. Westview Press, Boulder, Colorado.

Johnson, A.E. and R.J. Molyneux. 1986. The pyrrolizidine alkaloid free base and N-oxide content of toxic range plants. *Journal of Toxicology: Toxin Review*, 5: 256.

Kingsbury, J.M. 1964. *Poisonous plants of the United States and Canada*. Prentice-Hall, Englewood Cliffs, New Jersey.

Kummer, Anna P. 1951. *Weed Seedlings*. The University of Chicago Press, Chicago.

Looman, J. and K.F. Best. 1987. *Budd's Flora of the Canadian Prairie Provinces*. Agriculture Canada, Ottawa.

Majak, W. et al. 1980. Seasonal variation in the cyanide potential of arrowgrass (*Triglochin maritima*). *Canadian Journal of Plant Science* 60: 1235-1241.

Montgomery, F.H. 1964. *Weeds of Canada and the Northern United States*. Ryerson Press, Toronto.

Moss, E.H. 1983. *Flora of Alberta*. Second edition, rev. by J.G. Packer. University of Toronto Press, Toronto.

Muenscher, Walter Conrad. 1980. *Weeds*. Comstock Publishing Associates, Ithaca and London.

Mulligan, Gerald A. 1979. *The Biology of Canadian Weeds*. Contributions 1-32. Publication 1693. Communications Branch, Agriculture Canada, Ottawa.

Mulligan, Gerald A. 1984. *The Biology of Canadian Weeds*. Contributions 33-61. Publication 1765. Communications Branch, Agriculture Canada, Ottawa.

Mulligan, Gerald A. 1976. *Common Weeds of Canada*. McClelland and Stewart Limited.

Osweiler, G.D., W.B. Buck, and E.J. Bicknell. 1969. Production of perirenal edema in swine with

Amaranthus retroflexus. American Journal of Veteran Research 30: 557-566.

Panter, K.E., R.F. Keeler, and D.C. Baker. 1988. Toxicoses in livestock from the hemlocks (*Conium* and *Cicuta* spp.). *Journal of Animal Science* 66: 2407-2413.

Porsild, A.E. and W.J. Cody. 1980. *Vascular Plants of Continental Northwest Territories, Canada.* National Museums of Canada, Ottawa.

Schlaphoff, Elmer and Ellsworth Carlson. 1968. *Nebraska Weeds.* Bulletin No. 101-R. Nebraska Department of Agriculture, Lincoln, Nebraska.

Scoggan, H.J. 1978-79. *The Flora of Canada*, vol. 1-4. National Museums of Canada, Ottawa.

Schmutz, Ervin M., Barry N. Freeman, and Raymond E. Reed. 1968. *Livestock-poisoning plants of Arizona.* University of Arizona, Tucson.

Smith, R.A. and S.P. Crowe. 1987. Fanweed toxicosis in cattle: case history, analytical method, suggested treatment, and fanweed detoxification. *Veterinary and Human Toxicology* 29: 155-159.

Starreveld, E. and C.E. Hope. 1975. *Cicutoxin* poisoning (water hemlock). *Neurology* 25: 730-734.

Thornberry, Halbert Houst. 1966. *Index of Plant Virus Diseases.* Agricultural Handbook No. 307, United States Department of Agriculture, Washington, D.C.

United States Department of Agriculture. 1970. *Selected Weeds of the United States.* Agriculture Handbook No. 366, USDA Agricultural Research Service.

Walters, Dirk R. and David J. Keil. 1996. *Vascular Plant Taxonomy.* Fourth edition. Kendall/Hunt Publishing Company, Dubuque, Iowa.

Watson, Allan K. (ed.). 1985. Leafy Spurge. *Weed Science Society of America.* Champaign, Illinois.

Whitson, T.D. et al. 1991. *Weeds of the West.* Western Weed Science Society, Jackson, Wyoming.

Whitson, T.D. et al. 1987. *Weeds and Poisonous Plants of Wyoming and Utah.* University of Wyoming, Laramie.

Wilkinson, R.E. and H.E. Jacques. 1959. *How to Know the Weeds.* Second edition. Wm. C. Brown Company Publishers, Dubuque, Iowa.

Vance, F.R., J.R. Jowsey, and J.S. MacLean. 1977. *Wildflowers Across the Prairies.* Western Producer Prairie Books, Saskatoon.

Index to Common and Scientific Names

About the Authors

France Royer and Richard Dickinson have been
working together since 1989. Richard graduated
from the University of Alberta with a B.Sc. in
Physical Geography, while France is a self-taught
photographer. Together, they operate a botanical
and photographic service company.

France lives in Edmonton, while Richard now lives in
Toronto. When they are not working, they both
enjoy travelling and exploring the diverse plant
habitats of Canada.

France and Richard have previously written *Wildflowers
of Edmonton and Central Alberta* and *Wildflowers of
Calgary and Southern Alberta*, volumes that describe
the rich variety of flowering plants in the region.
They have a number of other writing projects in the
works.